TRAVER ON FISHING

Other Books by Robert Traver

Trouble-Shooter

Danny and the Boys

Small Town D.A.

Anatomy of a Murder

Trout Madness

Hornstein's Boy

Anatomy of a Fisherman

Laughing Whitefish

The Jealous Mistress

Trout Magic

The People Versus Kirk

TRAVER
ON FISHING

*A Treasury of Robert Traver's Finest Stories
and Essays About Fishing for Trout*

ROBERT TRAVER

Edited and with a Foreword by
NICK LYONS

The Lyons Press

Guilford, Connecticut

An imprint of The Globe Pequot Press

Printed in the United States of America

1 3 5 7 9 10 8 6 4 2

Library of Congress Cataloging-in-Publication Data

Traver, Robert, 1903–1991.
   Traver on fishing : a treasury of Robert Traver's finest stories and essays about fishing
for trout / Robert Traver; edited and with a foreword by Nick Lyons.
      p.   cm.
   ISBN 1-58574-296-1 (hc)
   1. Trout fishing. 2. Fishing stories. I. Lyons, Nick. II. Title.

SH687 .T698 2001
799.1'757—dc21

                                                                2001022457

Contents

Contents

from
Anatomy of a Fisherman (1964)

from
Trout Magic (1974)

Some Early, Some Late

Contents

Two Profiles

TRAVER ON FISHING

At that moment Parnell looked almost indecently happy; like a man about to cast a fly over the steadily rising granddaddy of all trout.

—*Anatomy of a Murder*

So I went fishing and my heart was carefree and gay. At dusk I snapped my leader on two trout of voting age and finally, just at dark, latched on to grandpa and the fight was on. "Come, come, sweet lover darlin'," I coaxed and wheedled. "Come to daddy, come to daddy." Twenty minutes later I went into the familiar daisy hoop and slipped the net under him. "Ah...." It was my biggest brook trout of the season. It looked like a dappled and dripping slice of sunset in the wavering light of my flashlight. But best of all, for twenty whole minutes I had managed to forget all about the Manion case.

—*Anatomy of a Murder*

. . . the Upper Peninsula of Michigan—in sprawling Marquette County—a remote region lying farther north than many points in Canada, a wild, harsh, and broken land sculptored and carved by a procession of ancient glaciers, a rugged land alternately pounded and caressed by two of the world's largest inland seas, Superior and Michigan, a land compounded of many hills and rocks and swamps and endless waterways. In my bailiwick dwell three of nature's noblest creations: the ruffed grouse, the whitetailed deer, and the brook trout. I occasionally hunt the first, stoutly ignore the second—except to admire him—and endlessly pursue the lovely brook trout and his sly cousins, the rainbow and the brown. This is the land where I was born. This is where I live and fish. This is where I hope to await eternity.

—*Anatomy of a Fisherman*

Testament of a Fisherman

I fish because I love to; because I love the environs where trout are found, which are invariably beautiful, and hate the environs where crowds of people are found, which are invariably ugly; because of all the television commercials, cocktail parties, and assorted social posturing I thus escape; because, in a world where most men seem to spend their lives doing things they hate, my fishing is at once an endless source of delight and an act of small rebellion; because trout do not lie or cheat and cannot be bought or bribed or impressed by power, but respond only to quietude and humility and endless patience; because I suspect that men are going along this way for the last time, and I for one don't want to waste the trip; because mercifully there are no telephones on trout waters; because only in the woods can I find solitude without loneliness; because bourbon out of an old tin cup always tastes better out there; because maybe one day I will catch a mermaid; and, finally, not because I regard fishing as being so terribly important but because I suspect that so many of the other concerns of men are equally unimportant—and not nearly so much fun.

Introduction

He called them "yarns" and that's what he wrote—his own unique mix of true or fictional narrative, mingled with wise upcountry wit, home-spun and down-to-earth philosophy that never truly hid the canny D.A. and brilliant judge he had been. He understood people shrewdly, brooked nothing bogus or deceitful, loved wilderness and solitude, and was just mad for bourbon from a tin cup, stogies, and brook trout fishing.

John Voelker made a world of his "Frenchman's Pond"—a swampy half mile ballooning of the East Branch of the Escanaba River on Michigan's Upper Peninsula, some two hundred feet across in place, two beaver ponds crossed by a bridge with two church pews on it, surrounded by his hundred and sixty acres of forestland. It's not Yoknapatawpha County but its characters, all real, give it a flavor that is as distinct as it is pungent.

"Wading or floating rivers never was my bag," he wrote to Harry Campbell in 1978; he preferred to fish the pond, perhaps sitting on a wood-and-metal milk case on one of the carpeted wooden ramps he'd built, and roll casting out for native brookies. He loved best these jewel-like emblems of what was native to his beloved Upper Peninsula, which he called that "wild, harsh, and broken land ... a land compounded of many hills and rocks and swamps and endless waterways." He said that in his "bailiwick dwell three of nature's noblest creations: the ruffed grouse, the white-tailed deer, and the brook trout." He endlessly pursued the "lovely brook trout."

He wrote to Harry Campbell: "I sometimes feel I'm missing out on a lot of fun, sticking to 'uncle's'"—his affectionate name for the ponds—"and my little brookies, but I sashayed around the U.P. for years after every kind of trout before coming home to my favorite." The little brook trout could be picky about the flies they wanted, but John once said that "pictures of too many bugs tend to make me wonder why I fish." He preferred a much simpler vision of fly fishing, with fewer bugs. Lloyd Anderson tied many of John's flies and Pete Peterson others; a #18 was fairly large for the ponds and he frequently used #20s and #22s. The Slim Jim was a favorite. Art Flick got him interested in the Grey Fox Variant, Flick's favorite fly. But the clear water and wild fish sometimes made the fishing better than the catching. When he caught some, John generally ate them—often roasting them on an open grill.

John's yarns about fishing the ponds remind us of a kind of fishing far removed from more public brands of fly fishing today, often accompanied by cries of "ripping some jaws," Latin entomology, techno-jargon, exotic locales. He is a poet of the near at hand. John was more content to hunt the woods for morels in morel season, blueberries in their time, play cribbage with a batch of local friends, and roll cast into the clear waters of Frenchman's. In fact, he spent a full thirty seasons after the publication of his best-selling novel *Anatomy of a Murder,* and the subsequent Otto Preminger movie with Jimmy Stewart, Lee Remick, and George C. Scott, doing just that. After the success of his book he retired from his position as Associate Justice of the Michigan Supreme Court almost at once, to fish and to write his deceptively simple yarns.

Introduction

John's themes are especially poignant and challenging today, when fly fishing has become so high-tech, such big business: keep the roads to your private pond unimproved, respect the myriad mysteries of the natural world, avoid cities, avoid deceit and pretension, don't put too much trust in technology, lie only to protect your favorite spots. Elihu Winer, who made a charming film about John at Frenchman's, told me a marvelous story about one of the images in which John is sitting on a log smoking one of his little stogies and looking so contemplative he might have the great matters of the world on his mind. They had been filming for several days with an expensive crew and had caught no fish. It happens. Someone suggested that the film needed some action sorely and that they might hook John's fly to a stick and fake a fight. John sat down to think about that for a while; Elihu caught him contemplating the matter—fully aware of the cost of the production. And then John said that he simply could not do it.

In 1981 he wrote to a friend that it would be best to "muzzle the computer technicians who have moved into fly fishing. Actually, the bastards make fishing sound like an overtime session at the office to listen to a pep spiel from the head man—just what it *ain't!*" His story "Morris the Rodmaker" shows how much he valued what was simple, well-made, and elegant—and Kushner bamboo rods were just that.

How I loved to get those long letters from John on yellow legal-pad paper, double-spaced, in green ink, always interspersed with his never-ending corrections, often corrections of corrections, always seeking exactly the right word, his words saucy, vinegary, wry. Yet for all his fussing there was nothing "literary" about the hundreds of letters I got when I was editing *Trout Magic*, just a nagging love of the right phrase. Nor is there literary pretension of any kind in his yarns.

Often he seeks the simpler word, or some puckish word, or an earthy phrase to replace an abstraction. Look at his famous "Testament of a Fisherman" for the kind of prose he was after—and for the values that were so deeply a part of him. Without blushing, he uses words like "love" and "fun"; he quietly champions the "delight" he finds in fishing while scoring crowds, television commercials, cocktail parties; he whimsically speculates that he may some day catch a mermaid; he does not sententiously call fishing a religion but says it is as unimportant as most of the other concerns of men, and that those other concerns are not nearly so much fun. Elsewhere, he adds that fishing is "one of the few pursuits left to man that it is fun even to fail at." And fly fishing, as distinguished from all other ways of fishing, "is oddly akin to the difference between seduction and rape."

Arnold Gingrich, who had published some of John's legal opinions in *Esquire*, says in *The Fishing in Print* that John's prose "gives you that wonderful relaxed, lazy, unhurried and unflustered, comfortable 'old shoe' feeling, page after page." Yes, it does, but the precise tone of his work did not come without a lot of green felt-tip pen correcting.

Charles Kuralt, a longtime friend after Kuralt made John the centerpiece of an "On the Road" segment, said that John was "about the nearest thing to a great man I've ever known." I think he was, too—but he wore the mantle "great" very lightly, for he was eminently human. Here's how Harry Campbell saw him in action, at Frenchman's, and reported in *Riverwatch* after John's death. The passage is worth quoting at length.

> Cocktails at Frenchman's were legendary. Only one style of drink was offered—or permitted—and it was prepared with meticulous care and devotion by the host. John would solemnly ring an iron farm bell to announce the commencement of the five o'clock cocktail hour—although on unseasonably hot afternoons, when the fishing was particularly slow, he might set his watch ahead to an earlier head start on the evening's festivities.

Once the summoned were assembled inside the cabin, we would witness his ceremonial preparation of libations. John's recipe is straightforward enough: in a very large jelly glass mix a cube of sugar, a dash of bitters, and a handful of ice from the cooler, a generous jigger (or, oops, two) of sour mash, a spalsh of water, a thin slice of orange, and a maraschino cherry. Then, drink the booze and toss the fruit to the chipmunks.

Storytelling at Frenchman's was world class. Punctuated by laughter and the tinkling of ice-filled glasses, John would spin yarns, recount past exploits, tell jokes, and generally hold court with all the grace and humor which marked his career on Michigan's highest bench. We would often laugh until our sides ached, and only when the booze ran out and the sun began to set would we reluctantly head for home.

Which is why it was so difficult to say goodbye to John Voelker last March in the somber setting of an Ishpeming funeral parlor, with all his old fishing pals wearing neckties, and everyone looking so sad. We all sat there on the folding chairs and just felt worse and worse, knowing we'd never see him wink or crack a pun or erupt with laughter again.

He looked and even walked a little like John Wayne, without the machismo. He was a spellbinding and hilarious public speaker—I heard him captivate a huge crowd at a Theodore Gordon Flyfishers' dinner when he won the Arnold Gingrich Angling Heritage Award. He loved fly fishing for his native brookies and eschewed both the strange words and laid-on complexity of too much of the modern fly-fishing world, driven by publicity and cant and pretending and egos run amok. And he wrote memorably about the activity he loved so deeply—once saying that it was the most fun one could have standing up. He was the kind of man of whom it is truthful to say, we shall not see his like again. And fly fishing is altogether the richer for being reminded of the elemental truths he championed.

I hope this collection of his yarns and observations—chosen

from his three fishing books, other books, and various magazine pieces—reminds us of his enduring values, catches the good old judge a raft of new readers, makes us laugh a bit more at ourselves and our fellow fly fishers, and invites us not to turn this happy pastime into a jargon-ridden cult.

—Nick Lyons
January 2001
New York City

from
Trout Madness
(*1960*)

Preface

There is a lot of amiable fantasy written about trout fishing, but the truth is that few men know much if anything about the habits of trout and little more about the manner of taking them. And still fewer of these occasional wise men will spare any time from their fishing devotionals to write about it. Our knowledge of trout is like man's tenancy on this planet: precarious and tentative. In a world where men scarcely know each other, and are at pains to fight endless wars to confirm this somber fact, it is perhaps a gratuitous display of ignorance for any man to pretend extensive knowledge of the sly and secretive trout. They are dwellers on another planet. I have fished for trout since I was a boy and I admit I still know little or nothing about them. Indeed this is one of the special fascinations of pursuing them. Perhaps it is also the beginning of trout wisdom.

This book is the story of a lawyer gone wrong; of a man possessed of a fourteen-carat legal education who has gaily neglected it to follow the siren call of trout. It has been wisely observed that many lawyers are frustrated actors, but I know of one, at least, who is simply an unfrustrated fisherman. For lawyers, like all men, may

3

be divided into two parts: those who fish and those who do not. All men who fish may in turn be divided into two parts: those who fish for trout and those who don't. Trout fishermen are a race apart; they are a dedicated crew—indolent, improvident, and quietly mad.

The true trout fisherman is like a drug addict; he dwells in a tight little dream world all his own, and the men about him, whom he observes obliviously spending their days pursuing money and power, genuinely puzzle him, as he doubtless does them. He prides himself on being an unbribed soul. So he is by way of being a philosopher, too, and sometimes he fishes not because he regards fishing as being so terribly important but because he suspects that so many of the other concerns of men are equally unimportant. Under his smiling coat of tan there often lurks a layer of melancholy and disillusion, a quiet awareness—and acceptance—of the fugitive quality of man and all his enterprises. If he must chase a will-o'-the-wisp he prefers that it be a trout. And so the fisherman fishes. It is at once an act of humility and small rebellion. And it is something more. To him his fishing is an island of reality in a world of dream and shadow. . . . Yet he is a species of unregenerate snob, too, and it pains him endlessly even to *hear* the name King Trout linked in the same breath with bass, pike, muskies, or similar representatives of what he is more likely to lump ungenerously as members of the lobster family.

All of these yarns are laid in the Upper Peninsula of Michigan, where I was born, a remote and sprawling region lying farther north than many points in Canada; a rugged land practically surrounded by the waters of two inland seas, Lake Superior and Lake Michigan. Many modest cities have larger populations than the whole U. P., a forgotten region which was virtually ignored in the westward surge of population. The canny lumber and steel barons, however, did not ignore the U. P., and they have doggedly hacked and clawed away at it for generations. Despite their best efforts, however, they still haven't quite been able to cut it down or blast it out. The brooding hills and gloomy swamps and endless waterways are still here. And the beaver. The people who inhabit the place are mostly from northern regions: Finns, Scandinavians, French-Canadians, with a generous sprinkling of the ubiquitous Irish, resourceful Cornish iron and copper miners, who were followed by the volatile Italians, and a mixed scattering of peoples from central Europe.

The simple truth is that the U. P. is one of the best hunting and fishing areas in the United States. It possesses three of nature's noblest creations: the ruffed grouse, the white-tailed deer, and the brook trout. Besides that there are sharp-tailed grouse, rabbits and black bears galore, some excellent rainbow and brown trout fishing, not to mention shoals of such tourist fish as bass, walleyes, muskies, crappies, bluegills and assorted stuff like that.

This fact, thank the Lord, is not yet widely known. It would be ironic—and a hideous thought to contemplate—if this little book should help bring about the discovery of the "forgotten" Upper Peninsula. Yet I take comfort when I reflect that the people who might find and deflower my native heath rarely hold still long enough to read books. And, I may ruefully add, they seem to have developed a special resistance to reading fishing books, like books of poetry, and somewhat like mosquitoes that finally learn to thrive on D.D.T. Apparently all that these people will willingly read are billboards, speedometers, funny books, road maps and signs proclaiming more Kozy Kabins five hundred yards ahead. They obediently race through here all summer long, sightlessly hissing along their labeled channels of concrete, bent only upon making five hundred miles a day, an achievement which somehow seems to ease the peculiar nature of their pain. They know not of the existence of the true U. P. They've never really been there.

In my view the best time to go trout fishing is when you can get away. That is virtually the only dogma you will be exposed to in this book. If you seek sage dilations on lunar tables, tidal impulses, wind phases, exotic fly patterns, tinted leaders, barometric pressures, and the like, then gently close this book and go fishing instead. Nor will you find herein any pictures of one big fish holding aloft another, the victor being identified largely by his triumphant grin. To this fisherman the fish in fishing happens to be what the onion is to onion soup: one of the main ingredients, yes, but far from everything. I fish mainly because I love the environs where trout are found: the woods; and further because I happen to dislike the environs where crowds of men are found: large cities; but if, heaven forbid, there were no trout and men were everywhere few, I would still doubtless prowl the woods and streams because it is there and only there that I really feel at home.

Successful fly fishing for trout is an act of high deceit; not only must the angler lure one of nature's subtlest and wariest creatures, he must do so with something that is false and no good—an artificial fly. Thus fake and sham lie at the heart of the enterprise. The amount of Machiavellian subtlety, guile, and sly deception that ultimately becomes wrapped up in the person of an experienced trout fisherman is faintly horrifying to contemplate. Thus fiendishly qualified for a brilliant diplomatic career he instead has time only to fish. So lesser diplomats continue to grope and bumble and their countries continue to fall into war. The only hope for it all, I am afraid, is for the Lord to drive the trout fishermen into diplomacy or else drive the diplomats to trout fishing. My guess is that either way we'd be more apt to have more peace: the fishermen-turned-diplomats would hurriedly resolve their differences on the trout stream so that they might return to their fishing, while the diplomats-turned-fishermen would shortly become so absorbed in their new passion they'd never again find time for war.

In this book I will lie a little, but not much, and I would prefer to hide my lapses under the euphemism "literary license," my excuse being that I find it difficult to inject drama into a series of fishing stories unless *somebody* occasionally gets on to a good fish. Quite frequently, you know, we fishermen don't.

The First Day

The true fisherman approaches the first day of fishing with all the sense of wonder and awe of a child approaching Christmas. There is the same ecstatic counting of the days; the same eager and palpitant preparations; the same loving drafting of lists which are succeeded in turn by lists of lists! And then—when time seems frozen in its tracks and one is sure the magic hour will never arrive—lo, *'tis the night before fishing!* Tomorrow is the big day! Perhaps it is also the time for a little poetry, however bad . . .

> *'Twas the night before fishing*
> *When all through the house*
> *Lay Dad's scattered fishing gear*
> *As though strewn by a souse . . .*

Dad will of course have been up a dozen times during the night, prowling the midnight halls, peering out at glowering skies, creeping downstairs and pawing through mounds of duffel for the umpteenth last-minute checkup, crouching over the radio listening to the bright chatter of the all-night disk jockeys, ritualistically tap-

ping the barometer—and perhaps even tapping his medicinal bottle of Kentucky chill-chaser. . . . It is this boyish quality of innocence, this irrepressible sense of anticipation, that makes all children and fishermen one. For after all, aren't fishermen merely
permanently spellbound juveniles who have traded in Santa Claus
for Izaak Walton?

Just as no Christmas can ever quite disappoint a youngster,
however bleak and stormy the day, so no opening day of fishing can
ever quite disappoint his grown-up brother. The day is invested
with its own special magic, a magic that nothing can dispel. It is the
signal for the end of the long winter hibernation, the widening of
prison doors, the symbol of one of nature's greatest miracles, the
annual unlocking of spring.

Since this fisherman dwells at Latitude 45 it should come as no
great shock to learn that on most opening days I am obliged to draw
rather heavily on this supply of magic to keep up my own drooping
spirits. It is sometimes difficult to remain spellbound while mired
to the hub caps in mud. *Our* big opening-day problem is twofold: to
know where to find ice-free open water; and then be able to get
there. During the ordeal we are sometimes driven to drink.

Our opening day is the last Saturday in April, ordinarily a disen-
chanting season of the year that finds most back roads badly
clogged if not impassable, and a four-pound ice chisel a more
promising weapon with which to probe our trout waters than a four-
ounce fly rod. Our lakes and ponds are usually still ice-locked; our
rivers and streams are usually in their fullest flood; and the most
sensible solution is to try to remember a partially open spring-fed
pond or beaver dam—and then spend a good part of the day trying
to get there. Hence it is that my fishing pals and I usually take several pre-season reconnaissance trips on snowshoes. But regardless of
the day, always we bravely go forth, come fire, flood, or famine—or
the fulminations of relatives by marriage.

On many opening days I have had to trek into the chosen spot on snowshoes. I remember one recent spring when I stood on the foot-thick ice of a pond on my snowshoes—and took eight respectable trout on *dry* flies from a small open spring-hole less than thirty feet away, skidding them home to daddy over the ice! If you don't believe it, don't let it bother you; I'm not quite sure that I believe it myself.

Since 1936 I have kept a complete record of every fishing trip I have taken. It is amazing how I can torture myself during the winter reading over this stuff, recreating once again those magic scenes, seeing again the soft velvet glitter of trout waters, hearing once again the slow rhythmic whish of the fly lines. . . . From these records one thing emerges rather clearly: past opening days were more apt to lean to the mildly tragic than the magic. Here is the actual depressing account, omitting only the technical data on barometric pressures, water temperatures, wind direction, and the like.

1936: Snowshoed into Flopper's Pond with Clarence Lott. Pond partly open. No rises, no fish, no errors. Two flat tires on way out. "Oh, what fun it is to run . . ."

1937: Same way to same place with Mike DeFant. Reluctantly kept five wizened fryers out of low peasant pride.

1938: Slugged into Werner Creek beaver dam with mudhooks on Model A. Same fellows plus brother Leo. Caught 3 small trout and a touch of double pneumonia.

1939: Hiked into Wilson Creek beaver dams on snowshoes with Bill Gray. No rises, no takers. Bill took 6 fryers on bait. Spent balance of day coaxing the old fish car back across broken bridge. Finally did it with oats soaked generously in rum.

1940: Louie Bonetti, Nes Racine and Leo and I to O'Neil's Creek dam. A beautiful day succeeded by an even more beautiful hangover. No rises, no fish, several errors.

1941: Tom Cole and Vic Snyder and I drove out to the "Old Ruined Dams." Roads open, ponds free of ice. Fair rise. Beautiful day. Tom (6), Vic (7) and I (9), all honest fryers. All day long wedges of geese honking over like crazy, sounding remarkably like the weirdly demented yowlings of a distant pack of coyotes.

1942: Same gang plus Leo, to same place, same conditions. I kept 5 fryers. Vic filled out on bait. Had fish fry that night in camp. Lost $2.50 at rum. Tossed and turned all night.

1943: (No fish and no entry of just where I went. My, my. Must have gone straight up! Maybe no gas coupons.)

1944: South camp with usual opening gang. Bucked drifts last 2 miles. High water. Picked arbutus on south hillsides. No fish in crowd. Drowned our sorrows in mead and wore twisted garlands of arbutus in our hair.

1945: To Ted Fulsher's camp with Bill Gray and Carl Winkler. Raw, cold. Northeast wind. Didn't wet a line. Won $17.00 at poker. Slept like a log.

1946: To Frenchman's Pond with gang. Our fly lines froze in the guides. Thawed lines and drove to South Camp where Leo broke out a bottle of rare old brandy. Evidently it was *too* old; after the third round I suddenly rose and clapped my hand to my mouth—and ran outside. Guess I had better stick to the reliable brands of medium rare one-year-old cookin' whisky, the kind designed for peasants of distinction—bent on extinction.

1947: Snowshoed 5 miles with Dick Tisch in to Nurmi's Pond. Snow still 3 feet deep in woods. Got caught in bitter cold mixed rain and snow. Came down with chills and vapors and spent three days in bed with a nurse. Enervating but fun. Must try same next year. Her name was Lulu.

1948: Chopped way through the winter's bountiful supply of windfalls into O'Leary's Pond with Gipp Warner and Tom Bennett. Saw 2 wobbly young bear cubs and 17 deer. Caught 2 nice trout right off bat. Chuckled mirthlessly and twirled my waxed mustaches. Then caught in sudden hailstorm, which ended all fishing. On to Birchbark Lodge, one of those quaint Paul Bunyanish roadside tourist-traps cluttered to the eaves with stuffed owls and yawning dead bass impaled on varnished boards—and possessing the cutest iddy bitty bar, made, we were solemnly assured, out of *real logs*. Next morning, snug in my doghouse, I suspected the whisky was, too.

1949: Snowshoed into Scudder's Pond with Joe Parker. Pond partly open over bubbling springs. Fish dimpling. Stood on ice and took 8 on tiny dry flies! 'Twas a miracle. Skidded them over the ice. *Skidding at Scudder's!* by George Bellows. . . . Joe took only 1 on spinning gear, the wrong medicine.

1950: To Alger County with Marquette gang. Felt like a midget. Out of seven men I was the shortest, at six feet. A tall tale! Snow, ice and high water everywhere. Didn't wet a line. Wet whistle instead. Excursion degenerated into a pub crawl. Lost count after the 17th. Heard 8 million polkas and hillbilly laments—all miraculously sung through the left nostril. Love and despair, your spell is everywhere. . . . The inventor of the juke box is a cross between a banshee and a fiend. May he and his accomplices roast in the bottom-most pits of Hell.

1951: Slugged way through deep snow into Scudder's Pond led by proud Expedition Commander Frank Russell and his new jeep. The man *searched* for snowdrifts to charge! There is a new form of lunacy abroad in the land, the victims of which are called Jeepomaniacs. They're afraid of nothing. . . . Pond ice locked as tight as a bull's horns, as the saying doesn't go. Al Paul caught 2 in outlet—trout, not bull's horns. Surprise-attacked by party of friendly natives. Entire expedition got half shot and retired in vast disorder.

1952: Mud-hooked way into Frenchman's Pond with Hank Scarffe and 2 boats. Nice intermittent "business" rise. Hank and I filled out, carefully selecting our trout. Fish fat and sassy. One of the most dramatic first-day rises I ever recall. Had but 2 bottles of beer all day. La, such a fine, contrite broth of a boy. Funny thing, I become a hell of a good fisherman when the trout decide to commit suicide. This is truly a fascinating pond.

11

And here is a later entry:

There have been 4 hauntingly lovely days in a row, the earth smoky and fragrant with the yeast of spring, the sky cut by the curling lash of endless flights of honking geese. Last night the wind swung abruptly to the east and the thermometer and barometer joined hands in a suicidal nose dive. Hank Scarffe, Al Paul, and I set out in 34° weather, the rainy sleet freezing to the windshield upon landing. All plans awry, we foolishly tried to reach the Moose Creek beaver dams, but got stuck up to the radiator in the first charge of a drift. We then retreated west and pushed and slugged our way through acres of rotten snow into Frenchman's Pond, where Hank and I huddled like wet robins and watched Al and his new telescope girder vainly test the pond with worms. Then came the snow, and there were *whitecaps* on the pond! Al folded his girder and we looked at each other and shrugged and slunk silently away. No one proposed even a drink. Once home I drained the fish car radiator, took a giant slug of whisky, and leapt morosely into bed, pulling the covers over my head. There I remained until nightfall, dreaming uneasily that I was a boy again and lo, it was Christmas—and I had just found my stocking filled with coal. I awoke to hear the blizzard screaming insanely outside. "*Whee-e-e-e* . . ." I crept downstairs in my bathrobe and drew every shade in the place, lit a roaring fire in the Franklin stove, built a foot-high highball, put on a mile-long piano concerto by Delius, and settled down with a book about hunting in Africa by a guy named, of all things, John A. Hunter. There were no pictures of fish! Was charmed to learn that the pygmies of the Ituri forest cure eye infections by urinating in the bad eye. Found myself wishing that the red-eyed weather man would just sorta kinda drop in. Ho hum, only 8 more months 'til Christmas.

But enough of this dreary recital of frustration, hangover, and rue. As you may by now suspect, the first day of fishing in my bailiwick is something of a gamble. Usually it is considerably more devoted to drinking than fishing, a state of affairs against which I maintain a stern taboo when the fishing really gets under way. *Then* any drinking—usually a nightcap or two—comes only *after* the fishing is over and done. To me fly fishing is ordinarily quite difficult and stimulating enough without souping up the old motor. . . . But the first day is different; it is mostly a traditional spring get-together of congenial souls, an incidental opportunity to try out and find the bugs in one's equipment, and a chance to stretch one's legs and expand one's soul. I regret that it also frequently affords an excellent opportunity to entrench oneself early and firmly in the doghouse. Then comes the time for all middle-aged fishermen to sow their rolled oats. All of which brings on a final seizure of dubious poetry.

> *'Twas the morning after the first day*
> *When all through the house*
> *Echoed the moaning and groaning*
> *Of poor daddy—the louse!*

The Fish Car

She was born on an assembly line in Detroit in 1928. After a bitter childhood involving many harrowing misadventures, she was found and adopted by me on a rainy spring day in 1935. It was then that I discovered my beloved orphan, forlorn and neglected, weeping silently in an obscure corner of a used-car lot. I stared at her and she stared mournfully back at me, dripping tears. With us I guess it was a case of love at first sight. Appraisingly squinting an eye and stroking my chin, I kicked her once on a rear tire—lo! there was air in it—and then told the man I'd take her. (Why do all prospective purchasers of used cars invariably kick at one of the tires?) The adoption papers cost me one hundred dollars. The superintendent of the used-car orphanage signed and gave me her birth certificate. We formally shook hands, and I somehow drove her away under her own power. Pedestrians paused and stared at us. Once home I broke a bottle of beer across her radiator and christened her "Buckshot."

She was a little two-door sedan with wire wheels and twenty-one-inch tires. (For my money she is also a mobile testimonial and

15

the most enduring monument I know to the mechanical genius of Henry Ford. How many cars of other make and like vintage does one still encounter regularly on the road?) When I got her she not only looked like a tramp, she was a tramp. Among many other things, her lights, brakes, horn, muffler, and charger didn't work; you could throw a creel through the leaky roof; a wildcat had evidently been let loose at her upholstery; the clanking engine sounded like the cardiac thumpings of an expiring thresher; a cardboard carton appropriately advertising a deodorant took the place of the glass missing from the driver's door; her windshield was cracked and completely fogged over, like a pair of dime-store sun glasses, giving the driver a wavering surrealist vision of the occasional larger objects he was able to behold.

But her heart and mind and spirit were essentially sound, and when I was done with her she was a glittering mechanical dream, a sight to behold. By that time, too, the original price I paid for her had faded into a Scotchman's tip compared to the national debt. As for her owner, he was poor but proud, and not unlike a widowed mother who takes in washing and sacrifices all to support a lazy daughter in indolence and sloth.

Since then my rejuvenated Buckshot and I have spent some of the best years of our lives together. We have hunted and fished together, explored and prospected for uranium, and gathered berries and pine knots together; there have been baseless dark rumors that we have even got drunk together. . . . But mostly we have fished; yes, year after year, season in and season out, come hell or high water, we have fished. Her radiator is adorned with two leaping tin fish I stole from my youngest daughter.

When Buckshot became old and discreet enough to vote, a few years back, I rewarded her coming of age by letting her rest after each bird season. All winter long I let her just sit in the garage, with southern exposure. There she basks like Man O' War let out to pasture. It is a kind of partial retirement, a sort of annual winter vacation with pay, in recognition of her long years of valor under fire. Now she is pure fish car and she loves it. When fishing season rolls around she snorts and trembles and backfires like an old fire horse at the sound of the bell.

She is loyal to me and in my way I am loyal to her. Last spring I had a chance to adopt a sturdy and handsome young jeep at a bargain price. I was jubilant; now I could ford rivers and scale mountains. But when it came right down to signing the adoption papers and getting rid of faithful old Buckshot on the trade-in, I fell to mentally reviewing our misspent youth together. Shortly I got all sentimental and choked up. We two had been through so *much* together. . . . "The d-deal's off," I finally told the astounded jeep man, sniffling and patting patient ol' Buckshot on the fanny. I felt so guilty for wavering that all summer long I fed Buckshot on nothing but the best ethyl gas. All was forgiven and I now suspect that our marriage shall last till old age—or jeeps—do us part. Not only is she cheap at half the price; she's a jeep at half the price.

I don't mean to imply that our romance hasn't had its darker moments. There were times when I could have reared back and given her a swift kick in the differential. No, Buckshot, I haven't forgotten the occasions when you sulked and pouted and even broke down and forced your poor old boss man to walk back to town from hell's half acre. 'Member the time you developed that—er—sudden female complaint way up north off the Yellow Dog plains? 'Member how I had to walk nearly twenty miles before I hitched a ride?—and then had to fetch a doctor from the garage, along with one of those expensive wrecker-ambulances to tote you in? And then paid nearly a hundred bucks for your operation?

Eh? How's that, Buckshot? What's that you just now said? Oh, that if I'd lay off swiggling beer when I was guiding you and watched closer where I was driving, you wouldn't develop nearly so many of those aches and pains and sudden fainting spells? Well I declare—now that's gratitude for you. My, my . . . I'm truly surprised at you, Buckshot. And in front of perfect strangers, too!

My fish car is probably one of the most complete fish cars in the world. Perhaps she is *the* completest, but then I don't like to brag. This I do know: All I have to do is to get into her and drive away—and we can stay out fishing for a week. There is no further preparation and nothing I can forget (unless I forget Buckshot herself) because I always leave all of my treasures in her custody. When she and I shove off we are a sort of Abercrombie & Fitch on the march. Here is only a partial list of the gear we *always* carry; it's standard equipment: Four fly rods and a spinning rod, all of which ride snugly on rubber slings suspended from the inside roof; binoculars, a camera, a magnifying glass (for studying the birds and the bees and the stomach content of trout), four sizes of flashlights (from pencil size to Lindbergh Beacon), and even one of those old Stonebridge candle lanterns for emergencies; waders and hip boots and low boat boots, and of course all the usual endless fishing gear (*that* would take a page itself), complete with patching cement, ferrule cement, and all the many odds and ends; eight miles of miscellaneous sizes and lengths of rope; a complete set of detailed county maps of Michigan based upon late air photos and showing all waters and side roads; a bedroll and spare blanket; rain clothes and a complete change of woods clothes; a tarpaulin and pup tent; a Primus stove and nesting cook kit with all the many trimmings; assorted water canteens; a small portable icebox; grub for a week, mostly bottled or canned; and, last but not least, always a supply of beer and a bottle or two of whisky—*always* when I leave, that is.

In addition I carry two spare tires and some extra tubes; enough small spare parts to start a neighborhood garage; a hand-cranked tugger that could yank a Patton tank out of a mudhole, complete with assorted logging chains and snatch blocks and "come-alongs" and U-bolts and towing cables, together with an old car axle to drive in the ground and use as a towing anchor in treeless terrain. I also carry enough tools and assorted junk to build and furnish a ranch house. On the roof I carry my rubber boat and inside the car the boat gear including anchors, jointed paddles, kapok cushions, air pump, etc. Then I carry two axes, one hatchet, one headhunting brush knife, two sizes of pruning shears for cleaning out difficult "hot spots," an all-size leather punch, two handsaws, nails and hammers, and enough pry bars and wrecking tools to convict me of intended sabotage and burglary. To keep in character for my felonies I usually tote a .38 special revolver. Then, to top it off, there is a six-volt overhead light bulb in the car that is so bright I can read the fine print on a bill of lading without my glasses.

And where does the driver sit? one may sensibly ask. Incredibly enough, I somehow manage to keep *both* front seats free for driver and passenger. Of course with this mound of equipment piled behind us we are usually obliged to converse in guarded whispers, lest our voices jar loose the poised glacier and bury us in the avalanche. Indeed, sometimes I have even managed to squeeze an adventurous small fisherman in the *back* seat, stashing the stuff around him, though I always thoughtfully furnish him a breathing pipe so that he does not perish on the way. "Fisherman drowned in tidal wave of fishing equipment!" is one headline we seek to avoid.

As I read over this modest inventory I am struck by the number of items I have left out. I haven't even hinted about the assorted barometers, thermometers, and depthometers, the toilet, gaming and first-aid kits, the fishtail propellers, transistor radios, and folding camp stools; nor yet about the red flares and collapsible canvas pails, the crow calls, Audubon birdcalls and Indian love calls—not to mention the aluminum waterscope I use leeringly to watch mermaids. And when my pals and I really go on a prolonged expedition and take along the trailer and all *three* of my boats, that is something to behold. Then I pile most of the gear in the flat-bottomed trailer boat, and lash the third boat on top. *Ship ahoy!* Admiral Dewey is about to steam into Manila harbor.

Last summer as I was about to shove off on big safari, Grace came out on the back porch to see me off. She studied the caravan rather thoughtfully for quite a while. She spoke slowly.

"You look," she said quietly, "you look like the addled commander of a one-man army about to launch a rocket invasion of Mars."

"Nope," I corrected her. "I'm the Ringling Brothers on my way to merge with Barnum & Bailey. Good day, Madam. Giddap, Buckshot!"

Big Secret Trout

No misanthropist, I must nevertheless confess that I like and frequently prefer to fish alone. Of course in a sense all dedicated fishermen must fish alone; the pursuit is essentially a solitary one; but sometimes I not only like to fish out of actual sight and sound of my fellow addicts, but alone too in the relaxing sense that I need not consider the convenience or foibles or state of hangover of my companions, nor subconsciously compete with them (smarting just a little over their success or gloating just a little over mine), nor, more selfishly, feel any guilty compulsion to smile falsely and yield them a favorite piece of water.

There is a certain remote stretch of river on the Middle Escanaba that I love to fish by myself; the place seems made for wonder and solitude. This enchanted stretch lies near an old deer-hunting camp of my father's. A cold feeder stream—"The Spawnshop," my father called it—runs through the ancient beaver meadows below the camp. After much gravelly winding and circling and gurgling over tiny beaver dams the creek gaily joins the big river a mile or so east of the camp. Not unnaturally, in warm weather this junction is a favorite convention spot for brook trout.

One may drive to the camp in an old car or a jeep but, after that, elementary democracy sets in; all fishermen alike must walk down to the big river—*even* the arrogant new jeepocracy. Since my father died the old ridge trail has become overgrown and faint and wonderfully clogged with windfalls. I leave it that way. Between us the deer and I manage to keep it from disappearing altogether. Since this trail is by far the easiest and closest approach to my secret spot, needless to say few, secretive, and great of heart are the fishermen I ever take over it.

I like to park my old fish car by the camp perhaps an hour or so before sundown. Generally I enter the neglected old camp to look around and, over a devotional beer, sit and brood a little over the dear dead days of yesteryear, or perhaps morosely review the progressive decay of calendar art collected there during forty-odd years. And always I am amazed that the scampering field mice haven't carried the musty old place away, calendars and all. . . . Traveling light, I pack my waders and fishing gear—with perhaps a can or two of beer to stave off pellagra—and set off. I craftily avoid using the old trail at first (thus leaving no clue), charging instead into the thickest woods, using my rod case as a wand to part the nodding ferns for hidden windfalls. Then veering right and picking up the trail, I am at last on the way to the fabulous spot where my father and I used to derrick out so many trout when I was a boy.

Padding swiftly along the old trail—over windfalls, under others—I sometimes recapture the fantasies of my boyhood: once again, perhaps, I am a lithe young Indian brave—the seventh son of Chief Booze-in-the-Face, a modest lad who can wheel and shoot the eye out of a woodchuck at seventy paces—now bound riverward to capture a great copper-hued trout for a demure copper-hued maiden; or again, and more sensibly, I am returning from the river simply to capture the copper-hued maiden herself. But copper fish or Indian maid, there is fantasy in the air; the earth is young again; all remains unchanged: there is still the occasional porcupine waddling away, bristling and ridiculous; still the startling whir of a

partridge; still the sudden blowing and thumping retreat of a surprised deer. I pause and listen stealthily. The distant blowing grows
fainter and fainter, *"whew"* and again *"whew,"* like wind grieving in
the pines.

By and by the middle-aged fisherman, still gripped by his fantasies, reaches the outlet of the creek into the main river. Hm . . .
no fish are rising. He stoops to stash a spare can of beer in the icy
gravel, scattering the little troutlings. Then, red-faced and panting,
he lurches up river through the brambles to the old deer crossing at
the gravel ford. Another unseen deer blows and stamps—this time
across the river. *"Whew,"* the fisherman answers, mopping his fore-
head on his sleeve, easing off the packsack, squatting there batting
mosquitoes and sipping his beer and watching the endless marvel
of the unwinding river. The sun is low, most of the water is
wrapped in shadow, a pregnant stillness prevails. Lo, the smaller
fish are beginning to rise. Ah, there's a good one working! Still
watching, he gropes in the bunch grass for his rod case. All fantasies
are now forgotten.

Just above this shallow gravel ford there is a wide, slick, still-
running and hopelessly unwadable expanse of deep water—a small
lake within the river. I have never seen a spot quite like it. On my
side of this pool there is a steep-sloping sandy bank surmounted by
a jungle of tag alders. On the far opposite bank there is an abrupt,
rocky, root-lined ledge lined with clumps of out-curving birches,
rising so tall, their quivering small leaves glittering in the dying sun
like a million tinkling tambourines. But another good fish rises, so
to hell with the tambourines. . . . For in this mysterious pool dwell
some of the biggest brown trout I know. This is my secret spot.
Fiendishly evasive, these trout are not only hard to catch but,
because of their habitat, equally hard to fish. The fisherman's trouble is double.

A boat or canoe invariably invokes mutiny and puts them
down—at least any vessel captained by me. My most extravagant
power casts from the ford below usually do the same or else fall

short, though not always. The tall fly-catching tag alders on my side discourage any normal bank approach consistent with retaining one's sanity. (Hacking down the tag alders would not only be a chore, but would at once spoil the natural beauty of the place and erect a billboard proclaiming: BIG TROUT RESIDE HERE!) Across the way the steep rocky bank and the clusters of birches and tangled small stuff make it impossible properly to present a fly or to handle a decent trout if one could. The place is a fisherman's challenge and a fisherman's dream: lovely, enchanted, and endlessly tantalizing. I love it.

Across from me, closer to the other side and nicely out of range, there is a slow whirl-around of silky black water, endlessly revolving. Nearly everything floating into the pool—including most natural flies—takes at least one free ride around this lazy merry-go-round. For many insects it is frequently the last ride, for it is here that the fat tribal chieftains among the brown trout foregather at dusk to roll and cavort. Many a happy hour have I spent fruitlessly stalking these wise old trout. The elements willing, occasionally I even outwit one. Once last summer I outwitted two—all in the same ecstatic evening. Only now can I venture coherently to speak of it.

I had stashed my beer in the creek mouth as usual and had puffed my way through the tangle up to the deep pool. There they were feeding in the merry-go-round, *both* of them, working as only big trout can work—swiftly, silently, accurately—making genteel little pneumatic sounds, like a pair of rival dowagers sipping their cups of tea. I commanded myself to sit down and open my shaking can of beer. Above and below the pool as far as I could see the smaller brook trout were flashily feeding, but tonight the entire pool belonged to these two quietly ravenous pirates. "Slp, slp" continued the pair as I sat there ruefully wondering what a Hewitt or LaBranche or Bergman would do.

"They'd probably rig up and go fishin'," at length I sensibly told myself in an awed stage whisper. So I arose and with furious nonchalance rigged up, slowly, carefully, ignoring the trout as though time were a dime and there were no fish rising in the whole river, dressing the line just so, scrubbing out the fine twelve-foot leader with my bar of mechanic's soap. I even managed to whistle a tuneless obbligato to the steady "Slp, slp, slp. . . ."

And now the fly. I hadn't the faintest idea what fly to use as it was too shadowy and far away to even guess what they were taking. Suddenly I had *the* idea: I had just visited the parlor of Peterson, one of my favorite fly tiers, and had persuaded him to tie up a dozen exquisitely small palmer-tied creations on stiff gray hackle. I had got them for buoyancy to roll-cast on a certain difficult wooded pond. Why not try one here? Yet how on earth would I present it?

Most fishermen, including this one, cling to their pet stupidities as they would to a battered briar or an old jacket; and their dogged persistence in wrong methods and general wrongheadedness finally wins them a sort of grudging admiration, if not many trout. Ordinarily I would have put these fish down, using my usual approach, in about two casts of a squirrel's tail. Perhaps the sheer hopelessness of the situation gave me the wit to solve it. Next time I'll doubtless try to cast an anvil out to stun them. "The *only* controlled cast I can possibly make here," I muttered, hoarse with inspiration, "is a *roll* cast . . . yes—it's that or nothing, Johnny me bye." If it is in such hours that greatness is born, then this was my finest hour.

Anyone who has ever tried successfully to roll-cast a dry fly under any circumstances, let alone cross-stream in a wide river with conflicting currents and before two big dining trout, knows that baby sitting for colicky triplets is much easier. For those who know not the roll cast, I shall simply say that it is a heaven-born cast made as though throwing an overhand half-hitch with a rope tied to a stick, no backcast being involved. But a roll cast would pull my fly under; a decent back cast was impossible; yet I had to present a floating fly. *That* was my little problem.

"Slp, slp, slp," went the trout, oblivious to the turmoil within me. Standing on the dry bank in my moccasins I calmly stripped out line and kept rolling it upstream and inshore—so as not to disturb my quarry—until I figured my fly was out perhaps ten feet more than the distance between me and the steadily feeding trout. And that was plenty far. On each test cast the noble little gray hackle quickly appeared and rode beautifully. "God bless Peterson," I murmured. Then I began boldly to arc the cast out into the main river, gauging for distance, and then—suddenly—I drew in my breath and drew up my slack and rolled out the fatal business cast. *This was it.* The fly lit not fifteen feet upstream from the top fish—right in the down whirl of the merry-go-round. The little gray hackle bobbed up, circled a trifle uncertainly and then began slowly to float downstream like a little major. The fish gods had smiled. Exultant, I mentally reordered three dozen precious little gray hackles. Twelve feet, ten feet, eight . . . holding my breath, I also offered up a tiny prayer to the roll cast. "Slp, slp . . ." The count-down continued—five feet, two feet, one foot, "slp"—and he was on.

Like many big browns, this one made one gorgeous dripping leap and bore down in a power dive, way deep, dogging this way and that like a bulldog shaking a terrier. Keeping light pressure, I coaxed rather than forced him out of the merry-go-round. Once out I let him conduct the little gray hackle on a subterranean tour and then—and then—I saw and heard his companion resume his greedy rise, "Slp, slp." *That* nearly unstrung me; as though one's fishing companion had yawned and casually opened and drunk a bottle of beer while one was sinking for the third time.

Like a harried dime-store manager with the place full of reaching juvenile delinquents, I kept trying to tend to business and avoid trouble and watch the sawing leader and the other feeding trout all at the same time. Then my trout began to sulk and bore, way deep, and the taut leader began to vibrate and whine like the plucked string of a harp. What if he snags a deadhead? I fretted. Just then a whirring half-dozen local ducks rushed upstream in oiled flight, banking away when they saw this strange tableau, a queer man standing there holding a straining hoop. Finally worried,

I tried a little more pressure, gently pumping, and he came up in a sudden rush and rolled on his side at my feet like a length of cordwood. Then he saw his tormentor and was down and away again.

The nighthawks had descended to join the bats before I had him folded and dripping in the net, stone dead. "Holy old Mackinaw!" I said, numb-wristed and weak with conquest. A noisy whippoorwill announced dusk. I blew on my matted gray hackle and, without changing flies, on the next business cast I was on to his partner—the senior partner, it developed—which I played far into the night, the nighthawks and bats wheeling all about me. Two days later all three of us appeared in the local paper; on the front page, mind you. I was the one in the middle, the short one with the fatuous grin.

Next season I rather think I'll visit my secret place once or twice.

Lost Atlantis

It was a hot lazy afternoon in mid-August. The small fry had the radio turned on full blast, blaring out the first game of a double-header between the New York Yankees and, I guess, the Green Bay Packers. The game had reached a pretty pass: there were two down and the bases were loaded; some character or other from Gap Tooth, Kentucky, was coming to bat; the din was terrific. I was enchanted to learn that this man of destiny weighed 193 pounds, stood 5 feet 11, had been rejected by the draft for night sweats, and boasted a batting average of .315. But horror of horrors, he had popped out in the last two times at bat. . . .

I retreated to the side porch, dark with hatred of all organized sports in general and Sunday afternoon baseball in particular. "Try that favorite brew of millions!" the announcer bawled after me. "Try a cool bottle of Pssst's mellow, golden, *homogenized* beer!" Ah, science had invaded even the beer vats . . . I made a mental note forever to avoid the stuff and sat staring morosely at the unkempt lawn, hot, bored, and fidgety. It was too torrid to go fishing, and anyway, I generously concluded, a responsible husband and parent owes a certain moral duty to share some of his leisure hours with his wife and children. Especially the poor kids. . . . Yes, during their formative and impressionable years a man's children need dear old dad around to—well—to sort of quietly set them an example. After all, *fishing* wasn't everything in life . . . I gave a virtuous little sniff.

Just then Grace came to the screen door and suggested that the lawn needed currying. "The place," she added acidly, "is beginning to look like an abandoned graveyard." Poor girl, she still cherishes the dream that I can ever be housebroken—at least during fishing season.

"Let's tether a goat instead and be the show place of the neighborhood," I said, ducking a withering look.

"Muskrat swings and pops up to center field!" the radio tragically proclaimed, as though announcing the fall of Rome. I squeezed my eyes shut.

Grace weighed the troubled situation. "Will you promise to mow the lawn tomorrow after work if I let you go fishing now?" she countered, trading slyly on a certain weakness she had observed in her husband.

"Madam, it's a deal," I answered brightly, already halfway out to the old fish car. With a flourish I swung open the garage doors, nearly tripped over a lurking lawn mower, and leapt into the fish car. "Giddap, Buckshot," I chortled, free as the wind, and in nothing flat I was rattling out toward Moose Creek, one of my favorite trout streams. Growing children, I mused between bounces, needed to balance their character development with the rare vitamins found only in freshly caught trout. Yes, I reflected, young ideals can best be nurtured in sturdy young bodies. Far from walking out on the kids, then, this fishing expedition, like so many others, was essentially a sacrificial labor of love.

Moose Creek is no great shakes to look at, being for the most part narrow and brushy, but the stretch where I usually hit it is a wide, shallow stream formed by an ancient inactive beaver dam which backs up the water for nearly a mile. I had been fishing there off and on for over fifteen years. The place harbors some nice brook trout but they are a temperamental lot, scary and hard to catch.

For years I had been hitting Moose Creek at this very same place—at old Camp Alice—about a half-mile upstream from the old beaver dam. I had almost always confined my fishing between the camp and the dam. While a good deal of the stretch was wadable, the margins of it were inclined to be swampy and difficult and there were also some interesting crannies and hideouts that could only be reached from a boat because of the varying depth of the water or accumulation of silt. Consequently I usually threw my rubber boat on the roof of the car whenever I planned to fish there. I had it along today.

Once or twice in recent years I had ventured upstream a little way from the usual point of embarkation, but this upper stretch was so choked and clogged with lily pads and some sort of matted and clutching water grass that I soon gave up and deeded it back to the Indians. Yup, there was no doubt about it: downstream toward the dam was by far the better place to fish. It was true that old-time fishermen used to tell me about a wonderful spring-fed beaver dam near the headwaters—"way up there in the foothills," they'd wave vaguely—but years ago, it seemed, some low genius in the conservation department had had a vision and blasted the dam out as part of some newfangled stream-improvement program. Here the old-timers would invariably choke up and dolefully wag their heads as though to say: "Mysterious are the devices of all game wardens . . ." So the word was out that the fishing upstream was all shot; and the fact was that the old fishing trails along the near bank had long since grown in and become choked with tangles of windfalls.

"Yep, yep," one old-time fisherman told me. "We'd only taken barrels of beautiful trout out of that there upper dam for nigh on to half a century—so those smart hammerheads in the State Capitol proved the fishing was bad—so they up an' blasts her out!"

Thus it was that on a hot Sunday afternoon I reluctantly

decided to go upstream and survey the historic ruins for myself. Boredom, not vision, was all that drove me to it. I leisurely wrestled the rubber boat off the fish car, gave the bladders an extra shot of air for my trip, loaded and strapped my .38 around my waist, threw my fishing gear and an old rod and a few cans of beer in my pack-sack, and shoved off. I paddled upstream slowly in the blazing sun, craning and listening, deliberately killing time. The voyage was on.

My first mild shock was to observe that the lily pads and thick water grass petered out before I had gotten around the second bend, the stream opening up into beautiful gravel-bottomed water in which I could see numerous small trout darting about. I had no doubt that their elders were lurking not far away. Naturally in the hot sun and the calm no fish were rising, but the spot was as trouty-looking as any stretch I had seen on the creek. "My, my," I murmured, "where has *this* place been all my life?" Of course my excuse was that I'd only been fishing the same creek for fifteen years.

I slowly pushed on and gradually the prevailing swampy shore gave way to higher land flanked in turn by low ridges, the creek narrowing and deepening, the banks now being lined with as lovely a stand of mature white pine as I had seen in many a year. Calm as it was, the soft whish and whine of the wind sifting through the tall wavy tops sounded like the muted strains of faraway violins. After another half-mile or so of this haunting vagrant music the creek narrowed down sharply.

Then I came to my first beaver dam. It wasn't much of a dam, as dams go, but the thing that quickened my pulse was the fact that it was a live dam, with fresh beaver cuttings very much in evidence. Could it possibly be? I mused, pondering what might lie above. Hm . . . let's go see.

I tossed the old rubber boat up over the dam, which didn't hold back much water, and sat perspiring in the bright sunlight sipping a can of warm beer. The big pines had now given way to a lush jungle of tag alders, the low ridges some distance away being adorned by spruces and balsams and a sprinkling of mixed second growth. I shrugged and pushed onward and upward.

In the next hour I negotiated three more fresh beaver dams, all about as modest as the first, the creek all the while getting so narrow that several times I was tempted to call it quits and head back downstream for the evening rise. But there is no lunatic quite like a trout lunatic, so each time I resisted temptation and doggedly pushed on.

Then I began to hit a series of big old white-pine windfalls lying plump across the creek. Most annoying they were, being too low to pass under and being sufficiently high, with their scorched and jagged old branches, to give me a bad time with my boat and gear. After scaling a round dozen of these fire-scarred old giants I finally scuffed a seat for myself among the layers of bird and animal guano on the last log and sat there sweltering and had another beer and wondered what in hell I was doing way up there on a narrow miserable creek in which any decent trout would have a hard time turning around. I mopped my brow and looked at my watch and figured I could still fish the evening rise below if I abandoned this foolish enterprise and made tracks. Yes, I'd turn around and flee this malarial bog.

Just then a slight breeze came up—I swear it was a miracle— and I heard the faint but unmistakable sound of distant running water, not a trickle, not the gentle splash of a little dam, but the dull steady moan of a considerable volume of falling water. Again I squatted in the rubber boat and paddled away and in a half-hour came to a beautiful live beaver dam, at least eight feet high, from where I sat crouched in the boat below and, it seemed, at least a hundred feet long. It was a gorgeous thing.

When I had excitedly clambered up the crisscrossed beaver cuttings and finally stood on the mud-packed crest of the vast dam, trembling like a girl, I felt like Magellan or somebody beholding a new continent. The dam was loaded to the scuppers, leaking over the top in some places, and backing up a beautiful expanse of mysterious deep water as far as the eye could see. Low ridges of jack pine fringed either side. The whole thing appeared to lie in a broad ancient beaver meadow, the dry margins still being lined with old water-killed trees reaching their rigid empty branches beseechingly into the air. It was plain that untold generations of beaver had dwelt and built their dams at this spot.

From this, and the occasional weathered old workings that I saw mixed with the fresh cuttings, I was pretty sure I was standing on the same old upper beaver dam blasted out years before by "those damned game wardens." The only trouble was that the oblivious beaver had ignored the fact that a dam in that place was officially *verboten*. Alas, they'd surely be arrested for violating . . . As I stood gaping, an exploring grasshopper foolishly lit on a sun-dried cutting near me. I caught and tossed him out in the dam. There was a quick swirl and a chunky trout whammed Mr. Grasshopper and flashed down and away. Hm. . . . Peering, I could see the wavering outline of a broad network of criss-crossed logs lying deep under water. The plot thickened.

Purely in the interest of science I rigged up my rod, tied on a number 12 Slim Jim—a quick-sinking wet fly—and pasted her out. *Clap!*—and I was onto a twelve-inch brook trout. Standing there in one spot on the dam in the blazing sun I took ten plucky brook trout running from ten to thirteen inches—missing twice that number—before my conscience smote me and I took down my rod. I sat and cleaned my fish, whistling while I worked, and then had my last can of beer to celebrate my new discovery. I then tossed my rubber boat over the dam, gave my bulging woven nylon creel a final loving pat, and pushed on. By then I couldn't stop and by that time, too, the sun was slacking off, and as I paddled upstream the trout were beginning to rise as far as I could see, some of them appearing larger than any I had taken or pricked. A pair of herons rose in noisy haste and flapped away in undulant flight. Ah, what a beautiful, isolated spot, I mused, delighted as a kid who had wandered into a fairy toyland.

from Trout Madness (*1960*)

I had not got two hundred feet above the splashing waters of my wondrous new dam before I heard something that made me nearly fall out of the boat—*the roaring rush of high-speed auto traffic!* Had mighty Magellan gone in circles and merely rediscovered Spain? I held my paddles to listen. There m-must be some mistake, I told myself, sick with dismay.

There wasn't. Another car rushed by, stridently sounding its horn. Frantic now with mingled curiosity and concern for my new dream spot, I paddled upstream in the lengthening shadows through one of the most dramatic rises of brook trout I had seen in years, the primeval calm of the spot being broken only by the ever-nearing roar and clash of car traffic and wailing horns. The combination of pristine peace and screeching mechanical din was positively weird. And in Heaven's name how, in this day and age, could there be such fabulous fishing within a stone's throw of a public speedway?

Up, up I went, like a man possessed, through perhaps a half-mile of sporty but narrowing water with lovely trout dimpling all around me. The invisible rushing cars now seemed to be practically alongside me. Pretty soon the dwarfed creek narrowed and shallowed to a rivulet so that I could no longer row. Shrugging like one of Roger's resourceful Rangers I got out and splashed upstream, dragging the boat by the anchor rope. Shortly the ridges narrowed, grown tight with jack pines, and I got into a series of shallow and intensely cold gravelly feeder springs. I then knew that I was at the headwaters of Moose Creek. But precisely where in hell was *that?*

By now it was getting dusk and I was running out of towing water, so I philosophically took my paddles apart and stashed them in my packsack, shouldered my boat, and sloshed up the dwindling main channel. All the time I could still hear the Sunday traffic rushing mildly by. A quarter of a mile of this and my creek became a mere trickle, so I veered left toward the car sounds and, with all the airy grace of a man carrying a folded double mattress, fought my pregnant rubber boat up through the thick spruce and tamarack to the jack pine on top of the ridge. There I rested and heaved and blew and mopped the sweat away and sneaked a reassuring look at my glistening trout—and longed for a beer. Then I heard the mutter of voices close by. Leaving my boat and pistol and packsack hidden in the jack pine I walked toward the voices and in no time came out into an opening—and upon a whole family of Sunday blueberry pickers, complete with picnic hampers, parked Chevrolet, and Grandma.

"Hello," I said, peering engagingly through my damp and sweat-matted locks.

The nearest picker, a kneeling, butt-sprung lady clad in revealing if scarcely becoming tight slacks, wheeled and squealed and nearly dumped her pail of berries. She stood regarding me in moist horror, as though she had seen a ghost emerge from the woods. I didn't much blame her. Another unseen car rushed by.

"Hello," I repeated. "I've been out looking for berries and I guess I got a little mixed up," I partially lied. "What road is that?" I said, motioning toward the sounds of traffic.

By this time a red-faced, perspiring man, presumably the lady's husband, quickly moved up to defend her be-slacked virtue from the hot maniac emerged from the swamp. I repeated my suave falsehood as he squinted an appraising eye at me. "The traffic you hear is on the main road between Ishpeming and Gwinn, on Highway 35," he answered warily. "You're right at the Moose Creek turn off." I blinked and shook my head at that, for I had just come over the same road on the way out fishing, and was therefore less than three miles from my car. And after all those years I was charmed to learn, for the first time, that since the dawn of man—or at least since the last glacier—my creek had always described a gigantic U. My chum kept staring skeptically at me. "What kind of berries you lookin' for in hip boots, fella?—cranberries? And what's in the bulging creel?"

Touché! I had forgotten to cache the telltale creel. I blushed prettily and piled on another whopper. "Oh, that . . . wa-water lilies! Yep, been out gathering water lilies, too . . . wife's crazy about 'em

. . . got all tangled up in that awful swamp." I tittered a trifle hysterically and waved vaguely at my New Spain. "Don't ever go near it," I warned darkly. "Full of snakes and things." The lady of the slacks sidled away from me as from a crazed leper. "Look," I rattled on, swerving abruptly from water lilies and reptilian swamps, "how would you like to make yourself a fast two bucks—and have a coupla cold beers to boot?"

"Hm . . . *cold* beer? How do you mean?" he parried, devoutly rolling his eyes and moistening his lips and stroking his chin. Plainly I was now talking his language.

"For driving me over to my car on Moose Creek—at Camp Alice. What do you say?"

I think the visions of the cold beer rather than mere money turned the trick; in a half-hour I was back at the fish car and had loaded down my pal with cool foaming goodies and his cab fare and sent him on his way. As he started to drive away he leered out the window of his car, winked, and fired this parting shot: "Those are certainly the gamiest-smellin' water lilies I ever smelt, fella. If I was you I'd go clean 'em off down in the creek!"

I grinned and waved as he gunned the Chev away, and then sat down on the running board of the fish car and opened a heavenly cold beer. "A-a-ah . . ." I looked up and saw a thin slice of yellow moon. I held up the beer. "You've had a busy day, little man," I whispered. "Fish, drink, and be merry—for tomorrow we must cut the grass. *Skoal!*"

Back-Yard Trout Fishing

It was one of those warm, soft, luminous summer evenings; the kind that commands fishermen to go forth and then makes them yearn for time to stop in its tracks. The sky was big and high and gloriously aflame, and the fanning shafts of sunlight sifting through the far-off piles of clouds looked like the very organ pipes of Heaven. I had stolen away after supper to get an hour or two of the evening rise on one of the nearby trout ponds. The old Model-A Ford and I were bumping along nicely down through the aquarium-green tunnel of an unkempt grove of second-growth maples, about three miles from my chosen pond, when—*pow!*—I had a flat, so I drew over bumpety-bump to the side of the dirt road, cursing softly as a stevedore.

Here was a nice kettle of no fish. If I stopped to change the tire I'd have little time left over for fishing, and if I hiked it, even less. What to do? I stood looking around. Hm ... that bald "selectively" logged hill to the left looked vaguely familiar. ... Then I realized that I was only about a quarter of a mile from Klipple Pond, a shallow and dying old mud puddle left from the ruins of an ancient beaver dam. I hadn't fished there since I was a kid. Should I give it a visit for old time's sake? The trout fishing in it used to be very good, yes, but that was true nearly everywhere in those distant days. Then there were dark rumors, too, that the pond had been dynamited and netted in recent years; and, anyway, none of the really *good* fishermen ever fished there any more or even mentioned the place. After all, how could a fisherman in his right mind expect to catch a decent trout these days less than nine miles from town, and only *six* miles by crow flight? Perish the thought.

Thus did I consider and mentally damn old Klipple Pond. I sighed and reached for the tire irons and then paused. *Must* I spend this enchanted evening wrestling with a flat? Here I had a night out and was dying to fish (I hadn't for a whole twenty-four hours!), so I shrugged and instead dug out the necessary tackle and gear and locked the car. At least I might as well go *look* at the place. . . . In less than ten minutes I had slipped and skidded down the old needle-covered deer trail on the steep root-lined hill and was standing on the soggy and twilit-margin of the old pond. Time had not stopped in its tracks; the organ pipes had disappeared.

The old pond lay in a deep glacial bowl scooped from between abrupt wooded hills. In the closing dusk its shallow waters looked as delicately thin and blue and uninviting as dairy milk in the bottom of a porridge bowl. It was the same old pond, all right: still no bigger than a small skating rink; still dotted with myriad islands of lily pads; still with the same old grass-grown water-logged raft that had once nearly drowned me still anchored to the near shore with the same weathered upright pole. Yes, and there was still the same dying sun shaded by the mixed spruce and maple hill across from me; still the same rhythmically persistent jungle drumming of the bullfrogs—*kwonky-kunk, kwonky-kunk!*—; and still the plaintive evening calls and ghostly dartings of the same mysterious birds whose names I had never sought nor ever cared to know. . . .

I sat there reflecting that under the surface of those placid waters endless battles raged, as fierce as any wars of men. Insects fought insects; bloodsuckers fought bloodsuckers, crayfish crayfish; salamanders salamanders; and all of them warred on each other; and the trout (if still there were any) fought all of them, all the while trying to avoid the fish ducks and gulls and kingfishers, the cranes and ospreys, and all the other swift dive bombers from out of the sky. And there was always the fear of the wily and undulant otter. And then, lo, a stray man now came along and sought to ensnare the trout with cunning little deceits contrived of feathers and fur. Yes, and he too was of the same species of lordly men who still stupidly fought each other days without end. . . .

I sat there reflecting that there was something ageless and timeless about a place like this; that it couldn't have changed much since the dawn of the world; that it would probably remain much the same after restless man, whose wisdom appeared unable to keep up with his brains, finally joined hands with his fellows and soared heavenward, propelled thence by the marvels of nuclear fission. Here, at this place, was primeval solitude: the patient unfolding pattern of a sublimely indifferent nature which doubtless regarded man as no more and no less important than a gnat.

As I sat there gripped by such lofty and poetic thoughts I heard the first splash. I crouched low and shaded my eyes against the waning sun and discerned an ever-widening wake not more than fifty feet out from me. Hm . . . Must have been a cavorting muskrat, I concluded, ready to flip my cigar pondward and flee the hungry mosquitoes. *"Plunk,"* it went again and this time—you've guessed it—I *saw* that it wasn't any mere muskrat at all, but the rise of a fine, careless, savage man-sized trout which was out after his supper and didn't give a tinker's damn who knew it.

With trembling hands I groped for my rod and clapped it together and threaded my line and tied on a leader and a pert little dry fly and teetered out a few feet in the muddy and treacherous ooze waiting for my ravenous friend to renew his challenge. All poetry, and mosquitoes were forgotten.

"Plash!" he went again, and by this time I became blissfully

aware of trout rises dimpling all over the pond. Roll-casting because of the halo of tag alders behind me, I began feeding out line to my near fish like a rodeo cowboy trying to lasso an escaping steer. Finally my stuff was out there, placed deliberately about ten feet to the right of him, so as not to put him down, and so that I might give it to him right on the nose the next time he rose—

"*P-lunk!*" he obediently rose, accepting the challenge, and I swiftly drew up the slack and rolled her like a hoop, the line rippling out like a fleeing serpent, the leader finally folding over, and the fly itself lighting upon the center of the feeding circle as gently as the wafted down of a thistle. There was a surge as my trout took it—*wham*—and I was on to him, fighting him, while all about me the frogs croaked—*kwonky-kunk*—, the birds darted and flashed and called, a ghostly owl hooted far up the valley, and the sun winked down out of sight. Then a fine rain started to fall. I stood there enthralled in the gathering gloom, my rod hooped and straining, the fisherman sunk in the ancient muck and ooze, ever so slowly fighting him up to the net. Give him line, take in line, come, darling, please come to daddy. . . . In ten ecstatic minutes—or was it years?—he lay gleaming in the net, as mistily colorful as a slice of rainbow robbed from the sky. Nearly a foot and a half in length he was, the loveliest native brook trout I had seen in many a year. And all this, believe it or not, within six miles of my own back yard!

It is seldom that rational men whistle when they must change a tire, especially in the rainy dark, but I know of one lunatic who did that night as he kept glancing up at the dripping creel of trout that sagged from the door of his car. . . . Since then my pal Henry and I have fished the old pond many times, but I must confess that never since have we found the trout as much on the prod as they were on that first magic night of rediscovery.

The unlikely old pond is truly enchanted; nowhere is it deeper than five feet, though the mud must go clean to Singapore. It crawls with bloodsuckers and the only fish in it are adult native brook trout. Even stranger, from opening day until about mid-season the place is teeming with trout; but along about the Fourth of July, as soon as the real summer heat comes along, they disappear as though someone had rung down a curtain or—worse yet—poisoned the pond overnight. The Lord only knows where or precisely why they go—but each spring at opening day they are back bigger and better than ever. There is a respectable inlet and a good outlet, and I keep promising myself that one day I must explore these unknown stretches, but my reason (sometimes the poorest of fishing guides) plus my aerial maps tell me there shouldn't be any decent open water anywhere near there. (But aerial maps can't show cool, deep, trouty beaver dams hidden away in the shade of enfolding trees.) At any rate, each year since then I give up the old puddle about mid-season and rattle off to other and greener pastures.

Perhaps next fall during bird or duck season I'll take my shotgun and my hip boots and explore the front and back doors of this queer old pond and try to discover where those smart trout go on their annual summer vacation. But perhaps that would spoil all the mystery of the pond; perhaps it is better to accept its favors humbly and without question; perhaps it is well to rest a lovely enchanted old pond that permits one to try for gallant and fighting native brook trout practically in one's own back yard.

Moral: Flat tire or no flat tire, pause once in a while in the summer madness of fishing; pause and take inventory and simply *make* yourself revisit some of those long-neglected and "fishless" old trout waters. There may be some big surprises in store. With me, at least, it has just about gotten so that my best and most exciting fishing is had at these forgotten old places that are totally ignored by those "smart" fishermen who day after day roar by them at top speed and, then, standing shoulder to shoulder like herd bulls, lash the more popular distant waters to a froth as foamy as an ad of their favorite beer.

Little Panama

My father, Nicholas Traver, was a tall man with big hands and the disposition of a bilious gnu. He was also the world's most successful saloonkeeper: that is, he hunted and fished all the time and only visited his saloon to raid the iron safe and cuss out the bartenders and lay in more hooch. He spent the rest of his time roaming the woods with his pal, old Dan McGinnis. Mostly he and Dan went to the favorite of his three camps, the South Camp.

Old Dan was a quick, wiry, mustached Scotch-Irish iron miner, turned trapper, who had violated the game laws so long and so well that they had finally given him a job and a star and called him a state trapper.

It was Dan's boast that he had never owned a game or fish license from the time, years before, when he had inadvertently stumbled into the county clerks's office and, not knowing just what else to do, had applied for a license. When the young man at the desk asked him the color of his eyes, he promptly replied, "Bloodshot," whereupon, Dan avowed, "the young whippersnapper commenced laffin' so hard he couldn't stop, so out I walks from the damn place, an' I ain't never been back. Of all the insultin' young bastards!"

Anyway, when Dan got to be a state trapper he was supposed to roam around the woods and trap wolves and coyotes and other predatory beasts; but when he got the star and the salary he quit trapping, and instead he and my father would go out to camp and fish and get a little drunk and play cards and argue.

My father and Dan would drive out of our back yard in the old buckboard with a barrel-bellied bay mare called Molly, the oats and a bale of hay in the back, a lantern clamped on the dashboard, and a battered water pail dangling from the rear axle. When they got to the gate my father, suddenly remembering, would call back to my mother. She would come hurrying out from the kitchen, wiping her hands on her apron, and quietly stand there on the back porch shading her eyes.

"We'll just be gone for the weekend, Bess," my father would say.

My mother would nod her head quickly and smile and wave her hand gladly, but sometimes when she turned away I noticed tears in her gray eyes. I guess it was because she knew that the weekend meant that she wouldn't see my father until the following Wednesday or Thursday, when they would return home for more food and whisky and beer, and then shortly depart once again "for the weekend."

But we boys said very little about my father being in the woods so much, because when he wasn't in the woods he was so crabby and bad-tempered that we wished he were. And he had two good bartenders, a Frenchman and a Cornishman, to run the saloon for him when he was gone. I have never in my life seen a man so crazy about the woods, about hunting and fishing, as my father. Unless it was old Dan McGinnis, the state trapper who wouldn't trap.

On my father's land there was a lake in which there were no fish. On the county map it was called Lake Traver, and I think my father was very proud of this—though he never spoke of it—because when they first came out with the big maps with Lake

46

Traver on them, he stuck one on the wall of the saloon, above the music box, near a gaslight, and made a big circle around his lake with a red crayon.

Lake Traver was the only body of water on his land. It was a deep glacial jewel, with its steep rocky banks on one side, above which towered straight Norway pine trees, their fallen needles lying thick on the moss-covered old rocks and in the crevices. The rest of the shore line was mostly wild cranberry marsh, with young cherry trees and poplars and maples reaching back to the pines. The lake was springfed, gravel-bottomed, without an inlet, and the water was very clear. It was always cool, even in the middle of the summer. But there were no fish.

From season to season my father and old Dan had planted barrels of brook trout in the lake—trout fry, fingerlings, even mature trout—but they were never seen again. Old Dan once suggested, during a feverish argument over this phenomenon, that the real reason the trout didn't survive was because they couldn't live in a lake owned by such a cantankerous, poisonous old buzzard as my father. But my father pounded the table and shook his head and shouted, "I'll make the bastards live in there yet." So the next spring would see him and old Dan lurching and tugging and cursing more cans of doomed trout into Lake Traver.

The funny part of it was that all they had to do was to hike over on almost any of the next forties, owned by the lumber company, and there the streams and ponds and beaver dams abounded with trout.

Just over the line, on the lumber company's land, in sight of my father's lake, was a big ancient beaver dam teeming with brook trout. My father tried to buy the land with the big beaver dam on it, but the lumber company wouldn't sell because there was a nice stand of young white pine coming along on it. They told him he could fish the dam all he liked, and treat it as his own, but they would not sell. So my father, overcome with humility and profound gratitude, roared at them to go plumb to hell. "You graspin' capitalist bastards!" The gnawing horrors of Wall Street were always a favorite theme of my father's.

My father was an independent man. He was in fact one of the most independent men I ever knew. And stubborn, too. He got so mad because he couldn't buy the beaver dam that he ceased to fish on any of the lumber company's land. Since they owned all the land for miles around his camp, this left him only his fishless lake to fish in. And he dearly loved to fish.

He couldn't somehow bring himself to believe there were no trout in his lake, despite the fact that old Dan, who could catch fish in a desert, had tried all kinds of bait, had flung flies all over the lake, and had even netted and dynamited to test the place, but nary a fish.

It really got pretty bad. He and Dan would hitch up old Molly and plod morosely out to camp for the weekend, and by and by, after a few preliminary drinks, old Dan would sneak over to the beaver dam with his fishing tackle, and then in a little while my father, cursing quietly to himself, would slip through the woods to his lake. There they'd be, in plain sight of each other, old Dan landing one beautiful trout after the other out of the beaver pond, and my father, no longer cursing quietly to himself, circling and circling his lake like a crazed water buffalo, his long legs buried in the cranberry marshes, wallowing and threshing, fishing like mad, with never a solitary rise.

Later, when they met back at camp, old Dan would cock his head sideways, comb his mustache with his fingers, and say, all pert and bright, "Have any luck today, Nick?"

"Hell, no. No bloody luck. They ain't risin' today. The wind ain't right—but I guess it'll change by night, Danny."

Then old Dan would dig in the damp grass of his creel and lay out the trout he had caught, smiling and allowing that the wind wasn't so bad over his way. "Let's build us a damn good drink, Nick," Dan might add, licking his mustache.

"Yes, Dan, we had a pretty hard day." My father would be staring at Dan's trout.

"You better come fishing with me tonight over on the beaver dam, Nick."

"You go high-dive to hell, you trespassin' ol' rum-pot," my father would say, stomping into the camp.

I knew that all this was going on because occasionally my father and old Dan would take me along, "for a fishing trip," they called it. My fishing consisted mainly of taking care of the old mare, Molly, front and rear; weeding the stunted vegetable garden— which my father evidently maintained to vary the diet of rabbit and porcupine—and of paring potatoes; filling lamps; hauling water and firewood; and making up the bunks.

And then there was the business of mixing those whisky sours for my father and Dan, which they never seemed to tire of. I learned to mix them before I learned to drink them. Whisky sours were one thing that my father and old Dan fully agreed upon. Never in my whole life have I seen two men who drank more whisky sours than my father and old Dan McGinnis.

It was on such a trip that the vision, the big solution, came to my father. It was a beautiful evening in the early spring, the trees were not yet in leaf, dusk was closing in, the whippoorwills had started, the mists were rolling up from the marshes. I had finished doing the supper dishes and had put fresh salt on the deer licks. Dan and my father were out fishing, old Dan as usual over at his beaver dam, my father gloomily stalking his lake. I was just getting out the fixings for the whisky sours.

Suddenly I could hear them shouting out there in the twilight, and then their stomping, and they burst into the camp.

"By the roarin' Jesus, Nick, I think you got it—*a canal's the thing!* We'll run the bloody beaver dam over into your lake—an' that'll freshen and change the water, jus' like you say—hell, an'— why then there'll be oodles of trout livin' at last in Lake Traver. Well, I'll be cow-kicked!"

My father seldom got excited unless he was drunk or mad. This night he was neither, but he was very excited. His eyes were shining and I saw how he must have looked when he was a boy.

"It come to me sudden-like, Dan," he kept saying in an awed voice.

He kept illustrating and waving with sweeps of his big hands how they would scoop out the canal and join the beaver pond to the lake; how they would build stop dams at either end to keep out the water while they were digging.

"Why, Dan—listen, Dan—we'll tell that bloody lumber company crowd to go run up a hemp rope." Then turning to me: "Son, mix up a mess of whisky sours—take one for yourself." And then I got excited, too, because it was the first whisky sour I ever had. It was not the last—not even the last that night.

Although it was only Monday and the weekend was barely half over, early the next morning we hitched up protesting old Molly and hustled her back to town. My father and old Dan could talk of and plan nothing but the new canal.

After that we didn't see my father around the house for days— not for a good part of the summer, in fact. The very day we got home, he and Dan visited all the saloons in town, rounding up out-of-work lumberjacks and thirsty bar flies to help dig the canal.

They bought boxes and boxes of dynamite, got secondhand scrapers and picks and shovels, and third-hand horses, and paraphernalia galore. With their motley crew they threw up a cook-shack and bunk-house tent—and then rooted and gouged and slashed away at their canal all the summer through. The leaves were tinted and falling, the fishing season was nearly over, when they had finally dug their ditch from the beaver dam over to Lake Traver.

All summer long fishermen came from miles around to view the proceedings; to watch my father, stripped to the waist, a fanatic with a shovel, throwing up vast clouds of dirt, shouting, sweating, straining at rocks—and at the same time carefully, tenderly feeding his sad-eyed bar-fly crew just enough whisky to keep them from deserting and yet not enough so that they would tumble into the ditch. He was foreman, engineer, laborer, wet nurse and all the rest, rolled into one.

And old Dan—here, there, and everywhere, like a hornet—cursing the teamsters, bullying the blasters, dispensing the drinks—occasionally falling into the ditch. But finally the great canal was dug and done and thirsting for water.

Labor Day was the big day, the grand opening. It seemed that half the town was lined up and down the big canal. My father had a bar set up along about the middle of the ditch. His two bartenders were there, aproned and sweating, working like mad serving free drinks. At noon my father got ready to fire his rifle, the signal for the blasters at each end of the canal to blow out the stop dams so that the prolific waters of the beaver pond would pour through the canal into the new trout paradise, Lake Traver.

As the noon hour drew near, everyone began to gravitate toward the middle of the canal. My father and old Dan stood out sort of in front of the rest, nearest the canal. Everybody was laughing and singing and talking.

Old Dan had a haircut and a red necktie for the occasion. He kept peering at a big silver watch and a soiled piece of paper which he held in his hand, clearing his throat. My father stood very tall and straight, his rifle ready in his hands. Then Dan raised his hand and glared at the crowd for silence. Squinting at the piece of paper which he held, he began to read, slowly and with dignity:

"This here is the dedication of Nick Traver's canal. We worked goddam hard on this here canal of Nick Traver's. You folks who is crazy about fishin' owe lots to the visions and leadership of my friend Nick Traver."

Dan turned to my father. "Let her go, Nick," he said, very quietly, and my father let her go, stepping back and handing the smoking rifle to me. Old Dan still stood peering at his watch. It took about half a minute for the short fuses to burn—the scampering blasters . . . and then two dull booms, practically together, and the stop dams were out. The hushed crowd pressed forward to the canal to watch.

For a moment nothing happened. Then we could hear a low rumbling roar, like distant thunder, growling and gathering; then we could see the water surging in from both directions in mighty waves, from the dam and from the lake, thundering, pounding, roaring and then—crash!—the two streams met in the middle of the canal, the ground trembled, and a great muddy wave burst high into the air, blotting out the sun like a typhoon, raining down all over—over Dan and my father, over me, the crowd, the bartenders, the whisky sours, over everything. And still the water roared in, hissing and boiling, while the dripping crowd stood there hunched and silent, like men at a lynching.

Then it happened. You could sense it before you could see it. There was an enormous flood of water coming from the lake, more and more and more, and then suddenly we saw—*we saw that the water was flowing in the wrong direction!* There was no mistake; it was roaring wildly past us from the lake into the beaver dam. We could see the dam rising and the lake lowering before our very eyes.

I looked at my father. He stood there dripping and mud-covered, shrunken-looking, his hair in his eyes, his mouth hanging open, watching the torrent pound into the beaver pond. Then we could see it before we could hear it, a cloud of earth and sticks and stones—it was war, a bombardment—then nothing but the pulsing surge of the water racing past us. And all the while my father and old Dan and the rest of us stood there, silently watching the fishless waters of Lake Traver emptying into the lumber company's ruined beaver dam. *The beaver dam had washed out.*

My father turned to me. He had closed his mouth. Looking like a little boy, he slowly wiped his muddy face with the back of his hand.

"Pa," I said very quietly, hoping the others would not hear. "Listen, Pa."

"What's that, son?"

"Pa, it looks like the whole trouble is your lake was higher than the beaver dam."

My father seemed to consider this. He pursed his lips and shook his head with little nods, thinking hard.

"Yes, son," he said finally, "it sure kind of looks that way."

Then someone tittered in the crowd. I heard it plainly. My father heard it too, for the look left his face in a flash, and he almost knocked me over as he leaped toward the crowd.

"Who done that?" he roared. "What dirty bastard done that?" He howled and danced before them, clutching out with his big hands, the veins standing out on his neck—a very bad sign. "I'll lick the hull mother-beating bunch of you!" he bellowed. The crowd gave ground as he advanced. "I don't give a rattlin' goddam for the hull snivelin' pack of you! I'll—"

Just then old Dan let out a whoop, and my father and everyone turned around just in time to see him sailing his big silver watch into the canal. He was acting like a drunken man in a beehive, leaping, laughing, cursing, shouting. He ran up to the boiling ditch, tore off his jacket, flung it in, turned and hollered, "Nick! Nick! It's a goddam swell idea—*a perfect swimmin' hole*!"

With that he took a mighty running dive, his thin legs crooked frog-fashion in the air, disappearing into the muddy water of the canal. My father and the rest frantically rushed up to save him. "Thar she blows!" someone hollered, just as old Dan came up spitting, snorting, splashing, looking like an aged walrus, threshing and trumpeting.

"Yoo hoo, boys!" he shouted, waving his hand. "Come on in—the water's fine!"

And, like the possessed swine of Gadara, every man jack of us, led by my father, went leaping pell-mell into what has been known, even to this day, as Nick Traver's Folly.

Paulson, Paulson, Everywhere

For many years I was district attorney of this bailiwick, and during that time I naturally had much to do with game wardens and, of course, with overzealous citizens who collided with the hunting and fishing laws. Indeed, I discovered some of my best fishing spots through these uneasy encounters; and while the following yarn is scarcely a fishing story, in any sporting sense, it *is* about trout and about some of the trout waters I found while plying my D. A. trade.

Up my way old township politicians never die; they merely look that way. Instead they become justices of the peace. It is a special Valhalla that townships reserve for their political cripples and has the following invariable rules of admission: The justice of the peace must be over seventy; he must be deaf; he must be entirely ignorant of any law but never admit it; and, during the course of each trial, he must chew—and violently expel the juice of—at least one (1) full package of Peerless tobacco. It is preferable that he speak practically no English, and that with an accent, but in emergencies an occasional exception is permitted to slip by. Sometimes I preferred the former.

I could write a lament as thick as this book about the grotesque experiences I have had trying justice court cases out before some of these rural legal giants. It is a depressing thought. Instead I shall tell you about the trial of Ole Paulson before Justice of the Peace Ole Paulson.

Ole Paulson of Nestoria township was charged with catching forty-seven brook trout out of season with a net. Ole Paulson was in rather a bad way because it is never legal to take or possess forty-seven brook trout in one day; to fish for them in any manner out of season; or ever to take brook trout with a net, in or out of season. Ole Paulson promptly pleaded not guilty and the case was set for trial before His Honor, Justice of the Peace Ole Paulson, also of Nestoria. I drove up there to try the case rather than send one of my assistants, not because I panted to sit at the feet of Justice Paulson, Heaven knows, but largely because I was dying to find out precisely where a man could ever *find* forty-seven brook trout in one place, regardless of how he took them. It was also a riotously beautiful September day, and afforded the D. A. a chance to escape from that personal prison he inhabits called his office.

"Vell, hayloo, Yonny!" His Honor greeted me as I entered his crowded courtroom, a high-ceilinged, plaster-falling, permanently gloomy establishment from which he ordinarily dispensed insurance of all kinds, assorted tourist supplies, game and fish licenses, live bait, not to mention various and sundry bottled goods and rubber accessories. "Ve vas yoost satting here vaiting for yew!"

"Was you, Your Honor?" I cackled gleefully, warming up disgracefully to this local political sachem, pumping his limp hand, inquiring about his rheumatism—or was it his flaring ulcers?—respectfully solicitous over his interminable replies, making all the fuss and bother over him that both he and the villagers demanded whenever the District Attorney came to town to attend court. It was understood that we two initiates into the subtle mysteries of the law had to put on a show for the groundlings.... The courtroom was crowded, every adult male in the community having somehow gathered enough energy to forsake the village tavern for a few hours and move across the street for the trial.

I turned to the People's star witness, the eager young game warden who had arrested the defendant. "Is the jury chosen yet?" I asked him in a stage whisper that must have been audible to a farmer doing his fall plowing in the next township. There could be no sneaky professional secrets in Judge Paulson's court—the penalty was swift and sure defeat.

"Yes," the game warden answered, "I struck the jury this morning. The list of jurors was prepared by Deputy Sheriff Paulson here. The six jurors are all here now."

It had not escaped my notice that I seemed to be getting fairly well hemmed in by Paulsons, but it was a trifle late to get into that now. I'd have to trust to the Lord and a fast outfield. I turned to Justice Paulson and said: "Very well, Your Honor, the People are ready to proceed with the trial."

"Okay den," His Honor said, rapping his desk with a gavel ingeniously contrived from a hammer wrapped in an old sock. He pointed to six empty chairs against a far wall. "Yantlemen of da yury," he announced, "yew vill now go sat over dare." Six assorted local characters scrambled for their seats, relaxed with a sigh, and were duly sworn by Justice Paulson. Allowing the jurors to sit for the oath was only one of his minor judicial innovations.

Justice Paulson, exhausted by administering the oath, opened a fresh package of Peerless and stowed away an enormous chew in his cheek. There was a prolonged judicial pause while he slowly worked up this charge. He spat a preliminary stream against a tall brass cuspidor. *"Spa-n-n-n-g!"* rang this beacon, clanging and quivering like an oriental summons to evening prayer. "Okay," His Honor said in a Peerless-muffled voice.

"The People will call Conservation Officer Clark," I announced, and the eager young game warden arose, was sworn, took the stand—and told how he had come upon the defendant, Ole Paulson, lifting the net from Nestoria creek just below the sec-

57

ond beaver dam in Section 9. "I caught him red-handed," he added.

"Do you have the trout and the net?" I asked the young warden, slyly noting the latitude and longitude of this fabulous spot.

"Oh, yes," he answered. "The net is in my car outside—and the trout are temporarily in the icebox in the tavern across the street. Is it okay if I go over and get them now?"

I turned to His Honor, "Your Honor, the People request a five-minute recess," I said.

Judge Paulson, moon-faced and entirely mute now from his expanding chew of Peerless, whanged another ringer, banged his homemade gavel on his desk and, thus unpouched, managed to make his ruling. "Yentlemen, Ay declare fi'-minoot intermissin so dat dis hare young conversation feller kin go gat his fish." He turned to a purple and bladdery bystander. "Sharley," he said, "go along vit him over an' unlock da tavern."

I gnawed restlessly on an Italian cigar while Charlie, the tavern owner and my sole witness, went across the street to fetch the evidence. The jury sat and stared at me in stolid silence. His Honor replenished his chew, like a starved Italian hand-stoking spaghetti. *"Whing!"* went the judge, every minute on the minute. A passing dog barked. The bark possessed a curious Swedish accent, not "woof" but *"weuf"*! I wondered idly whether "Sharley" and my man had got locked in a pinochle match when lo! they were back, the flushed tavern keeper appreciatively licking his moist chops over the unexpected alcoholic dividend he had been able to spear. The jury watched him closely, to a man corroded with envy. The young officer placed the confiscated net and a dishpan full of beautiful frozen brook trout on the judge's desk and resumed the witness chair.

"Officer, you may state whether or not this is the net you found the defendant lifting from Nestoria creek on the day in question?" I asked, pointing.

"It is," the officer testified.

Pointing at the fish: "And were all these fish the brook trout you removed from the net?"

"They were."

"Were the fish then living?"

"About half. But they were nearly done in. None would have survived."

"How many are there in the pan?"

"Forty-seven."

I introduced the exhibits into evidence and turned to Judge Paulson. "The People rest," I said.

"*Plink!*" acknowledged Judge Paulson, turning to the defendant. "Da defandant vill now race his right han' an' tell da yury *hiss* side of da story." It was not a request.

Ole Paulson was sworn and testified that it was indeed he who had been caught lifting the writhing net; that he had merely been patrolling the creek looking for beaver signs for the next trapping season when he had come across the illegal net; that the net was not his and was not set by him; and that he was just lifting the net to free the unfortunate trout and destroy the net when, small world, the conservation officer had come along and arrested him for his humanitarian pains. "Dat's all dare vere to it!" he concluded.

I badgered and toyed with the witness for several minutes, but it was an unseasonably hot September day and I could see that the fans were anxious to get back across the street to their hot pinochle games and cool beer, so I cut my cross-examination short. In my brief jury argument I pointed out the absurdity of the defendant's story that he was out prowling a trout stream in mid-September looking for beaver signs for a trapping season that opened the following March. I also briefly gave my standard argument that every time a game violator did things like this he was really no different from a thief stealing the people's tax money—that the fish and game belonged to *all* the people. . . . The members of the jury blinked impassively over such strange political heresy.

"*S-splank!*" went Judge Paulson, scoring another bull's-eye.

Had any man moved carelessly into the crossfire he would have risked inundation and possible drowning.

The defendant's argument was even briefer than mine. "Yantleman of da yury," he said, rising and pointing scornfully at the fish net. "Who da hecks ever caught a gude Svede using vun of dem gol-dang homemade Finlander nets? *Ay tank you!*" He sat down.

"*B-blink!*" went the Judge, banishing the jury to the back room to consider their verdict.

The jury was thirstier than I thought. "Ve find da defandant *note gueelty*!" the foreman gleefully announced, two minutes later.

"*Whang!*" rang the cuspidor, accepting and celebrating the verdict.

After the crowd had surged tavernward, remarkably without casualty, I glanced over the six-man jury list, moved by sheer morbid curiosity. This was the list:

Ragnar Paulson
Swan Paulson
Luther Paulson
Eskil Paulson
Incher Paulson
Magnus Carl Magnuson

I turned to Deputy Sheriff Paulson. "How," I asked sternly, "how did this ringer Magnuson ever get on this jury list?"

Deputy Paulson shrugged. "Ve yust samply ran out of Paulsons," he apologized. "Anyvay, Magnuson dare vere my son's brudder-in-law. My son vere da defendant, yew know!"

"*Spang!*" gonged His Honor, like a benediction. "Dat vere true, Yonny," he said. "My nephew dare—da deputy sheriff—he nefer tell a lie!"

I lurched foggily across the street and banged on the bar. "Drinks fer da house!" I ordered, suddenly going native. "Giff all da Paulsons in da place vatever dey vant!"

The Haunted Pond

When I was a kid there were no bass or German browns in our lakes
and streams and, as nearly as I can recall, few if any rainbows.
When a man said he was going fishing he meant he was going fishing for brook trout. Our waters were loaded with them. Then along
came the bass. The advent of these sea monsters was greeted with
shouts of wild delight by the bored native fishermen; here at last
was *really* a big fighting fish; and soon throngs of sleepy fishermen
were up all hours of the night greeting overdue trains, gaily acquiring assorted calluses and hernias as they unloaded can after can of
wriggling government bass fry and fingerlings into waiting buck-
boards and Model-T Fords and rushed them out and dumped them
into our lovely trout waters. It still makes me shudder to contemplate the fumbling midnight horror of this picture.

Needless to say, most of these fishermen lived to regret their
hot haste; and again needless to say, much of our good trout water
was permanently usurped by the bass and eventually ruined for *all*
fishing. It is only in comparatively recent years that state-directed
poisoning programs have removed the bass from some of our nat-

ural trout ponds and lakes and retrieved these waters for the fish that really belong there. The bass-infested trout rivers and streams present another and more difficult problem, but in general it is perhaps fair to say that nature saw to it that the bass soon died out or became a negligible factor in the true trout streams, while those streams and rivers in which the bass have thrived were probably doomed as trout waters anyway.

I personally don't happen to care a whoop for bass fishing or bass; in fact I loathe it and them; but I have no quarrel with the queer people who do, only a sort of bewildered pity. My big gripe is that I believe bass should be confined to bass waters, and I weep and grit my teeth and see red when I find the ugly brutes fouling up and crowding out our vanishing trout waters.

The point is that for their own scaly sakes bass should not be planted in trout waters; they not only ruin the water for trout, but they themselves are ultimately doomed. It is now known that bass will thrive in these trout waters for the first few years, growing to huge and awesome dimensions, but by and by, after all of the rough natural food is consumed, they will inevitably languish and grow stunted so that nobody is happy, not even the dwarfed bass.

Alas, my own father was guilty of more than his share of planting bass in our trout waters. He lived to regret it and I have forgiven him much in this respect, but I have never rightly forgiven him for planting bass in the lovely natural trout waters we used to fish.

One spring my father got authentic reports that the Winthrop boys had been winter-fishing the brook trout out at old Blair pond. "Aha, I'll fix 'em," my father said, so he and my older brother Leo quick got a load of bass and dumped them into the pond. (Bass mud down in the winter in a kind of quasi-dormant stupor and cannot readily be caught, at least up in this part of the state where winter doesn't fool.) At the time I did not know anything about this terrible deed, but it would not have done any good if I had because my father was not the kind of man who discussed his decisions with any man; he simply announced them.

My father indeed thwarted the Winthrop boys, all right, but it was a clear case of cutting off his nose to spite his face, because in two years not a single trout could be taken from the pond and after that it began to yield up the biggest and ugliest bass it has ever been my displeasure to look in the eye. For several years I used to lure bass fishermen out there with their chests of hardware in a vain hope that they might somehow fish the devilish monsters out. Many huge bass were winched in, and by and by they did disappear, only to be replaced by a race of midgets; and it shortly got so that one could take a mature undersized bass on nearly every cast, so stunted and hungry had they grown. At last I realized that the old place had been permanently ruined for all fishing. I nearly wept.

I should like to digress here and comment briefly on the various theories that account for what it is that makes trout disappear when bass take over their waters. For disappear they certainly do. One simple theory is that the bass eat all the trout (except for the very largest trout, who ultimately roll their eyes and die of loneliness); another that the trout perish of internal flat tires from eating the tiny spike-backed bass fry; another that the bass starve out the trout by their swinish consumption of all available food. And there are doubtless other theories. I rather lean to the first theory, but I am willing to concede that the other things are probably contributing factors.

The only places I have ever seen bass and trout persist together are in those waters where the trout have an opportunity to get away from the bass to spawn and get their growth before they come back down to vie with the bass. Lorraine Lake in this county (with its various springs and deeps and shallows—and many inlets) is such a spot; all of which rather lends force to the theory that it is the bass eating the smaller trout that causes the latter's ultimate extinction and not the trout fatally eating the smaller bass. But to get back to my haunted and ruined pond.

Along about the summer of 1940, perhaps fifteen years after the bass were planted, I first met Dr. Albert Hazzard. He was and is director of the institute for fisheries research, a branch of the division of fisheries of the Michigan conservation department working in cooperation with the state university at Ann Arbor. Doc Hazzard is not only a scientifically trained fish man and a good one but, I soon discovered, a swell modest guy to boot. I cornered him and chokingly told him the sad and harrowing tale of Blair Pond. He said he'd like to look at the place as the state was keenly interested in reclaiming all and any good trout waters for public trout fishing. I quick glanced at my watch and said when.

One way and another it was the summer of 1941 before Doc and his boys got out to Blair Pond. They did their stuff—caught bass, tested for plankton and other food content, took temperatures, etc.—and the upshot was that Doc wrote me that while the bass were both stunted and diseased, the pond was "highly suitable for trout," a conclusion which did not astound me since I had caught scores of speckled beauties out of it when I was a kid. Doc went on to say that they would not be able to make their poison survey until the following August, following which they could then poison out the bass and restock with trout within a month or so. He wound up his letter with these magic words: ". . . and there should be some trout fishing as early as 1943." I let out a whoop and turned three handsprings and went fishing.

Then along came Pearl Harbor, which unsettled more than fishermen, and I was not surprised when Doc wrote me the following June that the government had frozen all stocks of fish poison (rotenone) for the duration. However, there was one note of hope: Doc promised to complete the survey that summer so that the pond would at least be up near the top of the list when and if the stuff again became available. Thus were the villainous bass reprieved until the war ended.

In the autumn of 1946 Doc's boys (now mostly ex-G.I.'s) marched back and poisoned out the pond, but it developed that the first post-war poison released to the state was far too weak, and everything but a few minnows managed to weather the Borgia blitz. The thing was necessarily put off until the following year. In 1947 the question of poisoning out the pond struck a new snag over the further question of public access to the pond, once it was poisoned out and restocked. The objection was most reasonable so I swallowed my disappointment and cheerfully helped Doc and the conservation department to clear up this snag. Then in 1948, lo and behold, Doc's boys came and re-poisoned the pond and restocked it with nice clean little trout. At long last the thing was done.

I deliberately avoided the place until the 1950 season and I can best summarize the situation I then found by quoting from a letter I wrote Doc:

> You will be interested to receive a progress report on Blair Pond. I fished it this year for the first time since the planting. The first time I fished it I found both dams in good shape and the water well up. There were no rises and a short interval of worm fishing produced nothing. Last Saturday I tried it again with flies, spinning lures and finally, in desperation, with worms. Sitting on the rock part of the dam on the lower pond my partner finally got a good bite but missed the strike. Hearing his shout I joined him from the upper pond and threw in my porkchop and got a good bite and hooked the fish. It was an 11-inch brook trout full of fight and unusually heavy for its length. I would say it went three-quarters of a pound and was very "deep-chested" and literally hump-backed with flesh. There was no evidence of lice in the gills. A few minutes later my partner hooked and landed a slightly larger brook trout, and a few minutes later while retrieving my hook a heavy trout nailed the almost bare hook and after a splendid fight (I was using a bare fly hook, fine leader and fly rod) I landed a beautiful brook trout that went exactly 13 inches and was as plump as a partridge and must have weighed a pound and a half, most unusual for a trout that length.
>
> Yesterday I returned with 2 friends. There was a high wind which made fishing difficult and we finally settled down to worms. Right off the bat we caught 2 trout, both about 11 inches

and both unusually plump and full of fight. The flesh was salmon pink on all the trout. We saw no rises although both days should have produced rises towards evening. Yesterday we caught 3 shiners, and I can only conclude that they worked up over the bottom dam or else came out of some slough above. The beaver had dammed one of the two small inlets, one of the dams being practically at the edge of the lake and I am wondering if this will interfere with spawning.

We saw literally hundreds of minnows from an inch and a half to two inches but were unable to catch any although we chose to think they looked and behaved like trout fry. I am simply delighted with the way the trout appear to have taken hold although I am a little puzzled by the lack of rises. If you or your boys are up this way this summer I think it would be interesting to do a little seining to see how many survived the original planting. Certainly those that did are in excellent shape and there is every evidence that they will be propagating.

Little did I realize that I was whistling my way past the cemetery.

Doc replied, thanking me for my report and stating that he was "disturbed" by my report of the small minnows, as he suspected that they were young chubs or shiners and not trout fry. Following the 1950 trout season I wrote Doc partly as follows:

The place now has me baffled. In May, as I wrote you, we took five beautiful fat brooks, 11 to 13 inches, but all on bait. During the summer I haunted the place and never took or saw another trout—on bait or otherwise. There are hundreds of what we call shiners. The place is loaded with them. I did not see a single authentic trout rise. I fished late and early, on the surface and on the bottom and in between. In July we hauled a boat in there and scoured the place. Surface temperatures averaged 70 degrees. This occurred after a comparatively warm spell. We could not locate, from surface temperatures, the springs you once found during your surveys.

I am afraid the place may be one of those early and late season places, but the thing that dismays me most is my inability to see or attract a trout at or near the surface. Bait fishing leaves me cold. . . . If you get up here next summer I hope you and I can go and take a look. The boat is still there—and few fishermen appear to have been near the place. If we hadn't caught those five beauties I'd swear there were no trout in there.

Doc wrote back that he would personally make a check in the summer of 1951. This we did—and our nets showed that the ponds were infested with hundreds of chubs, shiners and suckers—but nary a trout. Doc concluded that the rough fish had survived and come in from tiny spring feeders above. That fall Doc's boys again poisoned out the ponds—and all feeders—and not a single trout showed up. *We had caught the only 5 trout that survived the 1948 planting of several thousand fish!* By then I was about ready for the gas pipe—but I reckoned without Doc Hazzard.

The pond was again poisoned out and replanted in the spring— a monument to the persistence and vision of Doc Hazzard. I have resolved not to fish there for several years—and then—so help me, following the first trout I take on a fly I swear I'll swallow a fifth of Old Cordwood and jump in with my clothes on. For that will be a day. And I wish my old bass-loving father could be there to see it.

The Intruder

It was about noon when I put down my fly rod and sculled the little cedar boat with one hand and ate a sandwich and drank a can of beer with the other, just floating and enjoying the ride down the beautiful broad main Escanaba River. Between times I watched the merest speck of an eagle tacking and endlessly wheeling far up in the cloudless sky. Perhaps he was stalking my sandwich or even, dark thought, stalking me. . . . The fishing so far had been poor; the good trout simply weren't rising. I rounded a slow double bend, with high gravel banks on either side, and there stood a lone fisherman—the first person I had seen in hours. He was standing astride a little feeder creek on a gravel point on the left downstream side, fast to a good fish, his glistening rod hooped and straining, the line taut, the leader vibrating and sawing the water, the fish itself boring far down out of sight.

Since I was curious to watch a good battle and anxious not to interfere, I eased the claw anchor over the stern—*plop*—and the little boat hung there, gurgling and swaying from side to side in the slow deep current. The young fisherman either did not hear me or, hearing, and being a good one, kept his mind on his work. As I sat watching he shifted the rod to his left hand, shaking out his right wrist as though it were asleep, so I knew then that the fight had been a long one and that this fish was no midget. The young fisherman fumbled in his shirt and produced a cigarette and lighter and lit up, a real cool character. The fish made a sudden long downstream run and the fisherman raced after him, prancing through the water like a yearling buck, gradually coaxing and working him back up to the deeper slow water across from the gravel bar. It was a nice job of handling and I wanted to cheer. Instead I coughed discreetly and he glanced quickly upstream and saw me.

"Hi," he said pleasantly, turning his attention back to his fish.

"Hi," I answered.

"How's luck?" he said, still concentrating.

"Fairish," I said. "But I haven't raised anything quite like you seem to be on to. How you been doin'—otherwise, I mean?"

"Fairish," he said. "This is the third good trout in this same stretch—all about the same size."

"My, my," I murmured, thinking ruefully of the half-dozen-odd barely legal brook trout frying away in my sunbaked creel. "Guess I've just been out floating over the good spots."

"Pleasant day for a ride, though," he said, frowning intently at his fish.

"Delightful," I said wryly, taking a slow swallow of beer.

"Yep," the assured young fisherman went on, expertly feeding out line as his fish made another downstream sashay. "Yep," he repeated, nicely taking up slack on the retrieve, "that's why I gave up floating this lovely river. Nearly ten years ago, just a kid. Decided then 'twas a hell of a lot more fun fishing a hundred yards of her carefully than taking off on these all-day floating picnics."

I was silent for a while. Then: "I think you've got something there," I said, and I meant it. Of course he was right, and I was simply out joy-riding past the good fishing. I should have brought along a girl or a camera. On this beautiful river if there was no rise a float was simply an enforced if lovely scenic tour. If there was a rise, no decent fisherman ever needed to float. Presto, I now had it all figured out. . . .

"Wanna get by?" the poised young fisherman said, flipping his cigarette into the water.

"I'll wait," I said. "I got all day. My pal isn't meeting me till dark—'way down at the old burned logging bridge."

"Hm . . . trust you brought your passport—you really are out on a voyage," he said. "Perhaps you'd better slip by, fella—by the feel of this customer it'll be at least ten-twenty minutes more. Like a smart woman in the mood for play, these big trout don't like to be rushed. C'mon, just bear in sort of close to me, over here, right under London Bridge. It won't bother us at all."

My easy young philosopher evidently didn't want me to see how really big his fish was. But being a fisherman myself I knew, I knew. "All right," I said, lifting the anchor and sculling down over his way and under his throbbing line. "Thanks and good luck."

"Thanks, chum," he said, grinning at me. "Have a nice ride and good luck to you."

"Looks like I'll need it," I said, looking enviously back over my shoulder at his trembling rod tip. "Hey," I said, belatedly remembering my company manners, "want a nice warm can of beer?"

Smiling: "Despite your glowing testimonial, no thanks."

"You're welcome," I said, realizing we were carrying on like a pair of strange diplomats.

"And one more thing, please," he said, raising his voice a little to be heard over the burbling water, still smiling intently at his straining fish. "If you don't mind, please keep this little stretch under your hat—it's been all mine for nearly ten years. It's really something special. No use kidding you—I see you've spotted my bulging creel and I guess by now you've got a fair idea of what I'm on to. And anyway I've got to take a little trip. But I'll be back— soon I hope. In the meantime try to be good to the place. I know it will be good to you."

"Right!" I shouted, for by then I had floated nearly around the downstream bend. "Mum's the word." He waved his free hand and then was blotted from view by a tall doomed spruce leaning far down out across the river from a crumbling water-blasted bank. The last thing I saw was the gleaming flash of his rod, the long taut line, the strumming leader. It made a picture I've never forgotten.

That was the last time ever that I floated the Big Escanaba River. I had learned my lesson well. Always after that when I visited this fabled new spot I hiked in, packing my gear, threading my way down river through a pungent needled maze of ancient deer trails, like a fleeing felon keeping always slyly away from the broad winding river itself. My strategy was twofold: to prevent other sly fishermen from finding and deflowering the place, and to save myself an extra mile of walking.

Despite the grand fishing I discovered there, I did not go back too often. It was a place to hoard and save, being indeed most good to me, as advertised. And always I fished it alone, for a fisherman's pact had been made, a pact that became increasingly hard to keep as the weeks rolled into months, the seasons into years, during which I never again encountered my poised young fisherman. In the morbid pathology of trout fishermen such a phenomenon is mightily disturbing. What had become of my fisherman? Hadn't he ever got back from his trip? Was he sick or had he moved away? Worse yet, had he died? How could such a consummate young artist have possibly given up fishing such an enchanted spot? Was he one of that entirely mad race of eccentric fishermen who cannot abide the thought of sharing a place, however fabulous, with even *one* other fisherman?

By and by, with the innocent selfishness possessed by all fishermen, I dwelt less and less upon the probable fate of my young fisherman and instead came smugly to think it was I who had craftily discovered the place. Nearly twenty fishing seasons slipped by on golden wings, as fishing seasons do, during which time I, fast getting no sprightlier, at last found it expedient to locate and hack out a series of abandoned old logging roads to let me drive within easier walking distance of my secret spot. The low cunning of middle age was replacing the hot stamina of youth. . . . As a road my new trail was strictly a spring-breaking broncobuster, but at least I was able to sit and ride, after a fashion, thus saving my aging legs for the real labor of love to follow.

Another fishing season was nearly done when, one afternoon, brooding over that gloomy fact, I suddenly tore off my lawyer-mask and fled my office, heading for the Big Escanaba, bouncing and bucking my way in, finally hitting the Glide—as I had come to call the place—about sundown. For a long time I just stood there on the high bank, drinking in the sights and pungent river smells. No fish were rising, and slowly, lovingly, I went through the familiar ritual of rigging up: scrubbing out a fine new leader, dressing the tapered line, jointing the rod and threading the line, pulling on the tall patched waders, anointing myself with fly dope. No woman dressing for a ball was more fussy. . . . Then I composed myself on my favorite fallen log and waited. I smoked a slow pipe and sipped a can of beer, cold this time, thanks to the marvels of dry ice and my new road. My watching spot overlooked a wide bend and commanded a grand double view: above, the deep slow velvet glide with its little feeder stream where I first met my young fisherman; below a sporty and productive broken run of white water stretching nearly a half-mile. The old leaning spruce that used to be there below me had long since bowed in surrender and been swept away by some forgotten spring torrent. As I sat waiting the wind had died, the shadowing waters had taken on the brooding blue hush of evening, the dying embers of sundown suddenly lit a great blazing forest fire in the tops of the tall spruces across river from me, and an unknown bird that I have always called simply the "lonely" bird sang timidly its ancient haunting plaintive song. I arose and took a deep breath like a soldier advancing upon the enemy.

The fisherman's mystic hour was at hand.

First I heard and then saw a young buck in late velvet slowly, tentatively splashing his way across to my side, above me and beyond the feeder creek, ears twitching and tall tail nervously wig-wagging. Then he winded me, freezing in midstream, giving me a still and liquid stare for a poised instant; then came charging on across in great pawing incredibly graceful leaps, lacquered flanks quivering, white flag up and waving, bounding up the bank and into the anonymous woods, the sounds of his excited blowing fading and growing fainter and then dying away.

In the meantime four fair trout had begun rising in the smooth tail of the glide just below me. I selected and tied on a favorite small dry fly and got down below the lowest riser and managed to take him on the first cast, a short dainty float. Without moving I stood and lengthened line and took all four risers, all nice firm brook trout upwards of a foot, all the time purring and smirking with increasing complacency. The omens were good. As I relit my pipe and waited for new worlds to conquer I heard a mighty splash above me and wheeled gaping at the spreading magic ring of a really good trout, carefully marking the spot. Oddly enough he had risen just above where the young buck had just crossed, a little above the feeder creek. Perhaps, I thought extravagantly, perhaps he was after the deer. . . . I waited, tense and watchful, but he did not rise again.

I left the river and scrambled up the steep gravelly bank and made my way through the tall dense spruces up to the little feeder creek. I slipped down the bank like a footpad, stealthily inching my way out to the river in the silted creek itself, so as not to scare the big one, *my* big one. I could feel the familiar shock of icy cold water suddenly clutching at my ankles as I stood waiting at the spot where I had first run across my lost fisherman. I quickly changed to a fresh fly in the same pattern, carefully snubbing the knot. Then the fish obediently rose again, a savage easy engulfing roll, again the undulant outgoing ring, just where I had marked him, not more than thirty feet from me and a little beyond the middle and obliquely upstream. Here was, I saw, a cagey selective riser, lord of his pool, and one who would not suffer fools gladly. So I commanded myself to rest him before casting. "Twenty-one, twenty-two, twenty-three . . ." I counted.

The cast itself was indecently easy and, finally releasing it, the little Adams sped out on its quest, hung poised in mid-air for an instant, and then settled sleepily upon the water like a thistle, uncurling before the leader like the languid outward folding of a ballerina's arm. The fly circled a moment, uncertainly, then was caught by the current. Down, down it rode, closer, closer, then—*clap!*—the fish rose and kissed it, I flicked my wrist and he was on, and then away he went roaring off downstream, past feeder creek and happy fisherman, the latter hot after him.

During the next mad half-hour I fought this explosive creature up and down the broad stream, up and down, ranging at least a hundred feet each way, or so it seemed, without ever once seeing him. This meant, I figured, that he was either a big brown or a brook. A rainbow would surely have leapt a dozen times by now. Finally I worked him into the deep safe water off the feeder creek where he sulked nicely while I panted and rested my benumbed rod arm. As twilight receded into dusk with no sign of his tiring I began vaguely to wonder just who had latched on to whom. For the fifth or sixth time I rested my aching arm by transferring the rod to my left hand, professionally shaking out my tired wrist just as I had once seen a young fisherman do.

Nonchalantly I reached in my jacket and got out and tried to light one of my rigidly abominable Italian cigars. My fish, unimpressed by my show of aplomb, shot suddenly away on a powerful zigzag exploratory tour upstream, the fisherman nearly swallowing his unlit cigar as he scrambled up after him. It was then that I saw a lone man sitting quietly in a canoe, anchored in midstream above me. The tip of his fly rod showed over the stern. My heart sank: after all these years my hallowed spot was at last discovered.

"Hi," I said, trying to convert a grimace of pain into an amiable grin, all the while keeping my eye on my sulking fish. The show must go on.

"Hi," he said.

"How you doin'?" I said, trying to make a brave show of casual fish talk.

"Fairish," he said, "but nothing like you seem to be on to."

"Oh, he isn't so much," I said, lying automatically if not too well. "I'm working a fine leader and don't dare to bull him." At least that was the truth.

The stranger laughed briefly and glanced at his wrist watch. "You've been on to him that I know of for over forty minutes—and I didn't see you make the strike. Let's not try to kid the Marines. I just moved down a bit closer to be in on the finish. I'll shove away if you think I'm too close."

"Nope," I answered generously, delicately snubbing my fish away from a partly submerged windfall. "But about floating this lovely river," I pontificated, "there's nothing in it, my friend. Absolutely nothing. Gave it up myself eighteen-twenty years ago. Figured out it was better working one stretch carefully than shoving off on these floating picnics. Recommend it to you, comrade."

The man in the canoe was silent. I could see the little red moon of his cigarette glowing and fading in the gathering gloom. Perhaps my gratuitous pedagogical ruminations had offended him; after all, trout fishermen are a queer proud race. Perhaps I should try diversionary tactics. "Wanna get by?" I inquired silkily. Maybe I could get him to go away before I tried landing this unwilling porpoise. He still remained silent. "Wanna get by?" I repeated. "It's perfectly O.K. by me. As you see—it's a big roomy river."

"No," he said dryly. "No thanks." There was another long pause. Then: "If you wouldn't mind too much I think I'll put in here for the night. It's getting pretty late—and somehow I've come to like the looks of this spot."

"Oh," I said in a small voice—just "Oh"—as I disconsolately

watched him lift his anchor and expertly push his canoe in to the near gravelly shore, above me, where it grated halfway in and scraped to rest. He sat there quietly, his little neon cigarette moon glowing, and I felt I just had to say something more. After all I didn't *own* the river. "Why sure, of course, it's a beautiful place to camp, plenty of pine knots for fuel, a spring-fed creek for drinking water and cooling your beer," I ran on gaily, rattling away like an hysterical realtor trying to sell the place. Then I began wondering how I would ever spirit my noisy fish car out of the woods without the whole greedy world of fishermen learning about my new secret road to this old secret spot. Maybe I'd even have to abandon it for the night and hike out. . . . Then I remembered there was an uncooperative fish to be landed, so I turned my full attention to the unfinished and uncertain business at hand. "Make yourself at home," I lied softly.

"Thanks," the voice again answered dryly, and again I heard the soft chuckle in the semidarkness.

My fish had stopped his mad rushes now and was busily boring the bottom, the long leader vibrating like the plucked string of a harp. For the first time I found I was able gently to pump him up for a cautious look. And again I almost swallowed my still unlit stump of cigar as I beheld his dorsal fin cleaving the water nearly a foot back from the fly. He wallowed and shook like a dog and then rolled on his side, then recovered and fought his way back down and away on another run, but shorter this time. With a little pang I knew then that my fish was done, but the pang quickly passed—it always did—and again I gently, relentlessly pumped him up, shortening line, drawing him in to the familiar daisy hoop of landing range, kneeling and stretching and straining out my opposing aching arms like those of an extravagant archer. The net slipped fairly under him on the first try and, clenching my cigar, I made my pass and lo! lifted him free and dripping from the water. "Ah-h-h . . ." He was a glowing superb spaniel-sized brown. I staggered drunkenly away from the water and sank anywhere to the ground, panting like a winded miler.

"Beautiful, *beautiful*," I heard my forgotten and unwelcome visitor saying like a prayer. "I've dreamed all this—over a thousand times I've dreamed it."

I tore my feasting eyes away from my fish and glowered up at the intruder. He was half standing in the beached canoe now, one hand on the side, trying vainly to wrest the cap from a bottle, of all things, seeming in the dusk to smile uncertainly. I felt a sudden chill sense of concern, of vague nameless alarm.

"Look, chum," I said, speaking lightly, very casually, "is everything all O.K.?"

"Yes, yes, of course," he said shortly, still plucking away at his bottle. "There . . . I—I'm coming now."

Bottle in hand he stood up and took a resolute broad step out of the canoe, then suddenly, clumsily he lurched and pitched forward, falling heavily, cruelly, half in the beached canoe and half out upon the rocky wet shore. For a moment I sat staring ruefully, then I scrambled up and started running toward him, still holding my rod and the netted fish, thinking this fisherman was indubitably potted. "No, no, no!" he shouted at me, struggling and scrambling to his feet in a kind of wild urgent frenzy. I halted, frozen, holding my sagging dead fish as the intruder limped toward me, in a curious sort of creaking stiffly mechanical limp, the uncorked but still intact bottle held triumphantly aloft in one muddy wet hand, the other hand reaching gladly toward me.

"Guess I'll never get properly used to this particular battle stripe," he said, slapping his thudding and unyielding right leg. "But how are you, stranger?" he went on, his wet eyes glistening, his bruised face smiling. "How about our having a drink to your glorious trout—and still another to reunion at our old secret fishing spot?"

These Tired Old Eyes . . .

These tired old eyes have beheld some fairly strange sights during the years they have guided this fisherman on his trout devotionals. Sometimes I suspect that fishermen while practicing their favorite vice are peculiarly well situated to observe nature with her hair down. Perhaps it is the very intentness and detachment of fishermen during their seizures. Perhaps their obliviousness to all but the business at hand somehow communicates itself to the rest of the forest and water dwellers so that they in turn are lulled into going about their normal pursuits with a calm they would rarely possess under the conscious search and scrutiny of the hunters or professional bird and animal watchers. At any rate fishermen are at least suffered if not accepted by the wild things of nature; and if they, the fishermen, would but look away more often from their fishing they would doubtless observe even stranger sights than they do. Here are some droll sights and experiences, just a few, that I have run across in my addled wanderings after trout.

On several occasions I have come upon a mother porcupine prone on her back nursing her young, a unique position which I have heard that the females of these prickly animals likewise maintain while begetting them—though my quill is somewhat uncertain on this latter point.

While on a fishing trip that I have mentioned elsewhere I have seen a skunk swim leisurely across a broad river, its tail arched proudly so as to keep its powder dry. I have also come upon rabbits and groundhogs nestling up in trees, an arboreal environment not normally associated with these creatures.

I have watched a pair of otter slip up over a beaver dam and assault and boldly gut the place of its trout while I stood there unarmed and helpless, trying vainly to drive them away with the few rocks I could find. It was a blitzkrieg and a harrowing spectacle to watch. One undulant otter patrolled the upstream escape outlet, flashing back and forth at incredible speed, while the other robber did the real dirty work, both chomping their jaws horribly each time they came up for air. Creation of panic and their lightning speed seemed to be their chief weapons. It was then that I learned thoroughly to loathe otter; so much so that I refuse to succumb to the obvious pun that there otter be a law against otter. If they would *only* confine their depredations to bass I'd start breeding them . . .

This was the same strange season that I swear I caught more birds and insects and assorted reptiles and flying things than trout. A typical entry follows:

"Caught a dragonfly on a 16 Trude on my back cast out at Frenchman's Pond. Kept pumping away at the forward cast and nothing happened, a creepy feeling. Looked back and there was the dragonfly, himself pumping away like mad, trying vainly to drag my fly and flyline in the opposite direction. Put down rod, donned my rubber gloves, and performed minor surgery before order was restored. Dr. T. Wellington Cole scrubbed with me. Suspect this may be as much evidence of the nearsightedness of dragonflies as a tribute to the expertness of my fly-tier."

This same thing happened *three* times that same season; though it never happened before and hasn't since. That enchanted summer

I also caught two bats and two unknown birds on my back casts, a swooping swallow-like bird on my forward cast, and three frogs, a fish duck, a snapping turtle and two garter snakes in the water. Toward the end of that season I find this wistful entry: "Must remember to start a zoo. It'll have everything but fish!"

On another expedition Gunnar Anderson, Tom Bennett, and Gipp Warner and I boated up the Big Dead basin. All of us were hilarious and feeling no pain. We put in at the eerily squawking heron rookery near the mouth of Wahlman's Creek to try for the big brook trout that sometimes lurk there. Long time nothing. Then I finally snubbed on to a fair trout on a sunken hair fly. Gunnar netted him and dressed him out and cast the entrails overboard, chortling, "This will bring the big ones around." Then he reached over to rinse off the trout. The trout slipped out of his hand—*pop*—and *swam* gracefully and deliberately down out of sight! We looked at each other wide-eyed and soberly weighed anchor and got the hell out of there. I know a little something about the possibility of muscular spasms, instinctive reactions, and habit responses and all that, but don't *ever* let it happen to you!

Here is another odd one for the book:

"At 5:30 this morning took a nice 13-inch brook at the high sand-bank-bend on the East Branch. Number 12 McGinty, dry. Had court that day so reluctantly quit at seven. Cleaned out my trout at gravel ford by washed-out bridge. Found partly digested bait hook in gut of largest trout. Met Gipp in town that morning and, since he and I fish that stretch a lot, started to tell him about finding hook. He stopped me and said: 'You caught the fish at the high sand bank, didn't you? He was over twelve inches. The hook was an eagle claw, about number 8, snelled, with red wrappings, with about two inches of leader left above the shank?' He paused. 'My wife lost that fish at 9:30 last night.'"

It was the same fish, of course, but the point is that a trout started feeding again within such a few hours after such a harrowing experience (contrary to many fish dopesters) and further, that during that short time he had nearly digested a hook that would loom relatively the size of a whale harpoon in our own bellies. Small wonder that the more one fishes for trout the less he pretends to know about them.

Here is an entry from my fish notes:

"My old fishing pal, Louie Bonetti, took me on another of his celebrated goose chases, this time down the Fifteen Hill Creek. 'Are you *sure* I can fly fish down there, Louie?' I cross-examined him carefully before we started, still smarting over past wild-goose expeditions led by the dauntless and irrepressible Louie. 'Sure, sure t'ing, Yon,' Louie grinned, 'you can fly lak ever't'ing!' He was right. We hadn't proceeded a hundred yards through this jungle before I realized wryly that the only way to properly present a fly in that creek was to fly over and drop it from a balloon. I could hear Louie ahead of me, threshing along like a bull elephant in must, pausing here and there to drop his bait into the murky waters. It was like trying to fish in a green barrel. After ruining one leader and losing three flies I shrugged philosophically and folded my rod and creeled my net and bowed my head in defeat. I longed only to get out of there. I had been taken again. . . .

"'Yon!' Louie shouted. 'Luke at dis! Come queeck, luke at dis!' I finally crashed into a clearing big enough to accommodate a telephone booth, and there was Louie proudly holding a ten-inch brook trout he had just taken on a big nightcrawler. From the mouth of the still-wriggling trout protruded four inches of another trout's tail! As I watched, Louie pulled on the tail and extracted what was left of a seven-inch trout! A cannibalistic ten-inch trout had eaten—or was eating—a seven-inch trout, and still had found the greedy appetite and room to cram Louie's porkchop bait on top of that! 'W'at you tink?' Louie asked me. 'Me, I think it's time for a drink,' I said, reaching in Louie's knapsack for his trusty pint bottle."

Another day Louie Bonetti and I were boating up a remote stretch of the Middle Escanaba, when hawk-eyed Louie spotted a little spotted fawn lying amongst the water-worn rocks that lined the exposed shore line below a high tangled bank. We assumed that it and its mother had come down for a drink or for respite from flies, so we went merrily on our way, the discovered fawn watching us out of sight with its soft liquid eyes. Many hours later, floating back down in the dusk, we saw that the fawn was still there. I was about to shrug and float on but Louie insisted that we put in. "*Non, non,* we stop. Somet'ing goddam a wrong a dis place, Yon," he said.

There was. As we approached the shore the fawn stood up on its spindly, wavering legs and bleated in terror, at the same time pulling out to the end of a chain which anchored a large double-spring trap, the rusty jaws of which we discovered were clamped tightly across the right foreleg just above the exquisite tiny hoof. I held the trembling creature from plunging while Louie tenderly released the jaws of the trap. We then carried the bleating fawn up the high bank and set it upon level ground. It continued to bleat and cry piteously. "Ma-a-ma!" it called. "Whew," answered the unseen mother from deep in the woods. *"Whew, whew!"* we could hear her thudding back and forth in the thick cover, running in quick thumping nervous trots.

The fawn took a few tentative limping steps in the direction of the woods and then *ran* on all *four* legs to join its mother, bleating gaily. Louie and I grinned and nodded and resumed our twilit float down the misty Escanaba, both of us swollen with virtue over the good turn we had done an otherwise doomed fawn.

"Damma dose coyote trappers," Louie swore darkly. "Why dey leave a dose set trap lay 'round for poor little fella catcha his foot in?" *This* burst of sentiment was from a man who had shot more deer than most men have ever seen. . . .

On still another day Louie and I were fishing a rather tangled but productive brook up near Silver Lake. When we met back at the car at dusk, a puffing and breathless Louie announced he had just met a "beeg" black bear on the trail. Louie, who always acted out everything that ever happened to him, crouched down on all fours.

"I coma down trail an' ducka my head under t'ick bush lak a dis—an' w'en I stan' up dere's dis beeg blacka bear stan' right dere on front of me—so close I can see even his little red eyes lak peeg, an' smell his bad breat'."

"What'd you do, Louie?" I said, wondering how the lucky bear ever got away from Louie.

"Hm . . . Wan time I hear some place, I dunno, some people he say if man say somet'ing to wile animal he liable get scare an' run lak a hell."

"Yes?" I prompted.

"Well, dis a here beeg black bear he stan' dere an' luke at me an' I stan' dere luke at him—so den I queeck remember w'at I hear. '*Say* somet'ing, Louie!' I t'ink. So I tip my hat lak dis, real polite, an' smile real nice an' I say reala loud, 'Gooda mornin', Mister Bear!'"

"What'd the bear do?"

"Hm . . . he get scare lak da people say an' run lak a hell nudder way."

"What'd you do, Louie?"

"Hm . . . Louie he *stay* awful scare an'run lak a hell dis a way. . . . Boy oh boy, le's have da beeg drink!"

To attempt to do justice to this rare man Louie would require a five-foot shelf of books. *Everything* happened to Louie—including the final awful day two autumns ago when the bullet from an old friend's deer rifle unerringly found its way into Louie's belly. Louie had been mistaken for a deer. He died the next morning and the whole county went into mourning. But the saga of Louie Bonetti will cling to his name for many years. I can only faintly suggest the pungent flavor of the man here.

Perhaps the most moving woods spectacle I have ever seen while fishing happened several years ago and the record of which I quote from my fishing notes:

"Yesterday on Loon Lake I saw the unfolding of a thrilling and saddening forest tragedy. I was prowling the north side of the lake when suddenly I heard a great commotion and squawking from the southwest corner, nearly a half-mile away. Looking I saw a wild duck and a great loon engaged in battle. It was a case of David versus Goliath, the little duck seeming to be the aggressor. I quickly put my binoculars on them. I cannot describe the fierceness of the combat; the incredible darting swiftness of it. At length the duck retreated, the loon following, the duck skeetering just over the top of the water as though wounded, always *just* out of reach of the pursuing loon. Then the truth dawned on me: this was a mother duck doubtless protecting her young and putting on the ancient lame-duck act. At any rate, the loon suddenly submarined and the duck, at the real risk of her life, still kept skeetering, flapping the very surface of the water, luring the loon on and away from her young, whose terrified cheeping now came thinly across the water. I never did see the young ducks. At length the mother duck rose in flight, and almost immediately the great loon popped out of the water where the duck had just been. The duck circled in low flight back to her young. She banked and skidded into a little bay and the terrified cheeping ceased.

"In the meantime I had ignored my fly and it had sunk to the bottom. I flipped the line to raise it—and was on to a good trout. While I was preoccupiedly landing this fish the loon returned to the ducks, and the very same battle ensued, except that this time the loon showed signs of giving up the pursuit and returning to the young. At this the lion-hearted mother duck again made a fierce frontal attack on the loon and again enraged it into following her virtually across the lake. And once again the loon rose from the water just as the duck lifted into flight and circled back to her young. Then I felt my rod bending and remembered I was on to a fish, my first trout on flies in tantalizing Loon Lake. I landed it. It was a plump fighting thirteen-inch brook. But I had lost all zest for fishing. I just sat and helplessly watched the distant drama, longing for a rifle to plug the bullying loon. Although the loon stalked the ducks all afternoon, schnorkeling in close, it evidently lacked the heart to again mix with the brave mother duck. At sundown I quietly folded my tent and stole away. There was no rise."

A few days later I returned, this time with a high-powered rifle with a scope sight. This is my entry for that day:

"Saturday back at Loon Lake I saw and heard a *pair* of loons giggling and cackling and diving, but no sign of the ducks. I fear the worst, namely, that the loons either ganged up and killed the gallant mother duck or else chased her away (though I think not) and ate her young. Certainly the young could not very well have flown or walked away. [NOTE: Since writing this I have indeed met a mother duck and her young walking along on land.] I was tempted to shoot the loons, but I was not sure there had been a murder or that they were the murderers. Anyway I was apparently too late. And, moreover, who was I to judge their guilt or appoint myself their executioner? I did not know that loons ate flesh, besides, possibly, fish, but now I am afraid they do. . . ."

Here I lapsed into a little gratuitous philosophizing which I shall throw in for good measure.

"The constant obscure savagery of nature seems always to lurk below the apparently placid surface of things. Probably even the lice on the loon's wings battle each other, while I know that the fish swimming below dwell in a subterranean welter of cannibalism. How can men hope for peace when combat and strife, not peace and calm, seem to be the basic norms of nature? In a real sense, then, peace is an unnatural state and all the elaborate plans of men to achieve it are, in this sense, in plain perversion of nature. Alas, peaceful men may be *unnatural* men, a fairly bleak prospect in the Atomic Age."

Spots Before the Eyes

Fishermen are a cultured and worldly lot; their broad and diversified interests make them delightful and even absorbing companions; they'll talk about anything under the sun so long as it concerns fishing—preferably with themselves in a stellar role. They take a trout's-eye view of the world and see everything darkly through their own wavering, distorted, astigmatic lens of broken beer bottles. Spots and speckles dance constantly before their eyes. When they aren't fishing they gabble and prattle about fishing much as clusters of idle women run on about babies and clothes—and the witch-like tendencies of *other* women. So it is that the following grab bag of trout prejudice and gossip concerns itself not so much with actual fishing as with the trivia of fishing, like the chatter of earnest boy scouts who temporarily forsake the solemn business of tying bowlines and rubbing dry sticks together, to sit around the campfire and compare the various wrenches and reamers and other burglar tools that adorn their respective scout knives. On with the small talk.

Outdoor Fish Fries: The flesh of the trout is a rare delicacy that comes from one of nature's most tender and perishable creatures.

Trout were never designed to be embalmed along with the steaks and ox joints of the aristocracy of the new Ice Age in their well-larded deep freezers. Trout should be eaten not later than twenty-four hours after they are caught, else one might better eat damp swamp hay crowned with chain-store mayonnaise. But by far the best time to enjoy your trout is beside the waters where they are caught. Take a fry pan along and some bacon or shortening, and a little cornmeal and salt, and have yourself a feast fit for a deposed king—or an ulcerated millionaire. But first take a trout. . . .

Competition in Fishing: A trout stream is a poor place for gambling and much of the reflective charm of fishing is lost by making a surly competition out of the undertaking. I will have no part of a fishing party made up of those fishing prima donnas whose very manhood seems to depend on being top rod. Yet my regular trout pals and I have worked out a standing wager on our fishing, and far from making us surly it is surprising how much added zest and friendly fun this adds to our sport. Anyone that does get surly about it is fired out of the lodge. This is our bet: we each pay the winner a dollar for the longest trout over twelve inches. The loser's ante jumps to two bucks a head if the longest fish goes fifteen inches or over.

The net result of this is good; we find ourselves more and more frequently returning a lot of legal-sized trout we might otherwise have kept; and when we meet and decide to quit "in just five minutes more" there is always the delicious uncertainty and the long chance that the Mister Tanglefoot of the day will make one last desperate cast and—*whambo!*—walk away with the honors. It has happened. Frequently, of course, no fish qualify, but there have been times when three or more of us have had to get out our calipers and crouch to see just who had won the two-dollar bet. These occasions have usually involved lunking browns or rainbows, but it has also happened with brooks.

Trout Sense: There is no substitute for fishing sense, and if a man doesn't have it, verily, he may cast like an angel and still use his creel largely to transport sandwiches and beer. I have friends whom I can mechanically outfish in practically every department of the sport yet who in their comparatively crude way still manage to tie into any big trout that happen to be lying about. They also continue regularly to relieve me of my wrinkled dollar bills. Then again I have fishing friends—several of them holders of enviable casting records—who can in turn outfish me in nearly every department but who sometimes even more sadly than I seem to lack that indescribable sixth sense that guides the flies of some fishermen into the very jaws of lurking "soakers."

Without growing mystic over this, some men seem to "think like a fish" more than others. They are the smart ones who can take one look at a pool or a riffle and sense immediately where to pause and plop their sloppy, ill-delivered casts, when all the while we Fancy Dans are posturing grandly over here or over there, unerringly sending out long whistling dramatic casts over the favorite lies of old tomato cans.

Once in a blue moon a fisherman comes along who combines this mysterious fish sense with superb casting ability and all the rest. I have known one or two of these diabolical fellows. He is the magician we other fishermen should take up collections for in order to persuade *him* to take up golf. There is no other way to keep the trout away from him. He can catch fish in a rain barrel. My current fishing pal, Henry Scarffe, is fast moving into this class. Some men are said to have sex appeal; *these* characters possess trout appeal, and I swear that many a happily married lady trout will forsake even her snug spawning bed to succumb to his lure. He is also the suave one who makes all the rest of us pedestrian fishermen look like slipping and fumbling political hacks out taking creel census in borrowed waders.

Glass Rods: I am now reluctantly satisfied that glass fly rods are mechanically the equal of and perhaps often perform better than the best bamboo rods. Not only that, they are more reasonable in price; require little or no care; and apparently last forever. I'll concede all that, but never will I let another glass fly rod darken my door. Put it down, if you will, to a burst of girlish sentiment of the heart or middle-aged sediment on the kidneys—I'll take split bamboo. To my mind there is no fairy wand in creation more graceful and beautiful than a good bamboo fly rod. They *look* so good; they *feel* so good. Like fingerprints, no two bamboo rods are alike; each is an individual possessed of its own unique character and one that a fisherman can really get to know.

But these gleaming impersonal glass rods that some chemist has conceived in a laboratory out of skimmed milk and old box tops, these synthetic concoctions that are turned out on an assembly line as much alike as two peas in a pod, simply aren't for me. I'd sooner cast over glass *fish* than use one. I love my bamboo fly rods and I choose to think they have a sneaking yen for me. But I'm afraid I can never quite fall in love with a chemist's incestuous brain child. In short 'tis a pox I wish on all glass rods. (Adv.: I'll sell you a dandy for five bucks.)

Creels: Conventional bulging wicker creels are handy to carry beer in, and they also look nice and woodsy when freshly varnished and hanging from the wall of a den. Aside from that they are clumsy, brush-snagging, foul-smelling nuisances. Get yourself a *flat*, loose-meshed matting creel, one that will nicely accommodate your landing net for travel or brushy going. If you *must* remain a slave to synthetics, then get a flat plastic one, damn it. Either variety is easily washable and thus does not attract the sea gulls and blow-flies for miles around.

Simple Refrigeration: One of those tightly covered round popcorn tins the kids keep trundling home together with some of those little cans of solution you pre-freeze solid in your icebox (and use over and over) make a non-messy and fine combination for cooling beer and keeping perishables. They are also nice to preserve that big trout you bought from Julius the guide to prove to your wife you were not out wading with squaws or dallying with blondes.

Guides on Fly Rods: They're way too small and they should be made of chromium or some other bland non-abrasive metal. I believe as many fly lines are ruined by the constant sawing and rasping through these niggardly conventional fine-wire snake guides as are ruined by the twin plagues of mildew and improper storage. Since there are from nine to thirteen of these wizened hacksaw guides on the average fly rod, I sometimes suspect that the line and rod people must have conspired to continue using them. I have a seven-foot glass combination spinning and fly rod, and when fly fishing with it—I rarely do—I use a lovely torpedoed-in-series Marvin Hedge silk fly line. In places where I can get a decent backcast verily I believe I can paste out nearly as much line in a controlled cast as I can with my best bamboo fly rod. Part of this is due to the rippled torpedo feature, no doubt, but a good part I believe is due to the larger, smoother, free-running spinning guides. At any rate I can really shoot the cast. Next winter I'm going to try an experiment and have a set of spinning guides put on one of my bamboo fly rods. Perhaps I'll still shame these unimaginative and smug medieval fly-rod makers into following suit.

On Getting Lost: If you are really lost and it is dusk, build a rough camp and compose yourself until the thundering horde comes to find you. Most people seem to display a morbid sort of missionary zeal in finding lost brethren. Conserve your matches for smoke signals. If it is still daylight follow a trout stream, if you are on or near one, and you should soon come to a broad trail beaten by the army of faithful fishermen. More lost men come to grief from panic and exhaustion than anything else. Remember, when you are lost you are only temporarily in a state that was permanent to your hardy ancestors. Keep your chin up and your temperature down, and above all use your head before your legs.

An obvious clue overlooked by many confused fishermen is secondary roads and trails. If a road or trail you are following forks off into two or more roads or trails, you may safely conclude that you are going the wrong way and that "civilization" lies the other way. All roads and trails fork off *away* from home plate. Simply follow the point of the V. Think it over. . . . Again, if you see car tracks on a road with water puddles you can easily tell the direction the car has gone by the tire marks. The tracks are visible entering the puddle but become obliterated by the splashing cargo of water as they leave. Follow the car. If it has gone to camp it shouldn't be far; if it has gone to town, that's for you, too. And if, while following the tracks, you come to a fork, you can also thus confirm which way the car was heading, town or woodsward.

Leaders: Leaders are the problem child of fishing; they are far and away the weakest weapon in the fisherman's arsenal. All leaders are necessarily an uneasy compromise between the fisherman's normal desire to hold a decent fish if he gets on to one and his awareness that it is neither sporting nor productive of rises to employ a logging chain. Theoretically a leader should be invisible, and the only way to approach this diabolic goal is to keep using finer leaders. The main drawback with this strategy, however, is that the finer the leader the less liable it is to survive the initial shock of the strike; yet, *once a fish is on*, it is surprising how much strain even the finest leader can stand.

I have found a simple way to lessen this frequently fatal initial impact on fine leaders and, good fellow that I am, I pass it on to you. It is especially good on still clear waters where one must employ hair-thin leaders. It is this: Simply affix a common rubber elastic band between the end of your fly line and the butt end of your leader. It's the neatest little shock-absorber on the market. Think it over—and then go forth and try it.

Not only does this stratagem help with the initial shock but it also helps greatly to reduce the danger of loss in play during those thrilling moments when you discover that your fish is heavier than you bargained for and it is touch and go whether you can hold on to him at all.

Slow Intermittent Rises: For good fishing give me these any time over the boiling and dramatic general rise. The latter is apt to be highly selective, and especially so on still waters. When trout are choosy every fly in the kit is apt to be the wrong one or else the right one is spurned if it is not presented and handled in precisely the right way. On the other hand a fairly steady but intermittent riser usually represents a fish gnawed by hunger and one more likely to snaffle any interesting morsel that drifts within its ken. Another thing, an occasional riser seems to range farther from his lie for food than does a rapid feeder on a particular fly hatch; hence the fisherman's cast need not be so delicately exact.

I remember a pair of such slow risers one evening at dusk on a deep, narrow run on the East Branch of the Escanaba. They were rising so seldom I almost passed them by. At first I tried approaching them from below but could not get within decent casting range because of brush and deep water. The approach from upstream was better but since they lay at the loop of a sharp double curve, the difficult slack-line downstream dry-fly float was not feasible. It looked as if I would practically have to go pat them on the nose to decently present a fly.

I did just that. I appproached them warily from above, the only way I could, inching along with infinite caution. When one would rise I'd move another foot closer. Finally they stayed down so long I thought I had put them down for good. Then both rose simultaneously. So, with scarcely more line out than twice the length of my rod, I dapped, not floated, a dry fly above the top riser. He immediately rose and nailed it. I powered him away from his cousin and fought him to net with only the leader showing. Without moving I tried the same strategy with the second riser—and also tied into him on the first try. They were a nice pair of fighting brook trout, but I perhaps wouldn't have had a Chinaman's chance to take either of them if they hadn't been hungry, less careful, and quite nonselective in their diet.

Another time I maneuvered for hours, it seemed, to get in casting position below a big intermittent riser on the Middle Branch. His lie was one of the many fisherman's headaches—inshore and directly under some low-lying tag alder branches—but I still saw a faint chance to float in a morsel over him. It was a delicate situation; one sloppy cast or false move would surely drive him down. In my mind's eye I could see him lying there just above me, fanning away and avidly watching everything, owly with hunger.

I concluded I had to do it on the first try or fail; it was all or nothing. So I made my false casts, back and forth, back and forth, measuring and calculating like a perspiring diamond cutter about to split a fabulous gem. Then, just as I released the business cast, the fly ticked a protruding tag alder twig and dropped like a sash weight, striking the water—*spat*—about four feet *below* my fish. Before I could let out an anguished yelp—or do anything else—that fish literally turned a somersault around and lunged downstream, nailing the fly. All hell couldn't have gotten it away from him! After a thrilling tussle amidst the awful tangle of half-submerged tag alder boughs I finally brought him to net. He was a monster brown with a yawning cannibalistic head like a tarpon. Part of his tail still stuck up out of the net, he was that big. And I *didn't* put him back. But the point is that I no more deserved to catch that fish than, I feel, I deserved to fail to catch so many others I have stalked and presented the fly to perfectly—only to have them spurn my most adroit and gorgeous offerings.

One-Man Boats: Most so-called one-man boats designed for trout fishing on inland waters could be better employed in harpooning whales off the storm-lashed coast of Newfoundland. These craft are usually far too big and heavy. Indeed, the average man would be hard put to trundle their *oars* any distance. And their designers evidently think that fly-fishermen mount and employ a windlass to crank in their trout; at least they build their monstrosities accordingly. In fact these builders possess a positive low genius for not knowing what in hell they're doing. The requirements for a one-man trout boat are few and simple: it should be small, light, safe, silent, and easily portable. But try and find one.

There are some new light metal one- and two-man boats seeping into the market that are in all respects the candy rig except for two bad features—they cost nearly their weight in gold and, worse yet, they make too damn much noise. Either the fisherman is forever accidentally banging the thing with his paddle or the varying water pressures are bulging and buckling the metal hide. *"Clank, clunk!"* I have a spendthrift friend, proud fellow, who possesses a new one, and a gleaming thing it is. The only trouble is that his clanging progress along a trout stream or pond sounds not unlike that rural legal giant, Justice of the Peace Paulson, whanging away at his tall brass cuspidor. Remember? All the terrified trout for miles around promptly go down and stay down. Now when we two go a-boating for trout I usually spend half my time getting to hell away from him.

I have three fishing boats: a light canvas-covered duck boat that I occasionally use on placid trout ponds; then a sturdy nine-foot cedar boat that I use on rougher ponds and lakes and rocky rivers and also when I use my fishtail propeller; and then an eight-foot rubber boat with twin inflatable bladders, sort of like pregnant hot dogs laid end to end. This last is my pet and is the best all-around one-man trout boat I have ever seen. (Isn't it nice that I like my equipment?) It is light, safe and silent; I can easily carry it and my fishing gear a quarter or half mile, inflated, if the going isn't too thick; and if it is I can deflate and pack it in and then inflate it with a hand pump or air cartridge. It is tough (I bought it way before the War) and has never once snagged or punctured.

I always prefer to wade when wading is feasible but so much of our glaciated country possesses such suicidally unwadable waters that I think my best fishing waters would be reduced by at least half if it weren't for my faithful old rubber boat. I have waded certain stretches of our rivers right up the middle and been only ankle deep, while only a few yards away yawned deep watery craters large enough to engulf a cathedral, pigeon guano and all, and leave not a trace. In fact I suspect some of them do harbor sunken cathedrals because on quiet evenings I sometimes seem to hear the stifled pealing of far-off watery bells. . . . At any rate, these hidden river caverns may be nice hiding places for big fish but they're rather wearing on the nerve ends of big wading fishermen.

The only trouble with my rubber boat is that it is getting pretty battered and old and leaky—like its skipper—and the first money I get ahead I'm going to send and get me an exact duplicate. It's strictly a honey and when this book is hatched and flutters soundlessly upon a heedless world I at least expect to be invited by the maker to pose for a sleek portrait in *Field and Fen* endorsing his brand of rubber sausage. "Folks," I'll say, "I've rid and spun around in and cursed this here now tough old sausage for nigh on to—" It'll be a labor of love.

The Strangest Trout Spot in My World: Of all the many weird places I know that harbor trout the Old Springhole on the Whitefish River in Alger County is the strangest of all. It is a veritable lake, a quarter-mile long and deep, set down in the middle of a shallow river and fed winter and summer from both sides by gushing ice-cold springs that tumble down out of steep crumbly limestone ledges. Both banks are crowded to the edges by a jungle of tangled cedars. It is a devil of a place to get a boat into and nine devils of a place to fly fish without a boat. There is one little fifty-foot catwalk of limestone on one side that a good roll-caster might cast from, provided he were only as tall as a midget. I once tried it on my knees and, in that prayerful attitude and doubtless due to divine intervention, was rewarded by taking a lovely trout.

Bait-fishermen naturally haunt the place, and on a good day the woods along both banks bristle with their protruding steel girders, much like the peering artillery of rival troops lined up for point-blank fire. I once came upon an old peg-legged local character who had hacked a hole in the jungle through which he was thrusting his girder, lowering a seven-inch fish into the inky water.

"Just ketch one?" I said, making low fish talk.

"Naw," he replied. "That's my bait. Can't ya see it's a chub?"

Lo, it *was* a chub. "Y-you mean you use *that* for bait?" I gasped incredulously.

"Damn right I do!" he snapped. "Caught a twenty-two-inch brook yesterday with a helluva bigger chub." He squinted up at me in my diving suit and endless paraphernalia. "And how many like *that* do *you* ketch with them there goddam little house moths?"

I gulped and fought my way on downstream.

In the July or August dog days when the temperatures rise and the water levels go down, all the big trout for miles around seem to congregate in this fabulous trout haven. Some of the most dramatic big-fish rises I have ever seen occur there. (I have never caught an undersized trout there nor seen one come from the place.) Yet the few times I have found the hardihood to tote my rubber boat in there one wouldn't think a trout ever had dwelt there. That's fisherman's luck, of course, but someday I'll hit. . . .

Bears I've Never Met: I've seen dozens of them from cars but I'm delighted to report that never yet have I met one face to face while on foot. Yet I've heard them and smelled them—they smell like an unmanicured pig—and one time I even contrived to get myself caught between a feeding bear and a muddy, unwadable beaver dam. Here's how it happened: Tommy Cole and I had gone up to the Salmon Trout Creek to fish a certain productive beaver dam. Tommy and I rigged up while we watched a sprightly rise. I then left Tommy and crossed on the dam and worked my way upstream through a tangle of brambles and raspberry bushes, intently fishing all the while. I had creeled two trout when at length I heard Tommy crashing through the thick brambles right behind me.

"Come on out here, Tommy," I said. "The going's much better out here." The crashing continued. "Tommy," I called more urgently.

"Woof," Tommy grunted in my ear, and then I heard the greedy slurping of the unseen bear feeding on the raspberries not more than two rod lengths behind me. He had been there all the while. . . .

"Taw-o-me!" I wailed like a banshee. The bear fell ominously silent.

"Halloo-oo!" Tommy answered, his voice floating thinly from far downstream, where I later found he'd gone to find a rumored new beaver dam.

"I—I'm a-coming!" I answered, and since I had successfully fished my way into this mess (the bear was doubtless just plain awed by my casting ability), I decided to fish my way out of it, though I'll admit I was glad no one was around making movies of my feverish casts.

This neck of the woods is crammed with black bears and yet I've heard of but two cases of a bear attacking a human—once from hunger (the bear stole a baby out of a forester's crib) and once because a man was molesting the bear's cubs. But I was plenty scared that day. The reason I had the hay up my neck with *this* bear was because I feared that he might think that I was challenging his possession of the raspberry patch. And raspberries were scarce that year. I wasn't, of course, and in fact I haven't ever been able to enjoy this wild fruit since—'though Tommy Cole still gives me the raspberry over the way I came charging pell-mell down creek to join him. He claims that on that day I joined the immortals: that I'm one of the few fishermen in captivity who ever made the 100-yard dash in ten seconds using hip boots for track shoes.

Getting Close to Trout: Wary as trout are, this can be done. It can be done because trout fishermen, including this one, constantly do it.

Some fishermen, like Hewitt, get real chummy and even manage to touch them with their hands—"tickling" it's called—but I've never got quite that far, or rather, come that close. All river and stream trout normally lie facing upstream. It is surprising how close one can come to them by approaching from below. But Indian stealth and infinite patience are two absolute requirements.

I have approached solitary feeding trout so close that I could have reached out and touched their feeding circles with my rod tip, and in fact had finally to *retreat* in order to make a presentable cast. The noise of the current, the fact that the fish is facing away, and his concentration on feeding are doubtless all factors making this possible. And if a relatively clumsy fisherman can get this close it is small wonder, then, that the lightning otter can sneak up and grab a trout.

Again, believe it or not, I have on a number of occasions suddenly found myself in the midst of a wild general rise of big feeding trout—maddening rises in which I could not possibly match the hatch—where I was morally certain I would have had a much better chance if I merely reached out and tried to take them with my landing net, I was that close.

The moral of all this, if there is any, is that a man needn't be a whing-ding tournament distance caster to present a decent dry fly. All he needs to do is learn to stalk up close and make an *accurate* short cast before his fish. In the meantime he isn't scaring the bejabbers out of the *other* trout and keeping down *all* the dormant but potential risers that might lie between him and his distant riser. Most rookie fly casters (and too many experienced ones) try to handle way too much line. I raise twice as many fish within thirty feet or less, in my dry-fly work, than I ever do beyond that distance. Forget the histrionics and dramatics and the business of trying to impress your fellows with what a hell of a power-caster you are. It's worth repeating: work up close and make a short accurate cast. If you must show off take up amateur dramatics next winter. That slinky Naomi Goldfinch is simply dying to have you hold her in your big strong arms.

Tying Your Own: Alas, I've tried and I've sighed and all but cried, but I simply can't seem to tie a decent fly. Apparently I fell on my head when I was a baby or something. All my flies come out like old feather dusters. And I really envy those fishermen who can tie a good fly because it seems to me there is a special satisfaction, not to mention a delicate massage to the ego, in luring a trout with one's own creation; something akin to playing a solo part in one's own symphonic composition and watching the glittering ladies out front heaving and sighing and swooning with emotion.

Aside from these intangible values, however, there is a definite practical value in being able to tie up precisely the fly you want. After all, *you* are the only person that really knows what you want— you were there and saw the wondrous sights. There are flies I still dream about that are apparently so filmy and fugitive—or simple— that I cannot seem to impart my dream to any tier I know. Perhaps I merely confess the limitations and poverty of my prose.

There is one big compensation I have observed in *not* being able to tie flies: the few good fishermen-tyers I know seem to spend most of the season manacled to their vises; they consume more time in tying flies than in fishing. And I doubt that many fishermen save any money tying their own; many of them seem promptly to develop an occupational malady that results in a sort of evangelistic fervor, a missionary zeal, to promulgate some particular pattern. Most of the fishermen-tyers I know *give* away most of their flies.

Despite these minor vices of the fly vise, however, I'll take the chance on being manacled and evangelistic and all the rest; I still long to tie a fly that doesn't always contrive to look like a motheaten Fuller brush. Then what a whiz-kid I'd really be on a trout stream!

Leader Sinks: Try lava soap. However dark remains your soul and buoyant your leaders you'll at least keep your hands clean.

Fly Dope: If you are hardy enough, smoke Italian cigars. They smell like a burning peat bog mixed with smoldering Bermuda onions but they're the best damned unlabeled DDT on the market; all mosquitoes in the same township immediately shrivel and zoom to earth. (Fellow fishermen occasionally follow suit.) However, if you are soft and effete, use formula 448. On the other hand one of the most popular fly dopes on the market is the best little varnish remover I've ever seen.

Domestic Relations: Invite your wife to go fishing during the height of fly time. Press her to join you. Tell her the *only* real canker in your fishing is missing her bright presence by your side. Put a quaver in your voice. "It's nice to go fishing with the fellows and all, Honey, but ..." is a good opening gambit. If successful in luring her give her sweetened water for fly dope. This harrowing experience will hold her nicely for a year. If she recoils in horror and refuses to go, still remembering the last time, she can nevertheless cherish the memory of that sweet generous gesture by her man. Either way you lay up red points and emerge as a real good guy. A sly fisherman can get a lot of domestic mileage from an occasional well-placed invitation of this kind.

Preservation of Fly Lines: Drunk or sober, always dry your fly line as soon as possible after leaving the water. In a pinch wind it around your whisky bottle, or else lay it out in loose coils in a shoe box. Even wrap it around yourself if necessary—or else mail it to me. More fishing equipment is ruined through thoughtless neglect than ever it is by use on laughing trout waters.

"You Shoulda Been Here Last Week!": Drill these whimsical characters between the eyes at forty paces.

Out-of-Town Guests Who Invite Themselves: Tell them you've given your fly rods to charity and taken up plug-casting for wormy bass—or else that, hurray, the doctor thinks those ugly spots on Junior may not be smallpox after all.

Out-of-Town Guests You Want to Come: Wire them that an eccentric old Finn west of here just showed you a secret pond where the trout measure three feet between the eyes—but that none of the bumpkins around here can ketch 'em, not even *you*. This challenge will fetch your man running every time.

Women Fishermen: Avoid them. One kind will quietly outfish you and generally get in your hair while another variety will come down with the vapors and want to go home just when the rise gets under way. Avoid all of them like woodticks.

Trout Fishermen: Most people avoid *them* like woodticks. They're regarded in many quarters as tricky and deceitful, subtle and full of guile, and as men who lie just to keep their hands in. But don't blame fishermen: after all they devote their lives to practicing these black arts on the stream, a topsy-turvy world where these vices are hailed as virtues. Be reasonable and reflect that fishermen just can't help acting the same way on the few occasions they mingle in the society of ordinary men. That is why so many normal people regard fishermen as being no damned good. Drat it, men, we're simply misunderstood.

The Old and the Proud

I heard the rhythmic whine and whish of his fly line before I saw
him.

It was late afternoon and I was sitting on the edge of a flood-
blasted high gravel bank overlooking a wide bend in the Big Escanaba River, leaning against one of a whispering stand of white pines,
sipping a tepid can of beer and waiting for the evening rise. The
sun was curving down and half of the river was already in shadow.
"Whish," sang the music of the unseen fly line, and I leaned forward
craning to glimpse the sturdy fisherman who had penetrated to
such a remote stretch on one of my favorite trout streams.

Then he rounded the bend below me, wading up over his
waist, breasting the deep powerful current, inching along, a tottering old fisherman supporting and pushing himself along with a
long-handled landing net which also served as a wading staff. As I
sat watching, a good trout rose between us. The old man saw it, too,
and paused and braced himself against the current. He then paid
out his line—false-casting to dry the fly and at the same time
extend his line—and then, when I had about concluded he would

103

never release the thing, whished out and delivered a beautiful curling upstream dry-fly cast. The fish rose and took the fly almost as it landed and I leaned forward watching the old fisherman as he expertly gathered in his slack, like a man harvesting grapes. He then suddenly whipped out his long-handled net and scooped in the fish as it passed him on its downstream run. It was a spanking beauty and I sat chewing my lip with envy.

The old fisherman held up his glistening fish and admired it and then creeled it. He then seemed to spend an interminable time selecting and tying on a new fly. He carried a little magnifying glass through which he peered at his fly boxes like a scientist bending over his retorts. In the meantime two more nice fish had risen between us, a circumstance which would have normally spurred me into action—not there, indeed, for this was now the old man's stretch—but I was held riveted to the spot by the sheer artistry and pluck of the old man's performance. The ritual of choosing and tying on the fly completed, it must have taken him another five or ten minutes to push and maneuver himself against the urgent river to assume his chosen casting position for the lower rising trout. Again there was the expert, careful, painstaking cast; again the obedient take on the first float; and again the sudden deft netting of the fish on its first downstream run. I thought the tottering old gentleman would surely founder and drown as he fought up through even deeper water to try for the third trout. He seemed to teeter in the current, like a wavering tightrope walker, and I restrained an impulse to shout a warning. Even *I*, a relative adolescent, had never dared wade up through this particular deep bend. . . . But the old man didn't drown and he calmly took the trout—again in as impressive a display of quiet fishing artistry as I had ever seen.

Here, I told myself, was a *real* fly fisherman, cool, deliberate, cagey, who for all the disabilities of his years could plainly fish rings around me and all the rest of my eager fishing pals. His performance was an illustrated lecture on one of the hardest of fundamentals for fishermen to learn: *easy does it*. But my heart went out to him as he continued to struggle manfully against the insistent current to reach still a new rise opposite and a little above me. On he came, like a man shackled by nightmare, still using his landing net as a staff. When he had fought his way opposite me I couldn't resist offering my nickel's worth of comment.

"Nice job of fishin'," I said, with all the foolhardy aplomb of the winner of a local dance marathon undertaking to compliment Nijinsky.

He glanced quickly up at me—one keen, appraising, wrinkled glance—and then away, as though I were a squirrel scolding and chattering on a bough. "Hm," he sniffed, that was all; just "Hm."

"Wouldn't it be a lot easier," I said, still filled with concern and still determined to take the fatal plunge, "wouldn't it be a lot easier if you fished downstream?"

The effect of this remark was as though I had deliberately impaled the old man with my fly or thrown a rock at his rising trout. His whole body seemed to shudder and recoil; then he stood stock-still and sighted me through his glasses, adjusting them, as though at last discovering that I was not a foolish squirrel but rather some new species of buzzing and pestiferous insect. "Harrumph," he snorted. "Listen, young fella," he said, "I'd sooner sit on my prat on the public dock at Lake Michigamme and plunk night crawlers for bass than *ever* fish a wet fly!"

Thus shriveled, I sat there red-faced and watched him teeter and struggle out of sight around the bend above. On the way he paused and took two more lovely trout.

This exchange of pleasantries between trout fishermen took place some fifteen years ago. Since then my anonymous old dry-fly purist has doubtless been gathered into the place where the meadows are always green and the trout always rising; but the lesson of our brief meeting was well learned. Ever since then my fellow fishermen may have at their trout from balloons or diving bells, for my part, without dredging up a single comment from me. And while I still fish the ignominious wet fly just as avidly as the lowly plunkers plunk for bass at Lake Michigamme, I have since learned that when dry-fly fishing is in season (alas, it frequently isn't in our chilly and temperamental northern waters) it is the most thrilling and rewarding—and exacting—of all methods of taking the fighting trout.

Whenever the day is dying and I find myself sitting on that particular high water-gouged bank on the Big Escanaba waiting for the evening rise, the brave words of that gallant old fisherman keep echoing and ringing in my ears—and lending them color, too. "Listen, young fella, I'd sooner sit on my prat on the public dock at Lake Michigamme and plunk night crawlers for bass than *ever* fish a wet fly!"

I have never forgotten this testy proud old man. In my mind's eye I can see him now. It is a still evening and he is breasting the deep celestial waters that run through green pastures. He is inching along with his glistening rod and his staff. A heavenly trout rises. He pauses and prepares to make one of his cool deliberate casts. His magic wand flashes and bends. "Whish," sings the line— "Whish," it goes, ever *"Whish."* . . .

The Last Day

Each year it is the same: this time, we tell ourselves, the doze and stitch and murmur of summer can never end; this season time will surely stand still in its tracks. Yet the hazy and glorious days glide by on golden wings, and presently here and there the leaves grow tinted by subtle fairy paintbrushes and flash their red warnings of impending fall. Even the trout become more brilliant in hue and grow heavy and loaded with spawn. And then, lo, one day we tired fishermen drag ourselves abroad only to discover that the stricken summer has waned into colorful northern autumn, like a beautiful woman flushed with the fevers of approaching death. It is the last day of fishing; the annual hibernation is once again at hand.

To this fisherman, at least, with all of its sadness and nostalgia the end of fishing is not unmixed with a sense of relief and release. No more is one oppressed by the curious compulsion of the chase; no more the driving sense of urgency that fills the eyes of fishermen with flecks of stardust shot through with mad gleams of lunacy. Reason is temporarily restored. The precious rods can now be leisurely gone over and stashed; the lines cleaned and stored; the boots hung up by their feet, and all the rest of the sad ritual. Yes, and with a little luck perhaps diplomatic relations can even be restored with those strange but vaguely familiar ladies with whom we have been oh so absently sharing our bedrooms all summer long.

For many years I have speculated on the precise nature of the drives that possess a presumably reasonable man and turn him into that quietly mad creature we call a fisherman. I am satisfied that it is not merely the urge to kill and possess. In fact I now think—like Messrs. Gilbert and Sullivan—that this has nothing to do with the thing, tra la, has nothing to do with the thing. Most fishermen I know are poor or indifferent hunters; as a class they are apt to be a gentle, tweedy, and chicken-hearted lot; and, let us admit it, they are frequently reflective and poky to the point of coma. But allowing for all this I sometimes wonder whether they are not a more atavistic and elemental crew than most of their fellow men—even more so than their bombarding second cousins, the hunters.

All hunters, unless they have got themselves too loaded with cookin' whisky, invariably first *see* their quarry and know precisely what it is, and then deliberately sight and hurl a projectile at it— bullet, arrow, rock or what you will—while the fisherman rarely "sees" his fish in this sense, but rather must expend endless ingenuity and patience in approaching and luring his game to its fate. And perhaps most important, when he is successful he is in actual, pulsing, manual contact with his quarry through the extension of his hand that he calls his line. The real combat only *begins* when he "shoots" his game, that is, sinks the barb. This, to me, marks fishing as at once a more subtle and yet basically more primitive pursuit than hunting, or selling cars or TV sets on time—or even excelling in the absorbing mysteries of corporate financing.

At this late hour I don't want to go in over my waders and poach on the preserves of the psychiatrists. Thank heaven I have never

been encouched and so am not qualified to. But sometimes I wonder whether the wild urge to pursue and lure a fighting fish isn't
connected somehow with the—er—sexual urges of the fisherman
himself. My, my, I've up and said it! Many frustrated and neglected
wives of fishermen will doubtless rise up at this point and shout
hoarsely, "*What* sexual urges?" Hm, let us see, let us see. . . .

Under the beneficent glow of our present pale tribal customs
courtship and marriage can get to be, so my runners inform me, a
pretty drab and routine affair; and I divine as though in a dream
that some men there are among us who doubtless rebel at constantly laying siege to an already conquered citadel; and unless
they are going in for collecting blondes of assorted shades and
varying degrees of moral rectitude, fishing and all that goes with it
may be the one pursuit that permits them to vent their atavistic
impulses and still preserve the tatters of their self-respect. I do not
labor the point, but smile evilly and cast my lure lightly upon the
troubled waters—and quietly rejoin the drabber subject of the
Last Day, the sad refrain upon which I seem to have opened this
swan song.

On the last day all fishermen are akin to pallbearers; worse yet, they
are pallbearers at their own funerals. Going out on the last day is a
job that has to be done, like burying the dead; but their hearts
aren't in the enterprise and the day is apt to be ruined by a future
that looms ahead as bleak and hopeless as the grave. They may
comfort themselves for the ordeal and brace themselves for the pur-
gatory of waiting by telling themselves that it is all for the best. The
fisherman's last-day funeral litany is a foggily beautiful and self-
deceiving thing and runs something like this: the fishing is no
longer sporting; the fisherman himself is dog-tired; the rise can no
longer be depended on; the spawn-laden trout are far too easy to
catch; and to take them now is to bite off one's nose. Amen.

Yes, on the last day we fishermen can try as we may to incant
ourselves into hilarity and acceptance, but our hearts are chilled and

our minds are numb. For what we fishermen really want is to go on fishing, fishing, fishing—yes, fishing forever into the great far blue beyond. . . . All that sustains us in our annual autumnal sorrow is the wry knowledge that spring is but two seasons removed. After all, we can sadly croak, it's *only* eight more months till the magic *First Day*!

from
Anatomy of a Fisherman
(*1964*)

Behold the Fisherman

To paraphrase a deceased patriot, I regret that I have but one life to give to my fishing. This is doubtless a curious confession coming from a man endowed with a four-carat education in the law, one who quit a more or less permanent job on his state's highest court—among lawyers the equivalent of winning the Pulitzer Prize—to devote himself to trout fishing and writing his yarns, but that's the way it is. What makes such a man tick? Well, that's what this book is all about.

Fishing, my research discloses, is older even than love and chess. In fact men have fished as long as there have been men and fish. Once they fished mostly for food, as some still do, but I suspect the reasons most fishermen now fish are nearly as varied as the kinds of fishermen who fish. And while all fishermen are probably a little mad, we shall here consider only fishermen for trout, who are mad in a special kind of way. But even this species of madmen differs among themselves.

Trout fishermen, like Gaul, may be divided into three parts: those who fish mainly to get fish; those who fish mainly to get away; and those who fish because they love the *act* of fishing and love to be where trout are found. This fisherman counts himself among the last breed, where I suspect most true trout fishermen belong. For trout, unlike men, will not—indeed cannot—live except where beauty dwells, so that any man who would catch a trout finds himself inevitably surrounded by beauty: he can't help himself.

Catching an occasional fish is to the enjoyment of trout fishing what encountering an occasional oyster is to the enjoyment of oyster stew: gratifying, yes, but far from everything. Now any fisherman likes to suspect that there is still a trout lurking around some-where in the same county, naturally, but a full creel every time out is not what he craves and would in fact spoil half the fun.

These old eyes have beheld the time when, fishing in Ontario, my wrist got so sore catching magazine-cover trout, and myself so bored with the whole enterprise, that I fairly raced home across the border where once again I might stalk my wary native trout, each of which I swear comes spawned into the world with a master's degree in evasion. What, then, is the mystic lure of fishing?

The Return of the Native

Gnawed with envy am I at those great-hearted fishermen who are forever returning their big trout to the waters from whence they came. Envious too am I of their subsequent shy accounts of their epic unselfishness in doing so, accounts which possess all the glow and sparkle of an unfilled application blank for life insurance, and usually run something like this:

"The great (*here insert name of species, whether brown, brook, rainbow*) trout lay inert and glistening in my landing net, eyes already glazing, gills yawping and working, gasping desperately for breath. Tenderly but firmly grasping him by the (*head, back, belly, groin, tail, upcuts*), I ever so gently worked the hook loose and finally removed it.

"My fly was a (*here insert pattern and type of fly and whether dry, wet or nymph*) tied on a (*here insert type, tensile strength and precise num-ber size of hook, ranging from ice tong to nit, that is from below 0 to 32*).*

"Then (*kneeling, standing, crouching in or beside*) my (*lake, river, pond, stream, sewage canal*) up to my (*choose your words, Buster!*) in the (*calm, clear, roiled, polluted torrential*) water, I submerged the great fish and gently held him upright.

---

* Here it is optional to pause and dilate on the history of the particular fly, giving thumb-nail sketches of its creator and local tyer, perhaps adding a modest little lec-ture on the canny fisherman's shrewd variations on the classic pattern, now revealed to a panting world for the first time.

"For a moment I feared I had tarried too long, but no—gradually I could feel the pulse and surge of renewed life awakening as it slowly regained the movement of its great tail and fins. Faster and faster worked the gills, stronger and more compulsive the sweep of the powerful tail and fins. Then I released it and, after a little pause, during which the gallant fighter seemed to roll its eyes up at me gratefully, it glided majestically down and away into the mysterious watery depths (*Sorry, standard form, no variations permitted*).

"Nearly exhausted now from my long struggle in landing him, which I estimated had lasted at least (*here insert not less than twelve minutes nor more than two hours*), I slowly trudged my way back up to my waiting (*motel, cabin, trailer, jeep, tavern, babe*) where with (*eager, numb, palsied*) fingers I poured myself a big (*shot, bumper, slug*) of (*bourbon, rye, Scotch, gin, vodka, buttermilk, Pepsi, Coke*). I held up my (*drink, glass, cup, dipper, bottle, jug*) against the (*dying, sifting, fading*) rays of the (*sinking, waning*) sun and solemnly toasted the gallant creature whose (*life, death*) I had just (*saved, spared, prolonged, averted, reprieved, paroled*).

"'Farewell, great-hearted old (*brook, brown, rainbow*),' I (*breathed, muttered, gargled, intoned*) with a (*catch, lump, frog, drink*) in my throat. 'Farewell until (*tomorrow, next week, next month, next season*), old (*boy, girl or, where gender is uncertain, pal is good*). Until then (*good luck, skoal, prosit, don't take any wooden nickels*).'"

For years I have been reading and listening to poetic dilations like this from the great-hearted giants among trout fishermen. In fact, some of these big trout have been caught and released so often they are losing their amateur standing. Fishermen of such heroic stature invariably fill me with awe and make me break out all over with little goose pimples of inferiority. I envy these Olympian fishermen their nobility of spirit—but I cannot emulate them. Alas, I possess the heart of a wood tick and the spirit of a gnat—*I keep my big trout!*

I try to comfort myself for my deficiencies by reflecting that since all trout are cannibals, and big ones almost exclusively so, I am really doing the remaining fish and my fellow fishermen a big favor by removing these monsters from our trout waters. I also try to tell myself that these noble grampaw returners are really nothing but a lot of high-toned masochists massaging their egos by doing a sort of Veblen in reverse, that is, getting a kind of perverse enjoyment out of their 'conspicuous humility.'

But it's no use, for I am aware that I will never qualify for membership in that most exclusive of fishing fraternities, The Ancient Order of Grampaw Returners.

The Other Side of the Coin

But all is not skittles and beer, as they say in merrie England, and the enemies of the fisherman are legion and invariably come equipped with two heads: natural and human. Natural enemies include but are not limited to—as lawyers love tersely to say in their 96-page leases—the inevitable hordes of insects, impenetrable fogs, too much rain, too little rain, the same for wind and sun, poor fly hatches, raiding otter, ospreys and fish hawks, drouths and floods, sluggish, sick, or dwindling fish—and many other assorted demons and goblins.

But man-made enemies are perhaps the most ubiquitous and frustrating to the fisherman, and they include: power companies who humorlessly persist in the notion that kilowatts are more important than trout, and who either blandly steal all the fisherman's water or else attempt to wash him out to sea; all beaver trappers, and especially those who break out precious dams to catch the beaver; neglected wives who accept dinner invitations on opening day or invite dreadful bores over for bridge on the last day; prowling monsters astride hernia-sized outboard motors, who invariably dash in on the crest of their own tidal waves to inquire sweetly how the fishing is ("Great, Buster, till you got here!" I someday long to say), and finally, a droll economic system that expects fishermen ever to work.

But as time passes perhaps the gravest threat to inland fishing of all kinds is from the water polluters and contaminators, who come in all shapes and sizes to fit all occasions. Wherever or whoever they are, the polluters spell despair to the fisherman and disaster to the trout.

Of these the industrial polluters, who seem to take perverse delight in using trout waters as their private sewers, are probably the most harmful to the fish and frustrating to the fisherman. For how does a tiny band of smelly improvident fishermen combat a jolly industrial giant so passionately devoted to the buck? Homicide might help, of course, but there is always the problem of how one goes about assassinating a corporation. So about all we have left is incantation and prayer—all fishermen are from infancy natural students of the hex—and perhaps some secret little stream these gay despoilers haven't yet found and deflowered.

Far down the rung of ruin, but still far too plentiful, are the campers and tourists and assorted outdoor itinerants who thoughtlessly use our trout waters as their personal garbage pails. These days one encounters the strangest objects while fishing. In fact the things I have fished out of trout waters could if I listed them bar this book from the mails. But perhaps the unkindest polluters of all are those fellow fishermen who themselves add to the growing mounds of beer cans and broken glass that increasingly adorn our lakes and streams. It is probably true that few fish were ever slain by flying beer cans, but their gleaming presence in trout waters surely kills enjoyment, the precious illusion of space and pastoral solitude and simple pine-laden cleanliness, and above all the wavering illusion that men were not entirely descended from the wild hog.

Shangri-La, Jr.

Trout, as I have said, inhabit some of the most curious places. I know a little shallow, rocky, malarial-looking pond on a tiny creek—

choked with weeds, lily pads, and the rather ostentatious calling cards of the cattle who drink there—that harbors some of the largest and loveliest wild brook trout I know south of Canada. For years I used to speed by the place hastening to some more distant Shangri-La. Then one fall evening on the way home I stopped in there looking for puffball mushrooms, which covet unkempt pasture lands. Instead I collided head-on with a spectacular rise of simply gorgeous brook trout—and swiftly forgot my precious mushrooms.

That night I had perhaps my finest hour, during which I was probably the best damn trout fisherman in Michigan. I rarely visit the place (you see, I'm still enslaved by the copyrighted wisdom of the outdoor magazines), and while I have never since quite had it so good as on that first night, never yet have I been skunked there, and last summer I tangled with and after a wild fight finally took the second biggest brook trout of my career. The name of the pond is—ah, but I never did learn how to spell that funny Indian name.

Portrait of Truth . . .

The most baffling natural enemies of the fisherman are the ever-present hordes of terrestrial insects, who regrettably show far less dietary discrimination than trout, and usually bite harder and more often. Ours come in the classic two varieties, the stingers and the biters, and include mosquitoes, of course, then deer flies, horse flies, black flies, wood ticks, enraged hornets and yellow jackets, and (my private plague) the tiny burning "no-see-ums." I ignore gnats and bats.

Fishermen are also occasionally beset by discerning bumble-bees—who doubtless mistake them for a rose. Under our competitive free enterprise system, of course, there are numerous fine insect repellents on the market, some of which are better than others, better, that is, at attracting insects. But by all odds the best fly dope I know—a kind that makes all insects vanish like magic—is a spectacular rise of trout.

On Trout Fishing and the Sturdy Virtues

Old fishermen never die; instead they write books about their passion, usually couched in a mournful, elegiac, Thoreauesque prose—withal larded with a sort of dogged jocularity—that old fishermen seem helplessly bound to employ when they put down rod and take up pen and look back on all the trout they slew. "Trouting on the Old Nostalgia" might well serve as the collective title of most of these wistful memoirs, some of which are best read to the throbbing accompaniment of an old movie Wurlitzer. Worst of all, too many of these books feed the myth that trout fishing promotes health, serenity and frugality in its disciples.

This is a lot of pious nonsense. Chasing trout is no less wearing and barely less complicated than chasing women. And more frustrating, too, because women, I have heard, are rather more readily overtaken and caught. As for the frugality bit, I swear my trout run me five dollars an ounce. Troy weight.

The truth is that trout fishermen scheme and lie and toss in their sleep. They dream of great dripping trout, shapely and elusive as mermaids, and arise cranky and haggard from their fantasies. They are moody and neglectful and all of them a little daft. Moreover they are inclined to drink too much.

The truth is that fishing for trout is as crazy and self-indulgent as inhaling opium. What, then, can be said for trout fishing? Simply this: it's got work beat a mile and is, if a man can stand it, indecently great fun.

Fish-and-Tell Fishermen

Any fisherman who will tell on the trout waters that are revealed to him possesses the stature of a man who will tell on the women he's

119

dallied with—exactly three inches high. I have a disillusioned chum who not long ago took one of these moral midgets to his favorite trout spot, a jewel of a beaver pond. That winter he was filled with anguish to read all about it in one of the outdoor magazines—complete with snapshots and maps. This deathless contribution to American journalism had the by-line of his literary pal, of course, who now languishes in the doghouse. But his pet beaver pond also languishes firmly on the tourist beat, and this perhaps is why fishermen become such secretive (and cynical) snobs.

Moral: Only take dogs, small children, and tested fishing pals to your favorite trout spots. Revised moral: On second thought, better only take dogs and small children.

Are All Fishermen Alike?

No, thank heaven. Fishermen vary as violently as do other men, and in their fishing they are just as apt to reveal their individual tastes and phobias and basic drives. For among fishermen, as in the stock market, there are the bulls and bears, the plungers and the timid souls, the lambs and the foxes, the avid ones and the dreamy fugitives from Walden. And each of us reveals it in his fishing. Perhaps it all boils down to just what men look for in their fishing.

Thus some fishermen seek only to catch enormous fish in far places where they must cast from here to eternity. Talking a mysterious professional patter, bristling with rod cases and passports, their fishing trips tend to be as big a deal as society weddings or African safaris. We can see their pictures monthly in the outdoor magazines, one big fish holding aloft another, the two being distinguished largely by a triumphant grin. These are the jolly "kill-kill" boys among fishermen, the tanned hearty lads whom I am at pains to avoid, and for whom I suspect the outdoors is but a suburb of their egos.

At the opposite extreme are the quiet anonymous fishermen who cling wistfully to their amateur standing, whose pictures rarely adorn the outdoor magazines, and who are quite content to seek more modest trout on fine tackle, perhaps on the comforting theory that it may take as much if not more subtlety and skill to fool their own heavily fished native trout than to engage a spotted whale on some virginal torrent in the Argentine. Perhaps this is only one man's small rebellion against this whole tedious bigger-and-better philosophy as it more and more afflicts our outdoors, indeed our very life. Perhaps it is pure envy. In any case, those easy uncluttered fishermen who do not weigh and calibrate their pleasure are the guys I like to fish with.

Possibly the most revealing difference between these two types of fishermen is what each does with his fish. The quiet fisherman either returns or eats the trout he catches; the kill-kill boys—after the photographs, of course—invariably clap theirs on the wall. There are times when I yearn to reunite them there.

Experts and Duffers

The main difference between experts and duffers in the world of fishermen—and perhaps also the beginning of trout wisdom—is that the expert *knows* he can't ever make trout feed when they don't want to, while the duffer keeps flailing away. That plus the fact that during those rare intervals when the trout are really in the mood for love, your expert being mechanically a little more adept is apt to get onto more fish faster than his fumbling neighbor.

Yet the old fishing hands have one big strike on them. They cling to their pet stupidities with all the zeal of Grandma to her old home remedies. Indeed, more than once I have seen the time when the duffers won all the glory and fairly fished rings around us old hands. They did so because in their innocence and uncluttered willingness to experiment they had stumbled upon the precise medicine—perhaps a ghastly old streamer that resembled half a pair of rusty ice-tongs that had grown a beard—and because they had possessed the humility that finally found nirvana.

Moral: Humility and open-mindedness sometimes catch far more fish than all the wise guys.

The Favorite Fly

We fishermen endlessly pride ourselves on our tolerance and lofty detachment, but in truth we are superstitious and goblin-ridden as any leaping witch doctor. And to a man we are slaves to the myth of the favorite fly. The syllogism is simple. A fly becomes a favorite, of course, because the fisherman once caught or raised a powerful lot of trout with it—probably on one of those rare enchanted evenings when they would equally have hit an old shaving brush; therefore it becomes a "good" fly, one in which the fisherman puts unbounded faith; therefore he fishes it more often and with extra loving care; therefore whatever trout he takes in the future are more apt to be caught on his pretty pet; and thus the more he is caught in the spell of his favorite fly.

It matters not that my favorite fly can prove nothing whatever about the relative merits of Hank's favorite fly. For how can either of us possibly appraise the worth of flies we so resolutely never cast? How can I possibly take a trout on a gray fox variant, say, if I am forever pelting out a spent-wing Adams? This is probably why most of the foxy old fishermen I know more and more lean toward favorite sizes rather than *patterns*. Yet all of us carry way too many flies of all sizes and patterns, and the truth is that far more flies are lost in the tangled and neglected forests of our fly boxes than are ever lost on trout. And the reason is that against all logic we still cling to that magic thing known as our favorite fly.

The Frugal Fisherman

The myth so common among non-fishermen that fly-fishing for trout is an expensive sport is sheer nonsense. As is well known to even the most fumbling tyro, all a fly-fisherman really needs to catch a trout are five simple things: a rod, a reel, a line, a leader, and a fly. Everything else is exhibitionism and mere frills. Of course if the fisherman is one of those pampered types he can shoot the works and indulge himself in a landing net and creel and perhaps even a pair of boots to keep his feet dry. But these refinements are not really necessary, and even the wiliest trout have been known to impale themselves upon the shabby offerings of the crudely-equipped fellows who lack these luxuries. Fly-fishing expensive? Utter nonsense!

Take my own case. Naturally I possess the five simple rudiments for fly-fishing, that is a rod and a reel, a line and a leader, besides a couple of old flies. Candor moves me to confess that I also have a net and a creel and a pair of old patched rubber boots. There are a few other odds and ends that I have accumulated over the years and usually lug along, but since they do not come readily to mind, I'll just rest the ballpoint a bit and slip out to the garage and take a quick inventory.

(*Two hours later*)

Ah, I got back. . . .

Some guys do seem to carry a little more tackle and gear than others. It's a kind of personal whimsey, I guess. But I must say it's amazing how the stuff does accumulate. Let's see now, where shall I start?

Ah, yes, first things first. . . . For example, while rummaging through the jeep just now I happened to glance through my fly vest. (It's utterly silly how *that* ever slipped my mind; of course I own a fly vest.) Fly vests, as the name implies, are designed mainly for carrying flies, but I seem to have added a few stray odds and ends. Quite a few, in fact. In or adorning this swollen garment I found a compass, a combination scales and measuring tape, a magnifying glass, a pencil flashlight, a tube of powdered graphite (to ease reluctant ferrules), a pair of scissors, tweezers, sun glasses, a combined leader nipper and hook disgorger, a nail file and clip, a weighted priest for conking languishing trout, a gadget for tying up tippets, a jar of line dressing, a bottle of fly dip, another of fly dope, five coils of assorted tippet material and, of all things, a gummy wad of old trading stamps.

I also came upon one bullet-hard, squirrel-gnawed piece of plug tobacco, a wizened artifact from some brave era when I had doubtless tried to forsake smoking Italian cigars—known among its addicts as the poor man's marijuana. This spurred the search. House cleaning could now be combined with inventory.

Diving deeper I found an aluminum soap box and bar of mechanics' soap to scrub out leaders; a wash cloth to dry my old paddies; a pocket knife; a carborundum hone to sharpen same and my fly hooks; also a miniature monocular for bird watching or casual window peeping when fishing palls, besides several miles of tapered leaders ranging from hawsers down to those as fine as a hair from the golden head of a Scandinavian princess. Alas, I found no princess. . . . I also appear regularly to carry between seven and eight hundred flies in a wild assortment of fly boxes, most of which I'd forgotten I ever owned. So much for a quick tour of the old fly vest.

What next, little man?

Pawing and tossing stuff around in the jeep at random, I was enchanted to learn that I carry 2 pairs of binoculars, 1 power scope, 2 cameras, dozens of rolls of overripe film, a raft of assorted flashlights ranging from pencil size up to the Lindbergh Beacon, a batteryless flashlight that works by some sort of ratchet, 2 old Stonebridge candle lanterns in case science should fail, scores of half-melted plumber's candles for same; 2 pairs each of waders and hip boots, 1 pair of detachable felt sandals, 1 pair of low boat boots; all sizes and types of rain gear; assorted vests, sweaters, gloves and ear muffs in case I should encounter a glacier. . . .

In addition, I found endless assorted nails and screws, nuts and bolts, $7.17 in coins, extra ferrules and guides, winding silk, eye bolts, an old gold filling, emery paper; assorted cements, glues, varnishes, ointments; a bedroll, 3 blankets, a set of detailed county maps, packsacks of all sizes, and an old ticket to a strawberry festival, an annual U. P. event. Also a tarpaulin, a silk pup tent—and a birthday card sent me ages ago written in the round hand of my oldest married daughter when she was nine. In addition, there are 2 axes, 2 saws, 3 hatchets, 1 fearsome brush knife that could cleave a charging rhino clean down the old spino; 2 sizes of pruning shears to clear out brushy "hot spots"; a hand-cranked tugger to supplement the jeep's winch when retreat seems the better part of valor; assorted tow chains, extra cables, snatch blocks; and enough wrenches and pry bars and hack saws and miscellaneous wrecking tools single-handedly to invade and conquer Fort Knox.

The cultural aspects of trout fishing are not neglected; I carry a small nature library: 2 illustrated books on wild mushrooms, 1 each on birds, wild flowers and trees, even some of my own books, besides the illustrated book of my friend Art Flick, his invaluable

The Fisherman's Streamside Guide, full to the gills with suave May fly patterns, natural and artificial, besides much other fishing lore. Since books suggest smoking, I recall I carry a battery of old pipes, reamers and cleaners, faded and forgotten boxes of tattered Italian cigars, matches, spare lighters, flints, spare wicks, packets of mildewed tobacco; playing cards and a cribbage board; 2 pin-on compasses plus 3 regular ones; 3 tiny transistor radios and a big powerful all-wave affair, including FM, to keep me abreast of the latest shaving creams and lotions and underarm deodorants, not to mention the state of the uneasy romance between the Russians and the United States.

Since fishermen occasionally must eat, naturally my jeep is an ambulant supermarket bulging with jars and bottles and assorted canned goods; fry pans and nesting cook kits; stoves and grills galore; 1 folding table, 4 folding canvas chairs, 1 luxurious folding rope chair for impromptu press conferences and coronations; 1 small ice box, 1 thermos jug, and enough wine, beer and miscellaneous booze to get half the county plastered. I also carry—but before chaos sets in I'd better set up some categories. On with the categories. . . .

FLY RODS: Like many another guilty trout fisherman, I own enough split bamboo fly rods to furnish buggy whips for most of the harness drivers of America. I possess at least one of every well-known make and quite a raft of others by rod builders one rarely ever hears of, possibly because many of them are dead and the rest have more work than they can handle. And like the man with a million ties on his rack, I usually "wear" only one, a gallant and battered old three-piece number that was old before our children, now grown, were even born. Most of my rods I no longer carry; some I reverently lug along but rarely use; two old favorites have won honorable retirement and are now set up like crossed swords in the tallest window of my den; others of late years I am giving to deserving youngsters; and recently I suspect my wife, Grace, of eying several others for curtain rods.

from **Anatomy of a Fisherman** (*1964*)

I own but one glass fly rod which I use only for wind casting, or fishing the heaviest weighted nymphs, or on rugged pack-in trips to unknown new territory. I must say it performs nobly and yet I wouldn't trade my oldest and creakiest split bamboo for all the glass fly rods in captivity—which is doubtless pure snobbery.

FLY LINES: After I had insured the economic survival of England by acquiring enough expensive torpedoed and double-tapered silk fly lines to reach from here to London, I discovered through my friend Art Flick a ridiculously cheap American fly line that does all that any fly line can be expected to do, only twice as well. It requires no dressing, no drying, no cleaning, no uncoiling, no storage, and no love. It positively thrives on abuse (last winter I inadvertently left one wound on a reel in the jeep in our unheated garage, and it leapt forth last spring eager and supple as a snake). Moreover, it floats and floats and floats. . . . If I wrote simply for money rather than for Art, I would reveal the name of it—but then we dreamy fishermen daren't commercialize our sublime sport, dare we?

Categories, categories. . . .

FLY REELS: I use only one make and it is made in merrie England. After all, the English were fly-fishing long before Columbus got himself lost. . . . It is strong and it is light and moreover it is reversible. I favor reversible reels because I happen to think every right-handed fisherman should reel with his left hand, and vice versa. (My fishing pal Hank Scarffe tipped me off to this one.) This banishes the need for ever riskily shifting the rod from one hand to the other during critical junctures. By 'critical junctures' I of course mean when you're on to a slob. Not that I ever play a fish off the reel, or recommend it, but a lot of loose and trailing slack line is frequently a hazard and always a nuisance, especially in flowing water, and again especially when a good fish works himself below you.

Most of the stuff I've listed up to now I lug along all the time, it's standard equipment, but naturally, for example, I don't drag all my boats along on every trip or always take my sleep trailer (hah, I'd clean forgotten the boats and the little old Tear Drop trailer!), so perhaps I'd better range out now amidst the fishing litter I just saw parked and lying around the new garage (see, I'd even forgotten about that nice new garage we had to build to house my boats and trailers and other treasures).

ASSORTED WATER CRAFT: Naturally I own a small fleet. Score: 3 wooden boats, 2 rubber boats, and an interest in a permanently cached metal canoe. Naturally, too, there is a fancy trailer (no, not the Tear Drop) to lug the wooden scows around. In the summer I spot these barges around the countryside, in strategic places, leaving them there until the trout season is over or the porcupines have devoured them.

Fly-casting out of a boat possesses all of the awkwardness and none of the eccentric charm of fishing out of a bathtub, and most fly-fishermen avoid it. But since I live in a rugged, heavily glaciated area where continuously wadable trout waters are rare and simply have to be learned at peril of dunking or drowning, boats are often a necessary evil.

Besides my regular flotilla I have a new rubber float (thanks to the generosity of an equally new fishing pal, Hal Lawin) that I call the Baloney Sausage, which is no more than an inflated truck inner-tube wrapped in a green canvas cover from which dangles a kind of droopy triangular diaper sling (like a child's bouncer-swing), from which in turn dangles the floating fisherman, exposing to an astonished world but a third of his former self.

This is perhaps the candiest fishing rig I own since it is readily portable, utterly noiseless, permits stealthy approaches and the most delicate controlled fly-casting, and opens up distant and intriguing trout waters theretofore regarded as unfishable save from a balloon. Since propulsion of this rig is a bit of a problem, especially in quiet waters, I have tied to it a junior sized wooden canoe paddle—besides wearing at times a pair of metal sculling flippers on my feet. When Hank Scarffe first beheld me encased in this contraption, along with its accessories, he thought I was an expec-

128

tant space man gone AWOL from Cape Kennedy. Now he's wooing Santa for one of his own.

Now I know I've overlooked lots and lots of stuff (for example, more sun glasses; barometers, thermometers, dephometers, my two harmonicas, my flute-like wooden recorder and my sweet-toned Italian clavietta; my bird calls and animal calls and assorted Indian love calls; the aluminum water scope through which I leer down at unsuspecting mermaids) but a man can't remember everything and moreover exhaustion is setting in. Anyway, you get a working idea.

At least I now dimly suspect why it is that when my pals and I take off on overnight trips people in the streets often stop and stare after us. First comes the groaning jeep, dripping waterbags dangling from either side (my, my, I forgot the water bags), gear piled clean to the roof, the roof itself carrying an inflated rubber boat, the Baloney Sausage roped to the rear. Next follows the Tear Drop trailer, hitched to the jeep, with another boat lashed to the roof, the inside clanking and awash with the overflow.

The summer before he died, old Danny McGinnis hailed us down as Hank and I were tooling out of town bent on a big trout safari. He drank in the spectacle, blinking at our cavalcade, rubbing his wire whiskers, tugging away at his tobacco-stained mustaches. Finally he squinted more closely and spoke.

" 'Fraid you got somethin' missin' there, Johnny," he said gravely.

"What's that, Danny?" I inquired in alarm.

"A little dog running behind."

Nevertheless, I still insist that the idea that trout fishing need be expensive is pure nonsense. Frugality is the fisherman's middle name. All one really needs is a rod, a reel, a line, a leader, and a fly. . . . The big trouble with fishermen is that most of us are help-less slaves to what that gallant old British lion, Sir Winston, once said about war: Nothing succeeds like excess.

And where do we put the fish? It's a good question. I often wonder.

Fellowship and All That

Do fishermen fish largely for fellowship, the comradely allure of later huddling with their fellow manics to brag a little and further cement their mystic brotherhood with bumpers of liquid glue? I rather doubt it, because fishing is essentially a lonely pursuit, and anyway the fisherman is generally far too pooped when his day's devotionals are over to crave anything but his lonely bed.

Or does he join forces with others so that he might commune with nature in the company of kindred souls? Again I rather doubt it, at least as a primary motive, for few things are more terrifyingly impenetrable than the oblivious concentration of a real-gone fisherman wooing a rising trout. He is almost literally out of this world. Perhaps we veer closest to penetrating the fisherman's troubled psyche when we remember that in all fishing there is a persistent pattern of pursuit, capture, and exhaustion. But before I get in over my waders maybe I had better leave to the Freudians the job of unraveling any lurking parallels . . . While fellowship there may be in fishing, in its essentials it is man against fish, man pitted against the creatures who inhabit the very element from whence he crept.

My Favorite Spot

Every fisherman has his favorite fishing spot, to which he returns with all the hypnotic fascination that lures the murderer back to the scene of his crime. This happens to be my favorite spot. We will call it Frenchman's Creek, for that is not its name. My pals shun and despise the place, as I do *their* favorite spots.

Trout are rather inconstant readers of the outdoor magazines, I suspect, for contrary to the sage fish wisdom there embalmed they sometimes inhabit the damnedest most unlikely-looking places. Frenchman's Creek is such a place.

Frenchman's reminds me of downtrodden Bill in the old ballad: it ain't much to look at but it's all mine. It isn't very deep, but I love it; the trout aren't very big or many, but I love it; it's scummy and weedy and isn't very pretty, but still I love it.

The fact is I haunt Frenchman's Creek like a boozer his favorite bar. Each new season I try again to break the habit and go straight, but few are the days I don't wind up there. I woo its disdainful trout as though each were Roxane and I the spurned Cyrano, because I love it. The old place has me hooked fast and far deeper than any trout I ever hooked there.

On Buying a New Fly Rod

Few sporting goods stores adjoin good trout waters, curiously enough, yet buying a fly rod in the average city store, that is, joining it up and sagely waggling it a bit, is much like seeing a woman's arm protruding from a car window: all one can really be sure of is that the window is open.

All you can tell about a new fly rod doing the routine waggling bit in a sports shop is whether it might have a wet or dry fly action and possibly whether the ferrules fit. The nodding clerk, incorrigible matchmaker, invariably assures you that this at last is the perfect union of man and rod. (He knows all about it, of course; on weekends he plunks for catfish with a collapsible steel girder.)

But the only sure way of telling whether or not a rod is perfectly balanced and really "right" for you while *fishing*—which after all is the name of the game—is to buy or bring along a line and leader and a fly and cast the whole blooming outfit over an expanse of water. (No rod, however expensive, is any better than the stuff that goes with it.) With city rents being what they are, few modern stores come equipped with casting pools. But buying a new rod any other way is sadly to press your fisherman's luck. Indeed, the amazing thing is not that so many fishermen plod along with woefully mismated and unbalanced outfits, but that so many of these "by-guess-and-by-God" outfits are half as good as they are.

Deceit, Dementia, and Fine Leaders
or Are All Fishermen Crazy?

All fishermen like to catch a *big* trout once in a while, naturally, but few experienced fishermen I know make it a way of life. We are quite willing to leave the pursuit of *that* will-o'-the-wisp to the younger guys. They'll learn. . . . For one thing, really big native trout these days are getting mighty scarce, they seldom feed on the surface and then rarely in accessible spots, and moreover they're wary as all hell. For another, compared to the average smaller trout, these slobolas are not nearly as good eating. For still another—let's face it—old fishermen are all a little crazy, and by the time they're fifty they are using such weird out-of-this-world tackle they can rarely hold a real lunker even if they get on to one.

Why should this be? The answer is simple. Because most of the old-time fishermen I know are constantly and deliberately under-leadered, that is, their leaders are as long and fine as the traffic will bear. This they do not simply out of good sportsmanship—though that's part of it—but because they have learned from long experience one simple fishing truth: the finer the leader the more rises and action the fisherman will get. There are few invariable rules in fishing, but I think this is one of them. And *action* is what your jaded old fisherman really craves, sometimes even more than fish. Here is our dark strategy unmasked.

If fly fishing is an act of subtle guile and high deceit—which it is—then the perfect leader would be perfectly invisible, like the emperor's new suit. For the whole point of the game is to entice a wild wary trout to take an imitation fly that is fake and no good. So deceit lies at the heart of the enterprise. But the trouble is that few natural insects I know come equipped with coarse feelers seven to twelve feet long. So trout wisely tend to avoid such curious puzzlements.

So it is here that the act of deception most often breaks down and why his leaders are the weakest weapon in the fisherman's arsenal of deceit. Regrettably, invisible leaders are not yet here—though I have my researchers working on it. Night and day, in fact. If all this is true, then it requires no piscatorial Einstein to perceive that the next best leader is one *approaching* perfection, that is, invisibility, which is naturally one as long and fine as he can possibly cast and still have a fighting chance to play and land a decent trout.

But all this is elementary to most crazed old fishermen, who've proved it time and again. I know a certain spring-fed pond near here that abounds in lovely wild brook trout almost constantly on the prod after tiny nymphs and midges and other wee invisible flies, both dry and wet. They have to feed often in order to get a square meal. But other fishermen also know about this, alas, and each season during the first week of fishing there is standing room only, with stoic pilgrims lining the banks imperturbably flailing away with their usual coarse store leaders evidently tied up from old hawsers, rusty cables, and frayed lassoes left over from "Gunsmoke." Occasionally they will take a crazed trout, but not often, because the pond is shallow and clear as gin and the trout are wild and wary. These fishermen are generally to a man badly overleadered. Only a starving or suicidal trout could possibly be fooled by their rigid unnatural lures.

I usually pretty well avoid the place during the first month—I'm afraid of being trampled—but by the time I start fishing there in earnest the old pond might as well be up in Labrador. The place is totally deserted: the stout-leader boys have had it and sadly coiled their hawsers and retreated back to the golf course, grousing about how lousy fishing has gotten.

This is my shining hour. Such is the advanced state of my fishing lunacy that here I always use 12-foot leaders tapered to 5-X merely as a starting base. To this I tie on tippets of varying lengths of still finer 6- and 7-X synthetic material (gut cannot be drawn this fine), depending upon conditions. For flies, rarely do I use larger than a size 18 on this pond, and last season I had a ball with 24's.

The only trouble is I may soon have to adopt a bright-eyed lad to tie on my tippets and tiny flies for me. The old eyes, you know. . . . This winter I'm negotiating with Oslo through Mrs. Paul H. Young for wee 28's, which is like plucking a "no-see-um" off your wrist and calmly fishing with it. Since all fishing seems inevitably to involve progressive dementia, next summer I'll doubtless do my fishing from a streamside padded cell, for diversion making up long languid leaders out of the dangling cobwebs.

Fisherman versus Hunter

Some of my best friends are hunters, but why they should so much want to hunt baffles me quite as much as why I should so much want to fish doubtless baffles them. For it is my belief that fishermen and hunters are two different breeds, comparative strangers who share only this in common: both happen to pursue their passions in the same environment, the woods. This no more unites them than sharing the same arena united the lions and early Christians. When hunters and fishermen do take a liking to each other, it is a clear case of the attraction of opposites. They are friends despite, not because of, their respective passions. As between friends everywhere, their trespasses are forgiven, their crotchets charitably overlooked.

In their monthly dilations the pundits of the outdoor magazines recognize that a difference exists. At five cents a word, they picture the fisherman as a reflective and fumbling fellow eternally wandering about the woods snagging his waders, misquoting Izaak Walton, pausing to pluck a wild flower, more often engaged in retrieving his flies from the tree tops—occasionally even catching a fish. On the other hand these same pundits picture the mighty hunter as a bronzed and steely-eyed chap, atavistic and elemental, one who lusts to kill simply because he must.

In their view, the effete fisherman cowers before violence and bloodshed and the loud noises of firearms; he is a kind of failed poet or strayed bird watcher; the hunter is a swaggering cave man inadequately disguised by Abercrombie. The pundits and I agree only that there is a vast difference between the two; we come to a parting of ways over what that difference is and what it signifies. After much pondering I'll plunge in over my waders and suggest that the true picture is quite the reverse: that it is the fisherman who is more nearly akin to man's earliest ancestors, the quiet one who in almost every sense of the word is more primitive.

Consider the hunter. Since the dawn of man he has sallied forth with his slings and arrows, stalked and spied his quarry and then, muttering a prayer to his tribal gods, hurled at it a projectile—rock, boomerang, poisoned dart, lance, arrow, or steel-nosed bullet. All hunters, ancient and modern, share one thing in common: once he has released his projectile the hunter has little or no control over it. He either makes a hit or he misses; if the former he's a hero, otherwise a bum.

Consider the fisherman. The quarry he stalks remains almost always hidden and unseen. Except where there are rising trout he can only wistfully hope; forever he pursues an elusive will-o-the-wisp. When he is lucky and gets a strike he becomes directly and personally engaged with his quarry by a pulsing extension of his arm—hand to rod to line to leader to fly. Unlike the hunter he is successful not when he smites a discernable victim who is usually fleeing both hunter and projectile in terror but, infinitely more subtle and deceitful, when his unsuspecting quarry eagerly seeks out and impales itself upon his worthless lure. His art is enticement; the hunter's annihilation.

One may pause and ask at this point, "Haven't you plunged into a semantic bog? If the hunter 'annihilates' as you say, doesn't this mark him as more brutal and primitive?" My answer is no;

more brutal perhaps, but not more primitive. By primitive I mean "pertaining to the beginning or origin, or to early times; original; primordial; primeval," to quote the very first entry in my doubtless primitive dictionary.

Early primitive man could annihilate nothing; puny in body and scarce in number he lived almost solely by his wits; simply to survive he had daily to elude and outwit the great swarm of fearsome beasts and reptiles and weird flying things that roamed and slithered and flapped about his ancient world. His boldness came later, much later, when through his cunning he had survived and multiplied, had contrived and perfected his aggressive weapons.

Indeed a good case can be made that only as man has evolved and come more and more to dominate his environment has he become more violently aggressive and brutal. Behold that finest flower of civilization, modern man, with his bristling arsenals of guided missiles and split atoms and—having failed to perpetrate enough mischief on this one—his dreams of invading other planets. Is he not the crudest of all, that is, less his old original pristine self, at once subtle and infinitely patient, cunning and curiously innocent? But that is another and sadder story. . . .

With the hunter the issue is rarely in doubt; either he hits and crumples his quarry or he misses and, shrugging and swearing, hopefully resumes the stalk. Once the fisherman becomes engaged to his fish the contest has only begun; throughout the struggle the adversaries are physically linked to each other; at any stage of the combat his quarry may escape; to the end the issue remains in doubt. Moreover, he stalks his quarry in that most ancient of elements, water, from which his remote ancestors originally crept; in a sense he is a wanderer searching for his past.

For those who associate "primitive" with elemental behavior and direct bodily collision, the fisherman is so utterly primitive he insists upon taking his quarry alive virtually with his bare hands. Short of wrestling a bear, what could be more primitive than that? Speak to me not of gentle fishermen.

"But what about those occasional characters who appear to love both to hunt and fish?" Ignoring those neurotic folk to whom all hunting and fishing is but a massage of their egos, and who might be far better off chasing golf balls or compliant Bunny Girls, I challenge the premise and suggest that there simply *aren't* any men who love *equally* to fish and hunt. Those fishermen who occasionally hunt are merely lost souls whiling away the vast Sahara of time between fishing seasons—and vice versa. Some even write books. . . . One thing seems clear: most of the dedicated hunters and fishermen I know are far more faithful in their fashion than ever her lover was to Cynara. Each in his secret heart scorns the other's sport.

Granted that hunters and fishermen are basically different; the *why* of their difference is another and subtler question the victims are probably as ill equipped to answer as the recumbent patient in the psychoanalyst's confessional is to analyze himself. Indeed Freud and Jung together might have had difficulty differentiating the fisherman from the hunter, though they might draw some fine analogy involving the difference between seduction and rape, *ya!*

I have my dark suspicions about what troubles the fisherman, but I hesitate to unveil them in a medium that might fall into the hands of women and innocent children. For one thing, my fellow fishermen might get powerfully irked over such treason; for another, their neglected wives might grow even more forlorn to learn that such a subtle form of infidelity has been going on behind their backs all these years. For wooing a trout with a fly is almost precisely akin to the slow and patient seduction of a proud and reluctant woman.

There, I've up and said it. Henceforth I shall have to fish in the Antipodes.

from
Trout Magic
(*1974*)

Sins My Father Taught Me

(With apologies to him and Dvořák)

1

To paraphrase a deceased patriot, I regret that I have but one life to give to my fly-fishing. I also regret all the years I wasted bait-fishing as well as all the trout I thereby unwittingly maimed or killed by these crude methods. For this is the "sin" my father taught me which I now wish to bewail—the wrong way to fish—though I suppose the way one learns to fish is just as chancy as the color of one's eyes or indeed that one was ever born at all.

In my father's favor I should add that he in turn probably learned his way of fishing from his own father, as I suspect most young fishermen do, and that this tends to happen for a variety of reasons: juvenile hero worship ("My old man's a better fisherman than your old man"); plain simian imitation; a lack of opportunity to learn any other way; and, more practically, the availability of his equipment when the old boy's off at work.

In any case, my youthful corruption began early and soon became total, and by the time I was ten I could wind up and heave a writhing gob of angleworms almost as far as my father could. My first fishing pole was an incredibly long one-piece bamboo number with an askew pigtailed tip, of the kind one used to pick out of bristling stacks that stood in front of hardware stores—your choice, fifteen cents. For I had bait fished many years before I graduated to the decadent luxury of having one of the new steel rods that magically telescoped, the kind my early fly-fishing hero Tommy Cole scornfully called a "collapsible girder."

In a canny effort to make myself indispensable so I'd never be left behind on fishing trips, I also contrived to become something of a neighborhood authority on the collection, preservation, and transportation of all manner of live baits, a dark art in which my father early schooled me. Though I haven't fished any kind of live bait in many years, I still remember most of those I gathered for my father and his fishing pals: chiefly angleworms and night crawlers, of course, and then a more esoteric and sometimes seasonal variety that included bloodsuckers, minnows, snaillike whitish things called grubs, and let's see, oh yes, grasshoppers and helgramites, to name the main ones.

I also learned that each species called for a special stalking and storing technique: night crawlers, as their name suggests, came much faster at night after a shower, especially when stalked like a footpad with a hooded-beam kerosene lantern with a sliding door (before flash-lights became common) of the kind refined ladies would today doubtless give their eyeteeth to get hold of to plant ivy in. My father also taught me that these crawlers, usually kept in a tub of rich black earth, became so python lively they would even avidly grab a reluctant trout if, the night before your next fishing trip, you cagily transferred the trip's supply into a container of damp caribou moss.

Grasshoppers were best gathered before sunup, I soon learned, when the lively devils were still numb from the chill of night. These were clapped into a wooden bait box with a screen at one end and a sliding door at the other which my father fashioned out of old cigar boxes from his saloon. Then there were homemade min-

144

now traps that one transferred to tricky buckets one was forever changing the water in. And there were the jars within jars for luring bloodsuckers, baited with liver, both a procedure and prey which gave me the creeps.

I pretty well stuck to garden worms and crawlers in my own fishing but my father played the field, using all the baits I've mentioned and others I've doubtless forgotten. He also had a macabre passion for all kinds of "boughten" dead baits, which I also failed to share (probably for economic as well as esthetic reasons), and he was a monthly pushover for the startling variety of pickled and embalmed baits that used to adorn the outdoor magazines, and still may.

A few years ago while I was rummaging through some of my father's old fishing gear I came up with a nostalgic prize: a bottle of what looked like the coveted remains of somebody's operation for tapeworms. Closer inspection of the faded label revealed that I was the proud inheritor of a virginal jar of pickled pork rind peddled by one of the early folk heroes of preserved baits, Al Foss. If any museum of ancient fishing tackle is interested, I'll cheerfully entertain bids . . .

My father had one hell of a time trying to switch from bait-fishing to fly-fishing, and he never made it. His youngest son also had one hell of a time making the switch, and he barely made it. My father's first discernible impulse to switch occurred when one of the earliest fly-fishermen I can remember moved to our town from the East. His name was August Ludington and he managed the local Singer Sewing Machine store—that is, when he managed to resist going out fishing with my father. I tagged along on their very first trip to our South Camp and there witnessed another fisherman fishing rings around my father. It was a rare spectacle.

To make it all the more humiliating, this feat took place on Blair Pond, one of my father's and my very favorite brook trout waters (also the setting of one of my earliest fishing stories, "Fishermen at Night," in case anybody gives a damn), though it was Mr.

Ludington's first visit. I suppose what happened was that an evening fly hatch had come along and the trout were feeding far above my father's inert and ignored gob of worms. It was a lesson I never forgot, and in later years I used to wince when I saw the trout start "jumping" (as we crude bait heavers called it), because this told me they would henceforth pretty much ignore any bottom-fished bait, dead or alive.

Back up at camp I went into my lantern-lit fish-cleaning act, and I still recall my father's look of pained incredulity when, after he had dug a few wizened fish out of his giant wicker creel, Mr. Ludington calmly poured out an avalanche of glistening trout. My father's eyes bugged and his jaw fell and his lower lip trembled.

"Well I'll be goddamned," he said when he could speak. "You mean you caught all *them* with a measly little fly that ain't even fit to eat?"

"That's right, George," Mr. Ludington said. "They were really on the prod tonight."

"My, my. Let's go have a drink—I guess I sorta need one."

When my fish-cleaning chores were done I got back into camp in time to make their third round of whiskey sours. I was also just in time to witness the event I'd all along been waiting for.

"Look, Lud," my father said as they clinked drinks, "where can a fella get hold of one of them there fly outfits?"

"Oh, Chicago or Milwaukee or almost any town back East."

"How much do they run?"

"Oh, twenty or thirty dollars should put you right in business, George."

"You mean the whole works—pole, reel, line—and some of them fake flies?"

"That's right, George, except we fly-fishermen call them *rods*, not poles."

"Hmm . . . Do you think you could get hold of an outfit for me?"

"Sure thing, George," Mr. Ludington said, glancing my way. "How about the youngster?"

"Nope, 'way too young for that there fancy new fangled fishing. How long will it take?"

"Should be here in a week, ten days," Mr. Ludington said, rising. "Here's bumps to the world's latest convert to fly-fishing."

"Thanks, Lud," my father said, glancing at me. "Step lively and take the man's glass, son—can't you see it's empty? Might so well freshen mine up, too."

But the world's newest fly-fisherman never quite made the grade, as I've said. In fact his grotesque attempts were a disaster from the start, perhaps because his main motivation was wounded pride rather than any genuine feel for fly-fishing. I still have his antique fly outfit: an awesomely long and heavy rod made of ash, I believe; an old level silk line virtually time-glued to the corroded reel; and, the richest prize of the lot, a fat leather wallet full of snelled English flies of unfamiliar patterns, most of them never used, some of them still curled away in their parched soaking pads.

I recently went over these ancient treasures and, as I did, recalled some of the highlights of his gallant efforts to make the switch. Mr. Ludington tried valiantly to show him how to cast but my father could not seem to get it through his head that fly-casting was not a matter of brute strength but rather of rhythmic, purposeful timing. And since he was a big powerful man with a magnificently short fuse, sometimes he looked like a man trying to beat up the water into a lathered vat of his brewer father's choicest beer.

When Mr. Ludington was with us, out of pride my father pretty well stuck with his flies, but when we two were alone he'd often come sidling over and sheepishly mooch some worms off his youngest son. When the sad day finally came that Mr. Ludington had to move away all pretense fled: the fly outfit was reverently laid to rest, without flowers, and the collapsible girder permanently reappeared.

My own conversion to fly-fishing, if not quite so dramatic or traumatic, was in some ways even more prolonged and uncertain.

147

By this I do not imply that all older bait-fishermen are too soaked in sin ever to switch to fly-fishing; in fact, I know two notable proofs that it can be done if one really wants to. One is my old friend, the late L. P. "Busky" Barrett, who was past seventy when we taught him fly-casting; the other, a younger fishing pal, Anthony "Gigs" Gagliardi, was in his mid-forties when he made the switch, last summer further reddening our bourbon-flushed faces by catching the largest brookie of the lot.

Another advantage I had over my father was that by my mid-teens I began to feel a vague but growing disillusion with the *way* I was taking my trout. For one thing, I was getting weary of all the fuss and bother and uncertainty of gathering, preserving, and fishing with live bait. But mostly I felt an increasing distaste for the tied, inert, plunking quality of the way I was fishing compared with the dash and singing grace of men like Mr. Ludington.

But still I did not forsake bait-fishing, and after Mr. Ludington left town I kept doggedly plunking away, more out of inertia and lack of guidance than anything else, I suspect. By the time I was ready for college my fishing went into sort of an eclipse, my summers being largely devoted to selling everything under the sun— "Good day, Madam, may I please demonstrate the wondrous new housewife-emancipating Mother Goose self-wringing mop?"—and also celebrating my belated discovery that chasing girls was almost as much fun as chasing trout. But one day my schooling was over and I was back home again clutching my diploma and looking around for my old fishing gear.

I found it and shortly after that I had the good fortune to meet Tommy Cole on a trout stream. I'd known about little old Tommy for years, of course, as one casually knows just about everyone in a small town. I knew him as one of the town's few dedicated native fly-fishermen as well as a bit of a choosy and aloof loner. Anyway, that day we fell to talking and discovered that both of us fished just about every day, so we made a date to go out together. We did, and hit it off from the start, and soon were fishing together almost daily.

from Trout Magic (*1974*)

As I look back on it, it seems both fitting and fateful that a chance meeting with a spunky fisherman on a remote trout stream not only changed my mode of fishing but in many ways, I suspect, my whole way of life. I'd now like to try to tell a little about this change and about the remarkable little man who inspired it.

2

Thomas Wellington Cole was a dark, slender little man of Cornish ancestry who had all the natural grace and gentility that as a boy I dreamed only dukes possessed. Though his formal education was both sketchy and brief, when he was not fishing or prowling the woods Tommy was an omnivorous reader and one of the most widely informed people I ever knew. Though I scarcely equate proficiency at word games with the highest cerebral flights, one of Tommy's more baffling feats was his ability regularly to solve the tough *New York Times* Sunday crossword without a dictionary, though I knew a fellow fisherman of his who couldn't even work the northwest corner of same with the help of five feet of encyclopedia.

As a young man Tommy also had a natural aptitude for mechanics and, like many Upper Peninsula of Michigan natives of that First World War era, was lured to the Detroit area to work on Henry Ford's budding assembly lines. Though he liked his job and the high wages, he keenly missed his Lake Superior bush country. When finally we got into the war to make the world safe for democracy (which world, ironically, became more and more totalitarian), Tommy promptly enlisted and was sent to the front in France where, after much harrowing action, the Germans gassed him and he was ultimately shipped home. Since with his ravaged lungs he could no longer do hard labor, he finally found a job in a nearby town chauffeuring a country doctor.

This chance job opened up whole new fishing horizons for Tommy, for it seemed that when Doctor Moll wasn't delivering babies he was out in the brambles delivering flies over trout. This was a daily ritual, in fact, and since the old doctor took quite a fancy

149

to little Tommy, he soon initiated his new chauffeur into the art of fly-fishing and even taught him to tie his own flies, including the Doctor Trude fly, whose creator Tommy's doctor long knew and had often fished with.

By the time I got to know Tommy the good doctor had transferred his trout fishing to some pastoral celestial realm and Tommy had returned home, resolved never again to bear arms other than a fly rod. This resolve included shunning all steady work and living on his modest disability pension and going trout fishing every day. By then I too was fishing almost daily, so we soon joined forces and started going steady. And from the very first day Tommy began a subtle campaign to wean me away from bait-fishing and win me over to the fly—a rather large, uncertain undertaking as it finally turned out.

Tommy was that rare combination, a gentle man as well as a gentleman, and so he sensibly proceeded not by ridiculing and running down the way I fished, but by trying to make me see that fly-fishing was simply a vastly more exciting, artful, and humane way of wooing a trout. From the outset he conceded that in its way bait-fishing responded as much to patience and skill as did other forms of fishing—something I already ruefully knew from years of fishing with such wily bait foxes as Edward "Bud" Harrington and, later, Bill Gray, a real wizard with bait.

At the same time, Tommy kept pointing out that since the whole strategy of bait-fishing was to let the fish swallow the bait while the fly-fisherman, upon pain of instant rejection, had to strike his fish at once, in practice this meant that the mortality rate of returned bait-caught trout was virtually total, while that of fly-caught trout was virtually nil. The accuracy of Tommy's shrewd observation was borne out later by the field studies of my old fisheries friend, Al Hazzard (with whom I had much exciting fishing while he was still stationed in Michigan), and many others.

Tommy also quietly reminded me—as well as demonstrated

almost daily—that the fly-fisherman was rarely plagued by catching such nongame fish as suckers and chubs and the like, though these trash fish were often the annoying bane of the bait-fisherman's existence. One evening after I'd caught such a monotonous procession of stunted perch that I'd run clean out of worms and had to quit, Tommy squinted over my way for a spell, rubbing his chin, and finally spoke. "Look, pal," he said, "if you play your cards right and also promise to clean out my trout I'll be glad to rent you the fly I'm using for only half a buck."

"Go to hell, Cole," I said, folding my girder and sitting there morosely batting mosquitoes while Tommy played and deftly netted still another trout.

During these propaganda sessions, which ran the gamut from the needle to the bludgeon, Tommy also pointed out that though the common angleworm could often be a savage killer when the trout were bottom feeding, there were frequent periods during a fishing day, especially during a good fly hatch, when virtually all the trout were cruising and feeding at or near the top.

"During these periods," he once said, "a plunking bait-fisherman might just as well heave out a stillson wrench."

"Yes, I know," I said, remembering.

He also gently kept harping, and finally made me see, that for a fisherman to restrict himself to fishing the same lure all day—which is essentially what the bait-fisherman does—is as dull and boring and foolishly self-confining as an eccentric fly-fisherman who would regularly go fishing with but a single fly.

"Unless you're a commercial fisherman," he ran on, driving home his point, "the main aim and fun of going fishing at all is the action a guy gets, not the goddam fish—which, like as not, he'll either throw back or give away."

"Yes?" I said, listening closely.

"And as I think I've already shown you, chum, the best way to get action trout fishing is to carry a varied assortment of flies—types, sizes, patterns—so that, if you're lucky, you might finally toss out something they really want." He widened his hands. "It's as simple as that, pard—or do you still fail to see the light?"

"I do *see* it, Tommy," I once all but wailed, probably while threading on still another worm, "but I can't seem to be able to convince myself that a hungry trout will continue to spurn something that's good to eat in preference for grabbing a bare hook adorned with assorted fluff that's fake and no good." I sighed, groping for words. "It seems you're making me a fly-fisherman in my head, Tommy, but not yet in my heart."

"That will come," Tommy solemnly promised.

A whole season passed this way, and part of the next, with Tommy eloquently preaching the gospel of fly-fishing while I kept doggedly pelting out my "pork chops"—Tommy's scornful generic term for all live bait. Along about mid-season of the second year Tommy seemed to take a new tack: he talked less about the joys and advantages of fly-fishing and instead seemed bent on demonstrating them. Meanwhile, I wondered whether he'd given up on me or was instead trying to shame me into the paths of virtue. Whatever he had in mind, one thing rapidly became clear—almost daily he monotonously beat hell out of me fishing.

It must have been sometime around mid-August (this was before I started keeping daily fishing notes) that Tommy got a tip from a retired fishing pal that there used to be some fabulous late-summer brown fishing on a certain remote stretch of the upper reaches of the Bogdan River, somewhere above the third wooden bridge, and that maybe the place was still worth a shot.

Our own fishing was in a bit of a late-season slump, so the next afternoon we threw my little cedar boat on top of the old Model A (which the tipster had said was needed to reach the place), and headed for the third wooden bridge to have a look. Once there we quickly unloaded the boat and hid the Model A (against the prying eyes of rival fishermen) and were soon pushing our way upstream, using canoe paddles for oars.

We swiftly saw that Tommy's informant was at least partly right:

the place was indeed isolated and hard to reach and, after a half-mile or so of maneuvering our way between the lush growth of overhanging tag alders, I was about ready to drown Tommy's tipster, having already accumulated quite enough material to write two books about all the phony fishing tips I'd followed.

Then came a spell of faster and shallower water, during which we several times had to get out and pull the boat, then a long stretch of more depressing tag alders. Then, rounding a slow bend, we came upon a wide, deep, open stretch, really an enormous pool, bounded on both sides by grassy natural meadows—"My friend says the Finnish farm kids used to swim here," Tommy explained—and suddenly we were beholding one of the most spectacular rises of big trout I've seen anywhere, before or since.

"Head her inshore," Tommy tensely whispered, and, once beached, we grabbed our gear and began rigging up with trembling hands. This was back in the gut leader and silk line days so, amidst all the plashing of big rising trout, meticulous Tommy had to go through the daily ritual of dressing out his line and scrubbing his leader and all the rest while all I had to do was uncollapse my girder and impale a crawler on my harpoon and quick plop it in.

At least bait-fishing has one small advantage, I thought as I made my first plop, but this advantage rapidly waned. By the time Tommy was rigged up and ready, I had caught several wriggling chubs and one gasping sucker and was towing in another.

Tommy moved upstream a decent distance and made his first business cast as I was disimpaling my latest sucker. Almost instantly he was on to a tail-thwacking, rod-bending brown, which he quickly creeled. By the time my harpoon was freed and rebaited he had caught and returned two more lovely browns and was fast to another.

Doggedly I arose and flung a writhing new gob of crawlers far out into the steadily dimpling pool. Something grabbed it before my hook had settled and almost wrenched the girder out of my hands as it roared off and away, and I found myself engaged to a threshing tiger.

"It's a real *dandy*!" I hollered, bringing all my bait lore to the playing of my prize, my straining girder almost bent double, while Tommy held his fire and watched me land my epic fish.

"Boy oh boy!" I hollered, deftly thrusting my net under him (my sole concession to Tommy's way of fishing) and straining to hold high, for all the world to see, the slobbiest, yawpiest, most repellent sucker either of us had ever beheld. "Oh," I said in a small voice, abruptly sitting down. "Oh," I repeated, and then I just sat there, dully watching the crazily rising browns.

"If you'd only thought to bring your watercolors," Tommy said after a bit, "you could paint some mighty purty trout spots on it."

"Go to hell, Wellington," I murmured, on the verge of tears, heaving the mammoth sucker far back in the meadow.

Tommy reeled in and moved down my way and thrust out a supple, tanned hand. "Here," he said sharply, motioning with his fingers, "hand over that goddam girder."

"Yessir," I said, surrendering my treasure and watching him collapse and toss it clattering into the bottom of the boat.

"Take this," Tommy said, thrusting his precious fly rod out at me, "and go sit your ass in the front of the scow."

"Yessir," I said, automatically obeying.

"Tonight I'm going to make a fly-fisherman out of you," Tommy quietly vowed as he squatted in the stern and grabbed up a paddle, "or you'll never in hell ever make it."

"What d'you mean?" I said, bristling.

"Just what I said. Now shut up and pitch out that fly—without my good eye on it, if you'll please kindly try and manage that."

Before we left the pool I had busted off on two beauties and finally landed a third. Then in the gathering dusk Tommy slowly paddled me down through the narrow lane of tag alders, which by now seemed a boiling cauldron of threshing fish, during which I caught four more browns and lost some more of Tommy's flies, one lost brown seeming almost as large as an overfed water spaniel.

By the time we reached the third wooden bridge my little cedar boat carried a dedicated new convert to fly-fishing. "Tommy," I said, grabbing and pumping his hand when we landed, "thank you for turning your back on one of the most sensational trout rises we've ever seen, just to turn a stubborn bait-fisherman into a fly-fisherman. Tonight, my friend, you really made it and I thank you from the bottom of my heart."

"Cut out the corny sentiment," Tommy said gruffly, "and hold that bloody flashlight steady so a man can see to clean out these trout. Quit shaking, will you?"

"Yessir," I said, watching the kneeling, blurred figure of Tommy through the dancing columns of insects and trying to hold back my convulsive sobs of joy that tonight, thanks to this gallant little man, I was not only a fly-fisherman in my head but at last in my heart, the only place I guess it really matters.

A Flick of the Favorite Fly

1

'Twas the night before Christmas when all through the house not a sound could be heard above the interminable caroling and trilling over the radio about some free-spending lover boy who kept pelting his adored with the damndest assortment of Christmas junk I ever heard of, winding up with, of all things, a partridge in a pear tree—for which coveted yuletide prize, as anybody knows who's ever owned one, she must surely have long been panting. Then the phone rang and I gratefully dove for it.

"Michigan's mightiest piscator," I said, prolonging the first syllable of the last word beyond any shred of decency, thinking the call was from one of my local fishing pals.

"Merry Christmas, mighty fisherman," a strange voice said. "This is Art Flick."

"Oh, I'm so sorry, Mr. Flick," I mumbled contritely, feeling my ears burning. "I thought you were one of the local boys I fish with. We carry on that way."

"What's that?"

"I mean I thought you were somebody else . . . What I mean is

157

I didn't mean to sound so braggy . . . Oh hell . . . Merry Christmas to you, Mr. Flick. You must have got my letter about your book."

"Yes, my publisher just forwarded it, hence the delay in thanking you. So tonight on an impulse I thought I'd phone and say hello and tell you how tickled I am to get such a nice fan letter from the author of *Trout Madness*, which I too greatly enjoyed. That makes us even."

"Not quite," I said, "because I write only in winter, while you sacrificed three whole summers of fishing to gather the dope for your book. Your book is based on solid fact while some of my more caustic critics call my fishing tales my best fiction. You wrote your book the hard way while I suspect that if I could always have fished all winter I'd probably never have written a line."

"You're making me purr," my caller said, chuckling. "I also wanted to tell you I'm thinking of accepting your kind invitation to come out your way fishing."

"*Now?*" I shrilled, glancing out at the windrows of drifted snow that almost reached our windowsills.

"Scarcely," Art said. "Probably not till late June or early July, depending upon the water level of my own Schoharie, which usually gets pretty low about then."

"Simply wonderful," I said. "I don't mean about your favorite river pooping out but about your coming out here fishing."

"*What's that?*"

"I mean how would you plan coming?"

"I'll probably drive and come by way of Canada so I can maybe stop and fish any likely spots I see along the way. My maps show Canada may be the shortest route."

"I think it is," I said, "and surely more pastoral. I believe you cross over near Buffalo and repatriate in Michigan almost within casting range of my back door."

"Your three minutes are up," the operator chimed in—which may furnish some small clue about how many Christmases ago our deathless conversation took place.

My caller took the hint, clearing his throat for a quick farewell. "Well then," he said, "I'll be seeing you next summer if all goes well."

"Great. And I'll be rereading your book and making up a list of trouty spots for us to hit. Merry Christmas."

"Happy New Year," Art Flick said, varying the formula. "Until next summer, then, good-bye."

After hanging up I strained to hear that clucking partridge in his pear tree but, lo, he'd gone to roost. I longed to follow him there but felt I ought to wait up to see that Santa did not get himself stuck crossways in our chimney while delivering that new fly rod I'd so thoughtfully helped him pick out.

Meanwhile, I reached for a slender volume lying on my reading table. It was called *Art Flick's Streamside Guide to Naturals and Their Imitations*, the book that had smoked out my first fan letter ever. And since Santa as usual was running late, there seemed no time like the present to start my refresher course. So I turned to Chapter One, "Selectivity of Trout," and read on and on until, with a jolly ho-ho-ho, Santa suddenly dropped in and broke it up—my reading, I mean, not that fragile split-bamboo fairy wand he kept waving about.

The big thing I liked about Art Flick's little book was that at one stroke it had brought order out of the prevailing chaos of flies and fly patterns. Naturally I had tried many times to dispel the mystery by reading large esoteric tomes on this murky subject. But by the time the love life of the hundredth fly was revealed, pinned down, and identified, both in English and in Latin, the sedative effect became so overwhelming I sometimes had to be shaken awake. Since I couldn't ever seem to remember a hundred fly patterns, I usually compromised by remembering none.

This is the common lot of a surprising number of fly-fishermen, I'd guess—even those who've written nostalgic fairy tales about their passion—many of whom would be lucky to be able to name even a tenth of the patterns that lurk among the neglected forests of flies they cart around, much less hazard a guess what naturals they are supposed to imitate. Overnight, Art's book changed all that.

The man had done this by the simple expedient of cutting to the bone the number of working mayfly patterns he felt any sane fisherman needed to carry. To learn what these were he had devoted three summers to prowling his beloved Schoharie in upstate New York armed only with an insect net and pickling bottles—catching, sorting, and ruthlessly weeding out.

Most of the scores of species he finally rejected lost out because Art felt their hatches were either too seldom or too small or too fleeting or too nocturnal or a combination of these. When he'd boiled down the survivors to less than a dozen he tied up his own imitations of this small elite, furnishing sketches and photos of both as well as charts of their average annual emergence dates, and called the result simply *Streamside Guide.*

That winter, besides working on a new fishing book of my own, I read and reread Art's book several times. And each time I marveled over how any fisherman could possibly possess not only the stamina but the awesome character to be able to quit fishing cold for three seasons running simply to chase bugs, no matter how helpful the results might be to his slothful fellow fishermen who so merrily fished away their own summers. Like a small boy learning his ABCs, I learned by heart all the popular names of Art's selected, patterns—Quill Gordon and all the rest—getting so carried away that I even took to mispronouncing their scientific Latin names.

"March Brown," I'd chant my way down the list, intoning their Latin equivalents with the sonority of a cardinal. *"Stenonema vicarium!"* When in late June a note came from Art that he was just taking off and would probably arrive by the afternoon of the twenty-ninth his zealous Midwest disciple was all primed and ready.

Several droll coincidences attended the arrival of Arthur B. Flick. One was that it so happened another fishing pal was already visiting me, photographer Bob Kelley of *Life* magazine, who had flown in to work on the final layout of our own forthcoming word-and-picture book, *Anatomy of a Fisherman*, since duly published but now long out of print, alas.

Bob thought he needed a few more "snaps" for our book, and since the twenty-ninth dawned with a rare total overcast we decided over breakfast to make a quick dash out to Frenchman's Pond in my jeep and get our pictures and thus be rid of all distracting chores by the time Art arrived.

The occasion also happened to be my birthday, but this macabre circumstance failed to dampen our spirits as the jeep dropped off the edge of the last improved road with a thump and began bouncing its way over an endless series of jack pine roots lying exposed in the sandy ruts. As the trees grew larger and more plentiful the bouncing became so frequent and violent that our talk became a kind of breathless stutter.

"Wa-wa-what's that?" Bob inquired as we felt a sudden definitive jolt in the rear of the jeep, which grated to an abrupt stop as we sat curiously watching a lone automobile wheel go languidly bouncing past in a cloud of dust and head gracefully for the woods.

"I'm afraid that, Robert," I said wearily, "is a rear tire and wheel off the vehicle we are—or rather were—riding in."

"What do we do?" Bob said when, after searching among the tall ferns, we finally retrieved the wayward wheel—including also, I pensively noted, a rusted brake drum from which peeked a small gleaming section of broken axle.

"We flip a coin," I sighed and said, "to see who hoofs it to hell out to the nearest phone to call a goddam wrecker."

Bob held out for cribbage, a game he'd monotonously been taking me at since his arrival, but fortune smiled and I won, which so relieved me that the new cribbage champ fixed Bob a king-sized belt of bourbon to speed him on his way, pouring one for himself for company.

"I'll phone your Grace, too, so she'll know what's cooking,"

Bob said, downing his drink and shedding the last of his cameras and starting off on his long dusty march.

"Give her my love," I called after him, shivering a little over the prospect of the domestic lecture this latest calamity would surely win me over the mounting cost of keeping my fish car ambulant.

It was nearly noon before Bob got back with Olaf the wrecker man, having sensibly waited for him at the roadside tavern from which he'd phoned and where both had obviously tarried to celebrate my birthday. After a few more rounds of birthday drinks Olaf spat on his hands and backed his wrecker up to the rear of the jeep and soon had it dangling from high aloft.

"All aboard!" Olaf leaned out his cab and hollered. "Ever'body yump in."

So Bob clambered aboard and I made as though to follow. "Only vun fella rides oop hare vit me," Olaf announced, holding up a warning hand.

"How come?" I said.

"Sompbody's got to ride in da yeep," he explained. "Ay clean forgot to brung dem goldang front-wheel towing bars, so Ay guess you gotta steer da ting."

"I see," I said, and somehow managed to scale my dangling jeep and wrestle my way behind the wheel. "Toot, toot an' avay ve goo!" I hollered out my window, suddenly falling into the Viking spirit of the thing.

Naturally over the years I've arrived home from fishing in a rather wide variety of states and positions, but the day I met Art Flick was the very first time I ever made it there backward. As Olaf slowed down for the turn into his employer's garage I glanced out at the knot of curious on-lookers and saw my wife, Grace, standing next to a strange man.

"Hi, Grace," I hollered. "Who's your handsome escort?"

"Your expected guest, Mr. Flick," she called back. "He's only been waiting around since shortly after you and Bob took off after breakfast."

"Sorry," I said as we rolled on into the garage and Olaf thoughtfully brought up a ladder so I could more quickly dismount and go greet my neglected fishing guest.

As Art Flick and I shook hands I saw a tall, tanned, crew-cut man who, although I knew we were virtually the same age, possessed the shy, diffident smile of a growing boy. After introducing Bob I tried to explain what had happened.

"Forget it," Art said, looking up at the lovely persisting overcast. "Fisherman's, luck. Anyway, I wrote you not to expect me so early. Who's for going fishing?"

"Hm . . ." I said, reflectively rubbing my chin and eyeing my wife's shiny new sedan. "Hm . . ."

"We'll take my old crate," Art said, swiftly appraising the brewing domestic crisis. "You boys go get your fishing gear while I clear out some space."

"Good-bye," I called out to Grace as we three rolled off; and she bravely waved us on our way and, I think, even managed a little smile.

2

One of the first rules in fishing is that there are few rules in fishing that resourceful trout do not manage to break. Indeed, if there be any they don't smash to smithereens at one time or another my top candidate is this one: if you want to make sure the fishing will turn lousy, just dare invite a fellow angler from far away; the farther, the lousier. Before the poor man's visit is over you can lay ten to one you'll be muttering some version of the classic lament of Pierre the Guide, "Mistaire, you shoulda been 'ere las' week."

Then, ah yes, there's that companion rule I almost forgot. The moment your fishless guest takes off the fishing will magically improve. This too I've seen happen so many times I've adopted an Italian switch on Pierre's old refrain.

It was taught me by an early fishing pal, priceless Luigi "Calla-me-Louie" Bonetti, an unreconstructed bait-fisherman who was forever luring me to join him on epic cross-country hikes into fabled fishing spots that often as not turned out to be either (a) nonexistent, or (b) fly-fishable only from a tethered balloon, or (c) just plain lousy.

On one such memorable day we'd slogged and hewn our way in so far that I felt like *both* Lewis and Clark. At last Louie paused on a ridge and pointed down in triumph at a shallow malarial puddle from which we proceeded to extract an endless procession of wriggling chubs. When exhaustion and disillusion finally made us both sit down in order to gather ourselves for the long hike out, Louie the eternal optimist tried to comfort me.

"My frien'," he declaimed, reaching over and patting my sweat-dampened shoulder, "you shoulda been 'ere *anexa* week!"

And so it was during the visit of Arthur Flick. We two fished morning, noon, and night. We fished rivers and streams and we fished ponds and beaver dams. We fished alone and we fished with others, including such wily local fly-fishing hands as Hank Scarffe and Bill Nault. But nothing helped, of course, for the visitor's hex was firmly glued upon the week.

During his six-day stay I don't think Art and I between us caught a dozen decent trout. In fact I know we didn't because my daily fishing notes, which I've kept since Depression days, tell the whole sad story. Here is a typical entry. "Another day of fruitless flailing, this on the beautiful stretch around Seem's Rock below the Hoist Dam. Bob Kelley sensibly gave up and took off this A.M. Art loved the water and gave it the old college try, but around 6:00 P.M. we got abruptly washed out by an advancing tidal wave as the goddam kilowatt boys began running their goddam dam. Maybe better luck tomorrow."

And so it went day after day until, in desperation, I personally guided Art to the very hottest spot in the very hottest fishing place I knew—the old beaver dam on Frenchman's Pond.

"Arthur," I said, pointing at a calm, inky stretch lying between the two gurgling outlets and shaded and protected by clumps of overhanging bushes, "this is the hottest spot in the whole pond as well as the deepest. It is also one of the toughest spots to cast a fly," I ran on, feeling like a realtor trying to peddle the place, "which probably explains why it holds such lovely brooks."

"Hm," Art said as I paused for breath, at the same time quietly appraising his best casting position.

"Bottom's a vast tangle of crossed logs," I continued, this time pausing only to grope for more adjectives. "Favorite hiding place of some of the most gorgeous native brook trout I've seen anywhere. Go get 'em, Arthur."

The sun had emerged during my declamation, so while we waited for more cloud cover I got my second wind and proceeded to give Arthur a free lecture on the desirability of using wee flies and fine leaders on this particular pond. I found the courage to dare counsel the sage of the Schoharie because I'd been haunting the pond for at least a hundred years during which, as I told him, I had yet to behold a hatching insect larger than a wizened split pea.

Art listened gravely to my further spurts of piscatorial wisdom, nodding occasionally as enlightenment dawned. By the time I was done the sun had again gone under so, aglow with virtue over my burst of unselfishness, I withdrew out of range and gave Art the stage. "Go get 'em, Arthur," I repeated.

Arthur wasted no time, already feeding out line, and as his undulant casts gradually lengthened I had the illusion he was whipping a small bird back and forth. "*Wheep, wheep!*" chirped the screaming birdie as I stood pondering its possible breed.

"Arthur," I whispered hoarsely, "what in hell kind of fly *are* you using?"

"Oh, a little something I happened to have on," he whispered back, keeping his eye on the ball. "Just thought I'd give it a quick try before switching to the small stuff."

Suddenly it occurred to me that I'd recently heard this same soaring creature somewhere before, especially when none of Art's

165

other patterns happened to be hatching. Then came the shock of recognition.

"You mean your Grey Fox Variant?" I whispered, my heart sinking, for this was probably his biggest pattern, something akin to pelting out a swooping condor, say, compared with the minute flies I'd just been extolling.

"Right-o," Art replied, raising his arm high for the final delivery. "Happens to be a real favorite of mine . . . sorta like those wee babies are with you."

"*Ephemera guttulata,*" I murmured, all but kneeling and crossing myself as Arthur released his cast.

I watched, frozen, as the line raced far out over the waiting dam like a lash, seeming for an instant to hang suspended over the magic spot, then the leader sleepily folding over and forward and the fly slowly drifting down on target with the dreamy languor of a falling leaf.

There was the sudden flash as of a shaft of lightning as a great dripping creature rose and in one savage roll engulfed Art's favorite fly. The canny fisherman struck, gently but firmly, and I winced my eyes shut as I heard the faint telltale *ping* that shouted to the world that my friend Arthur had just been cleaned out by the most glorious trout we'd beheld all week.

"*Wowie!*" Art hollered, grinning from ear to ear. "I see what you mean."

"Anyway, I was half right," I said. "There *was* a big one there— even if he was dumb enough to hit your feather duster."

"Think I'll rest the spot and try another," Art announced, flipping open a large fly box to expose what looked like a whole nodding field of feather dusters.

"Think I'll mosey along upstream," I said, after morosely watching him tie on an exact duplicate of the fly he'd just lost.

"Don't take 'em all," Arthur ritually said, carefully testing the new fly against the leader as I shook my head and silently moved away.

"Art," I said, suddenly turning back, all pride flown, "you wouldn't happen to have an extra *guttulata* on you you could spare a pal, would you?"

"Sure thing," Art said, tossing me his big fly box. "But there's one thing you've got a little wrong."

"What's that?" I said, making a flying catch.

"Actually, it's the Green Drake that's called *Ephemera guttulata*," he went on, feeding out line, "a fly I've personally found most difficult to tie a decent imitation of."

"My, my," I said, reciprocal enlightenment dawning.

"And while the large Grey Fox Variant doesn't really imitate the Green Drake—or indeed anything for that matter—it's a mighty good attracter fly that I've also found can be a darned effective substitute when the natural is hatching." He paused in his fly-casting and cast me a quick smile. "In fact it often works, I've found, when the Green Drake *isn't* hatching."

"So I've noticed," I said, prying open his aluminum treasure chest.

"Just help yourself and leave the box there," Art said, intent on his casting. "Carry 'em by the dozen. Favorite fly, you know."

"Sorta sweeps over me," I murmured as I snitched a couple of Art's feather dusters and moved upstream toward another likely spot. But the spell was broken and though we faithfully flailed away until hunger and dusk reprieved us, neither of us saw or raised another trout that could hold even a candle to the glorious one Art had earlier made love to and lost.

3

Though I wouldn't go so far as to say that I fish to improve my mind, I do think I learned a lot while fishing with Arthur Flick. In fact I suspect all fishermen learn something from every new fisherman, even from the clumsiest duffers. And Art Flick was no duffer, heaven knows, being one of the loveliest fishermen I've ever fished with, and there've been a few. By this I mean that not only was he a

167

superb fly caster but, possibly even more important, an observant stalker, a careful hoarder of his casts, and a subtle and endlessly patient wooer of the elusive trout.

One of the biggest lessons I learned from Art, or possibly had confirmed, is that catching an occasional fish is to the enjoyment of trout fishing what encountering an occasional oyster is to the enjoyment of oyster stew: gratifying, yes, but far from everything. Poor as our fishing was in the things one could weigh and calibrate, we two had ourselves a ball.

There were several other little tricks and handy things I learned from Arthur, of course, just as he probably picked up a stray thing or two from me, these little exchanges being a sort of small currency of good will among kindred fishermen. But by all odds the most comforting lesson I learned from Arthur was this: that even the master himself, the man who tracked down and dreamed up his own creations, was himself a helpless slave to a favorite fly—even as you and I.

Why a fly becomes a favorite is about as profound a proposition to unravel, I'd guess, as Calvin Coolidge's historic revelation to a waiting nation that when a lot of people are out of work unemployment results. A fly becomes a favorite, of course, because the fisherman happened to have the damn thing on that memorable day when they would have probably as avidly hit an old carpet slipper. Either that or, at the opposite extreme, he happened to have the "right" fly on during a highly selective feeding period and, moreover, happened also to have sneezed or tripped or something and thus given it just the right action at just the right moment . . .

Like a boy and his favorite toy, any fisherman naturally favors the fly he once had all that fun with. And fun to a fly-fisherman above all means getting action. The infatuation, you see, is cumulative: the more the fisherman fishes his favorite fly, inevitably the more favorite that fly becomes. It does so because naturally any fish he catches have simply *got* to be on it, but also because henceforth he fishes his favorite with greater confidence and extraloving care—

two imponderable but sometimes crucial factors in that enchanting woodland gambol known as casting the fly. Or is that word spelled "gamble"?

A favorite among flies is like the reigning favorite in a harem: neither is likely to be soon displaced by those veiled and neglected rivals who so seldom get the boss man's nod. Or as Calvin himself might have put it, were he addicted to fisherman's idiom, flies that so resolutely remain hidden in one's fly box aren't ever apt to catch a hell of a lot of trout. And Calvin would have said a mouthful.

Came the final evening when our fun and frolic was over and the next morning Grace and I walked our guest out to his car to say good-bye.

"Arthur," I said, shaking hands, "I've just dreamed up a theory why our fishing was so lousy."

"What's that?" Arthur said—after six days, perhaps a little warily.

"I'm afraid our local trout are just plain illiterate," I said. "Since they haven't been able to read our books, naturally they couldn't know how good we are."

"I have a more comforting theory," Art said as he thoughtfully climbed into his car. "Your trout aren't illiterate at all and they've avidly read both our books."

"Yes?" I said, rising to the fly.

"Consequently they *do* know how good we are, so naturally when they saw us both together they simply fled in terror." He smiled his boyish smile. "Thanks for everything, you two, and good-bye."

"Arturo," I murmured after him as he rolled away, "you shoulda been 'ere *anexa* week."

A *Kind of Fishing* Story

or, The Night I Lost to Jack Sharkey

I was wearing a pinstriped gray business suit the night of my memorable bout with Jack Sharkey, the former heavyweight boxing champion of the world. You don't believe it? Well, you'll believe it even less when I tell you that at the time I was running for judge.

It all happened back in the days when I still played at being a lawyer and politician—that is, before the trout had entirely captured me and taken over—and I was seeking to hold a job Governor G. Mennen "Soapy" Williams had earlier appointed me to fill when an incumbent judge had quit.

Now a candidate running for judicial office in Michigan finds himself in a bit of a bind. He can't hope to soar to victory on his party's coattails (although, for the particular job I was running for, he must first be purged of all politics by courting and winning a partisan political nomination), because of a droll state law making all judicial elections nonpartisan. He can't very well flay his opponent because that would betray lack of judicial temperament. He can't go around making glowing promises because in court cases some-

171

body's always got to lose. About all he can do is exude charm, try to keep his nose clean, and wish that his name was O'Brien.

After consulting the oracles I decided to concentrate my statewide campaign on Detroit. I did so for several reasons, one being that my personable young opponent hailed from there. Another was that Detroit's sylvan precincts harbored more than three times as many sterling voters as dwelt in my entire native Upper Peninsula. Yes, Detroit was clearly where the action was, so this displaced fisherman sought it and, I must say, he got it.

My campaign was slow getting off the ground. My own party dared not be nice to me, as I've said, and the other party wouldn't if it could. So it rapidly swept over me that the voters' rapture over my candidacy was remarkably containable. People stayed away from my meetings in droves, though I did meet some pleasant janitors who had to hang around and who at least didn't throw my campaign cards away until I'd said my piece and left. There was radio and television, of course, but who wanted to contribute to the campaign fund of such a resolutely forsaken political waif?

In desperation I started haunting the auto plant gates, and to my horror discovered I'd become an invisible man. Though a towering, handsome giant in a green polka-dot tie called Soapy might occasionally penetrate their collective consciousness, the boys at the plant gates looked right through me with a sort of incurious numbness as though I wasn't there. My campaign cards dropped from their nerveless fingers faster than I could deal them out—and I'd learned dealing early at Hickey's Bar. At the end of these spooky sessions I frequently went and peered in tavern mirrors to see if I was still there.

The more I campaigned the lower my spirits sagged. To add to my general depression, this was a springtime election and I was forced to miss the opening of trout season—perhaps the crowning blow. Things got so bad that only a kind of dogged loyalty and pride kept me from chucking the whole thing and fleeing north to my trout.

One night I sobbed in my beer and poured out my woes to my old friend and former college roommate Art Farrell, who worked on a Detroit newspaper. Good old redheaded Art loyally condoled with me but managed to escape before outright blubbering set in. The next morning he phoned before I was out of the sack, I having long since quit playing the role of card-dealing invisible man at the plant gate dawn patrol.

"I have a plan," Art said, and he proceeded to unfold it. Seems each spring his paper sponsored a mammoth indoor sports show, he explained, attended by throngs of sturdy citizens—and voters. One was coming up just a few days before the election and he was sure he could get me on.

"But what would I do?" I inquired glumly. "*Sing?* I'm already hoarse from shouting down the echoes of my own voice in empty halls."

"Give an exhibition of your fly-casting ability along with Jack Sharkey," Art explained. "You've already wasted most of your talents chasing trout and this could be the big vindication."

I chose to ignore Art's subtle thrust. "You mean the former heavyweight champ?" I inquired.

"Yup," Art said. "He's a boss fisherman and top fly caster now and travels all around. How about it?"

"Why not?" I said. "If I'm gonna lose the bloody election I'd sooner go down holding a fly rod than pumping the limp hands of perfect strangers."

So Art came and drove me out to the shop of my old rod-making friend Paul Young, from whom I freeloaded the loan of a balanced fly outfit for my bout, explaining to Paul that the several lovely rods I'd bought from him were naturally far away at home.

"Just think," Art mused aloud as we drove away, "you'll probably be the first opponent Jack Sharkey ever faced who's spent a whole lifetime training for a single bout."

"Planned it that way," I said, patting the slender rod case that held my secret weapon.

Came the big night and Jack and I met and shook hands in the center of the ring—I mean the casting pool—each holding his four-ounce fly rod aloft in lieu of gloves as we cagily eyed each other before the bell. Jack was a big soft-spoken guy and he chatted amiably to put me at ease while the crowd roared and the flashbulbs popped.

First Jack was introduced to the cheering multitude, and then I was. In all the din and general euphoria I quickly forgave the announcer for so mispronouncing my name that it came out sounding rather more like a brand of imported German sausage than that of any known sitting judge. Then the bell rang and we came out warily, his pinstriped Honor, I must say, feeling just a wee bit outweighed and overmatched.

First Jack, a really beautiful caster, sparred a little and threw out some conventional back casts; and then I did; then, standing toe to toe, we both flailed away. Swish, swish, back and forth, away we went in a ballet of sheer rhythmic poetry. First in solo, then in duet, we finally shot the works, doing flocks of dreamy roll casts, brisk haul casts, side casts, dramatic steeple casts—the whole exciting business—while the crowd roared and roared.

Our bout ended in a delirium of applause, and I wrung Jack's big paw and he threw me a playful punch and, rallying from that, I left with my manager, Art, fairly drunk with triumph. Later, as we broke training together over at Casey's Bar, I mistily thanked my old pal Art and he solemnly assured me that *this* had been my finest hour.

"I take it all back," Art said. "I mean about wasting your time fishing."

"S'nothin' at all, pal," I said, lifting my glass. "Heresh to your health."

But the political show must grind on, and the next day, however languidly, I was back on the campaign trail. While it may have been pure illusion on my part, it somehow seemed that this time people clung to my campaign cards just a little longer before flinging them away. As the few remaining days passed I even toyed with the thought that I might win. After all, I reflected, judges had been elected for less . . .

Election Day came down to the wire and late one soft May evening I found myself in a car loaded with my staunchest supporters as they whirled me from a downtown meeting to a final one of the campaign out beyond Eight Mile Road. It was nearing midnight, we were only an hour behind schedule, and I was utterly pooped and longed to be home. As we tore along through the balmy night the thought that I'd soon be quitting this vast anonymous human hive began to obsess me.

"God, fellows," I suddenly blurted, "I wish I were up home fishing."

"Oh," my driver inquired politely, "are you a fisherman, Judgie?"

"I *love* it," I wailed, trying not to break down.

"Then you sure should have been over the Armory coupla three nights ago. Guy there could cast a fly through the eye of a needle."

"Tell me more," I said, perking up, for after all, *I*, Judgie, had been over at the Armory only a coupla three nights before.

"Never saw anything like it," another supporter put in. "Sheer poetry, that guy."

"What guy?" I inquired hopefully.

"Why ol' Jack Sharkey, of course," still another chimed in. "You know, the former heavyweight champ."

There was a considerable pause. Then: "Wasn't there some other guy there with him?" I asked in a small voice.

"Well, let's see now. Hm . . . Yeah, there *was* some character there dressed like a banker. Couldn't quite catch the name—sounded kinda Polock or Krautish. Anyway, he couldn't hold a candle to good ol' Jack."

"I wish I'd been there," I managed to croak.

The election came and went. I won. And after Art and his Ruthie and I had celebrated I raced home to go fishing, and have never been back.

Fly Fishermen: The World's Biggest Snobs

"Fly-fishing is such great fun," I once took a deep breath and wrote, "that it really ought to be done in bed." While I stick with this seductive notion, such an opening understandably left me little room to explore any aspects of the sport beyond certain droll romantic parallels. This was a pity because, alluring as my theory may be, there is rather more to fly-fishing than *that*.

Consequently, I've often felt a pang that I there failed to unveil still another theory I've long held about fly-fishing and the curious people it afflicts. And since the longer I fish the stronger grows my suspicion that my theory may be happening to me, I'd better get on with the unveiling while I'm still able to.

I say "able to" because to my mind—and here's my theory—fly-fishing is a progressive and hopelessly incurable disease that leaves its victims not only a little daft but high among the world's biggest snobs. At last, I've finally up and said it! (And where, ah where, is my escape passport to New Zealand?) As for my qualifications to speak, by now I am so far over my waders in the terminal stages of the disease that I feel I've won the right to risk at least a passing comment on its pathology and some of its gaudier symptoms.

Snobbery has been defined as an insufferable affectation of superior virtue. Good as this is as far as it goes, to my mind it too much overlooks the disdainful air of condescension and outright intolerance that marks the breed. And it is here that we fly-fishermen really shine, resourcefully contriving to exhibit an unvarying intolerance toward the faults and foibles of other fishermen while remaining sublimely oblivious to our own. Fly-fishermen, in fact, have raised garden-variety snobbishness to heroic heights.

Being a crafty lot we often try to hide our true natures, occasionally going so far as to exude an air of benign indulgence toward those lost souls who fail to fish the fly. But our pose is as phony as the flies we fish, for in our hearts we regard all nonfly-fishers as meat-hunting barbarians. Why only last winter in the big corner booth at the Rainbow Bar one of our top local fly casters so far cracked up that he remarked out loud that there might be a little good in other forms of fishing. I was there and heard this astonishing heresy with my own ears.

In poor Hal's favor, I should add that we were a mixed bag of fishermen that day, including even "bait flangers," which was the way the late Tommy Cole scornfully lumped all heavers of angling hardware; Hal was caught in the benevolent glow of his third (double) bourbon; and one of the flangers present was his wife's brother—who, with the disarming guile of the breed, had already grabbed the tab.

But Hal lied, of course, and the moment the flangers left and we horrified fly-fishermen turned on him, the poor man hung his head and abjectly recanted—even to standing another round. "I was just carried away," he explained huskily, hiccuping and patting his heart. "S'matter of fack, fellas, deep down I've always known fly-fishing is to the rest of fishing what high seduction is to rape."

In his advanced stages your real-gone fly-fisherman grows critical even of his fellow fly casters, grading and calipering them as though only he held the key to some piscatorial Court of St. James's. Merely being a caster of the fly is no guarantee of admission to the sacred precincts; all *that* gets you is the right to stand in line awaiting your turn to face the inquisition.

"Is it true," a typical question might run, "that last summer you were actually seen using an automatic reel?" Should the angler confess, quick is his banishment back among the angling riffraff. A like fate awaits any poor soul ever caught using a level line, while a conviction of the major offense of using a fiber glass rod means a minimum sentence of at least five years hard labor among the girder-wielding bait casters.

Different fly-fishermen exhibit different symptoms of snobbish daffiness, of course, but my own case is sufficiently typical that I think I'll confess it as a warning to others. I was born and raised and happily still live among some of the country's most exciting and varied brown and rainbow waters. To sweeten the pot, coho and chinook salmon have lately been added.

Does lucky me daily go forth to stalk these glittering monsters? I do not. In fact I haven't even fished where they live in several years much less impaled one. Instead I pursue only the smaller and scarcer brook trout and these mostly in remote back-bush ponds and beaver dams. When ecstatic visiting anglers ask me what I think of all the assorted piscatorial treasures all around me I usually reply—with a snobbish sniff—that my main reaction is one of gratitude that their well-advertised presence has taken so much pressure off my own speckled darlings. This frequently makes them glance at one another and shrug and sometimes even wink, a look I've learned to interpret as meaning "How crazy can you get?"

But visiting fishermen don't know the half of it, for my snobbish decline is even daffier than that. Not only do I fish solely for brook trout but, worse yet, only for *wild native* brook trout. In fact, I'll detour miles if I hear even a rumor that a spot I'm headed for has been planted. One morning last summer I almost swallowed my

179

cigar when I caught up with a hatchery truck bouncing into French-man's Pond evidently bent on a planting spree. Both cigar and pond were spared when I learned that the driver had merely taken a wrong turn so, forsaking all thoughts of fishing, I got out my maps and helped speed him out of there.

A companion quirk is the crazy leaders I use. They must be as long and fine as I can possibly cast, so long and dreamy in fact that I await the day when I'll get so entwined I'll have to holler for help to get cut away. This means a 12-foot leader for a starter, tapered to 5X, invariably augmented by a length of 6X tippet to which, on cloudless days, I often add a wisp of 7. On real bright days I've longed for 8X but have so far put off using it because it will doubt-less also mean carrying a magnifying glass to tie the stuff on with. And one more gadget added to my swollen fly jacket could spell the difference between survival and drowning.

Speaking of fine leader material, I recently heard a rumor that the best of all comes from the golden tresses of Scandinavian princesses. While this sounds like a bit of a gag, so intense is the fly-fisherman's eternal search for the perfect leader that, come next winter, I'd be tempted to track the rumor down if it weren't for a companion rumor that the stuff is prohibitively expensive. This seems to be so, I gather, because genuine golden-haired princesses are not only getting harder to find but, in this age of Clairol, riskier to identify. Then too, I suppose, no matter how genuine or compli-ant the princess may be, once tracked down, a certain amount of hazard must accompany such a delicate royal foraging.

This brings me to a final shameful confession, one which I know I've simply got to make but have cravenly kept putting off. Maybe it would help if I led into it gently. The thing I'm driving at is this: snobbish as I know my fishing has gotten, I am aware that there are still other fishermen who've got me beat. This brings me to the brink of my confession: since it takes a snob to spot a snob, I now ruefully know I don't rate a place in the very front pew with the certified snobs. I don't for two reasons, either one of which could forever bar me from becoming a champ. One, I don't always fish a dry fly; and two, I sometimes fail to throw back all my trout.

Now I can rationalize my sins for hours on end, telling myself that it's sheer madness for any fisherman to keep forever pelting a dry fly up in this subarctic Lake Superior country, where both our seasonal and daily fly hatches tend to start late and quit early. Or again, I can repeat over and over that any guy who returns as many trout as I do—since I fish virtually every day all summer long—ought occasionally to rate keeping a few. But suave excuses get me nowhere because I know other more lionhearted fishermen who not only return all their trout but keep stoically pelting out a dry fly even on days so cold and resolutely riseless that they have to wear lined gloves to preserve a discernible pulse.

Many times I've tried to mend my ways and go straight, and sometimes I've made it for days on end. But two things usually seduce me back into sin: my corny passion for action when I go fishing and my low peasant craving for the taste of trout. After I've spent hours fishing a place I know is good and fail even to see a rise, much less get an offer at my dry, I'm apt to cave and tie on a wet or even a nymph and go slumming down where they live. Again when the pangs of hunger gnaw me, especially when I'm fishing alone, I'm often helplessly driven to creeling a few and going on a secret binge. The big thing that keeps me from becoming a genuine topflight snob is just lack of character, I guess.

Now that you've had a glimpse at the snobbish depths to which some addled fly-fishermen can descend, it sweeps over me that I still haven't come within a country mile of showing the real how and why of what makes us tick. What starts a dewy young fly-fisherman down the rocky road to snobhood? Is it all due to individual temperament or perhaps to some genetic quirk, or maybe even a constipated adolescence? Or is there something inherently snobbish in the sport itself? Anyway, pondering these prickly questions has made me recall a fishing incident of my youth which, if it doesn't quite explain all our queer ways, may give at least a revealing clue to how one snobbish fly-fisherman got started down his own path to perdition. If it needed a title, I think I'd call it simply "A Fly-Fisherman Is Born."

It all began over forty years ago on a lazy Sunday afternoon on the upper reaches of the lovely Jordan River in northern Lower Michigan. I had sashayed down that way from my Lake Superior bailiwick to court the girl I finally married. The poor girl should have been forewarned: on only the second day I had forsaken her to pursue the exciting new sport of fly-fishing, new to me, that is.

Though I'd been flailing away for several hours, diligently whipping up quite a froth with my spanking new fly outfit, my efforts had so far met with a remarkable lack of success. As I see it now, my failure was doubtless due to a lavish combination of two things: my own sad ineptitude plus the awesome outfit I was using.

This latter consisted of a sturdy three-piece split-bamboo fly rod for which I'd paid exactly $5.95, with postage thrown in, and which the longer I hefted the stronger became my conviction that its builder had cagily designed it to do double duty at pole vaulting. To this I had clamped an old Martin automatic reel carrying an equally venerable level silk line, both given me by one of my early fly-fishing heroes, Tommy Cole. Where I had dredged up the short bedspring coil of gut leader I was using I have mercifully forgotten, but I do recall it was strong enough to tow barges with. Upstream.

To this hawserlike leader I had tethered a giant buck-tail streamer and, thus armed, had managed to put down every rising trout I'd so far encountered. That took a bit of doing because, back in those days, one still saw far more fish than fishermen on the lovely Jordan—not to mention those latter-day armadas of clanking canoes monotonously firing off their salvos of beer cans.

Finally, after much floundering and splashing, I made my way down to a deep partly shaded pool at the foot of a long riffle, some-where, I believe, about Grave's Crossing. Being a little disconsolate as well as winded, I paused there to admire the view and take a five. Suddenly the mysterious calm of the pool was rudely interrupted. The biggest trout I'd seen that season exploded in its middle, sending out a series of tiny wakes. As I scrambled into position to hurl my feathered anvil, the trout again rose, and yet again.

Brandishing my rod like a knight his spear, I began whipping my huge fly back and forth, back and forth, paying out line as my gaudy harpoon screamed ever faster past my ear. Then, along with a wee prayer, I let her go and my fly plopped down into the pool with the thud of a landing capsule just as my trout rose. I struck; I missed; and I narrowly escaped losing an ear as my fly hurtled past me, successfully harpooning a lurking tree in its wild backward flight. Had I hooked the trout I have no doubt he would have landed across old Highway 66.

I had read somewhere, possibly in early Bergman, that canny fly-fishermen always rested a startled trout, so I splashed out of there and toiled up the steep bank and retrieved my fly from an overhanging elm. Then I composed myself under its shade to watch the pool. After ten minutes of craftily resting my prize, with still no rise, I debated getting the hell out of there and maybe at least raising a beer.

"Maybe I stunned him," I mused, perhaps not entirely an outside speculation considering the fly I was using. Finally I decided to give him another ten minutes, so I lit a cigar and pored over my lone fly box, admiring my dozen or so equally imposing flies, all decorated in various colors, all the time waiting for my trout to become unstartled.

Two low-flying ducks came hurtling upstream just as my giant trout rose. For a second I had a wild thought he'd risen for them, but no, they were wheeling round the upstream bend as he rose once again. So again I got out my fly box with trembling hands and pored over my feathered treasures, finally choosing and tying on another giant streamer of equal caliber and fire power but rather different hue. I had already learned, you see, that we crafty fly-fishermen had to vary our subtle offerings.

I glanced downstream to plan the angle of my new assault and my heart sank. Another fisherman was wading round the downstream bend, fishing as he came, headed straight for my private pool. As I sat watching him inch along, listening to the slow rhythmic whish of his casts, my feeling of resentment at his presence turned gradually to admiration and then to concern—admiration for his superb casting ability; concern lest at any moment he be swept away.

For as he drew closer I saw that my intruder was a very old man, incredibly fragile and spindly, looking as though he'd be far more at home in a wheelchair attended by a nurse than out here alone breasting a powerful stream. He was in water up to the limit of his waders, precariously teetering and balancing, pluckily bucking the current with a tall wading staff. As I watched with growing apprehension, the macabre thought flashed over me that if he sneezed about then he'd surely ship water and that if *I* sneezed he might even drown.

But on he came, slowly, coolly, apparently serenely unruffled by the glorious trout rising steadily between us. It was the only riser in sight, in fact, but still the old man did not hurry, fishing every inch of the riseless water between himself and the pool, delivering each loving cast as though it were his very last.

I leaned forward tensely when the old man had worked himself into casting range for *our* trout. But no, he still was not ready; instead, with cupped hand he was lunging at the surface, seeking (I sagely concluded with an assist from Bergman) a specimen of the floating naturals. Finally he caught one, which he studied at length through a little glass. Then, still using his glass, he began producing and poring over a series of fly boxes that could have stocked both Abercrombie's and Mills and Son. Then he found and pounced on his prize like a dieting dowager plunging for a bonbon. Then came the slow tying on of his new fly, then the hand testing of fly against leader. When finally he straightened and faced our steadily feeding trout, I sighed and weakly sat back.

"Wheesh!" went his line as he deftly fed it out in short side casts, gradually lengthening it and facing more upstream, the line now undulating like a fleeing serpent, even to a low screaming hiss. Back and forth it went, drawing ever closer, ever back and forth, lazily back and forth, in a kind of surrealist ballet.

Then came a forward cast during which he seemed subtly to stiffen and brace himself; then the sudden release, with both arms held high like a diver's, and I marveled as the line coiled forward like a lash high above the pool, seeming to hang poised for a moment before ever so gently descending, the leader dreamily curling forward like the unfolding of a ballerina's arm, the tiny fly itself settling last upon the water with the languid grace of a wisp of airborne thistledown.

The fly circled uncertainly for a moment and barely began its brave descent when the trout rose and engulfed it in one savage roll. The old man flicked his skinny wrist to set the hook and the battle was on. All the while I sat there tensely watching, hypnotized, drinking in the memorable scene, watching an old man's skill pitted against this dripping eruption of nature, watching the gallant trout's frantic rushes and explosions followed by periods of sulking calm as it bored deep, trying to escape its barbed tormentor, the throbbing line and leader vibrating like the plucked string of a harp, watching even the firefly winking as a succession of tiny spray-born rainbows magically came and went.

I do not know how long it was before the old man had lowered his net into the water and, almost before I knew it, was straining and holding aloft a glistening, dripping, German brown trout of simply enormous proportions. Again I watched closely as the old man turned his sagging net this way and that, admiring his catch, nodding at it, seeming even to be whispering to it, then carefully unhooking it and—here I almost fell off my perch—with both hands gently lowering his prize to the water where, with a sudden flash, it took off and away.

"Bravo!" I leapt to my feet and shouted, thrilled and carried away by the superb performance I had just witnessed.

I had startled the old man and he did a quick little balancing act during which he doubtless shipped some water because, as he peered up at me testily over his glasses, he emitted a grunting sound and, scowling, looked away.

"Look, Mister," I shouted, emboldened by this warm show of fishing camaraderie, "wouldn't it be much safer and easier if you turned around and fished downstream?"

This time I'd really shaken him; it was as though I'd struck him with a stone. Again the quick little jig from which he soon rallied to give me a withering glance, peering up at me as though studying some species of gnat, all the while making funny noises in his throat. Then it came.

"Young fellow," he quavered in a high falsetto voice fairly dripping with scorn, "I'd sooner be over on the Ironton ferry dock settin' on my ass plunkin' for bass than ever fish a wet fly downstream!"

"Yessir," I said, hanging my head, sneaking out of there with burning ears, making a wide detour downstream and then stealthily back to the river, where, from behind a protective clump of bushes I secretly watched the old man at his devotionals.

And as I watched and mused I was overtaken by a vision, and presently found myself dreaming a wistful dream that someday, some way, I would be able to fish and carry on like this magnificent old goat.

Size Is Not the Measure

The other day I ran across a fishing article in a Detroit newspaper that filled me with delight and melancholy. The part that particularly caught me was a reference to a recent claim made by a state fish biologist that, in his opinion, more and more fishermen were turning away from the pursuit of brook trout in favor of other species of trout and salmon, particularly the generally larger- and faster-growing brown.

My delight came from learning of the lessening of competition for what still remains *my* favorite fish, all state fish biologists to the contrary, the lovely brook trout; my melancholy over the realization that evidently our national passion for bigness for bigness' sake was now afflicting even my fellow fishermen.

The article went on to say—and I took no joy at all from this— that this growing obsession with bigger fish was already affecting many state planting programs and that, in response to mounting clamor for vaster piscatorial targets to pelt away at, fewer and fewer brook trout were being planted compared with burlier specimens.

Pondering this sad news it suddenly swept over me that, come to think of it, I hadn't seen a single picture of a brook trout adorning any of the outdoor magazines in many months—or was it years? Their places had instead been taken by gaping specimens of heavyweight trout or salmon—not to mention a growing variety of deep-sea monsters—being held aloft at risk of hernia by smirking fishermen who could often be distinguished from their victims only by their grins.

The more I brooded over this sad state of affairs the more my melancholy deepened, and it did so for a variety of reasons. First of all I felt that this new obsession with bigger and bigger fish was inevitably transplanting to our trout waters the whole competitive, strident, screechingly acquisitive world of business. Worse yet, that in doing so, fishermen were sacrificing one of the main rewards and solaces of going fishing at all, namely, that fishing is—or at least used to be—the world's only sport that's fun even to fail at. Further, by making an ego massage out of this ancient sport, these deluded souls were actually creating more not less frustrated and unhappy fishermen for the simple reason that the more fishermen there were who panted only after big fish naturally the fewer big fish there would be left to be caught. Finally it struck me as sad beyond words that fishermen themselves would let one of the world's oldest and loveliest contemplative pastimes turn into a competitive rat race much as we have allowed modern basketball to degenerate into sort of a commercialized polka played only by bored pituitary freaks.

All of which brings me to one of my own big-fish experiences. It all happened back in the distant days when you could still buy a decent split-bamboo fly rod for under thirty bucks. Hank and I had been fishing what I shall call Big River—for that was not its name—all that hot sunny Sunday with little luck. Toward late afternoon, bouncing out in the Model A, we decided to take a quick look at a certain slow deep bend at the foot of a long run of white water.

Nothing but juniors were rising, and we were about to

resignedly take off when Hank spotted some splashy risers a little way upstream, above the fast water. Immediately he began twitching and champing to have after them. Would I care to join him? he magnanimously inquired, his voice suddenly grown hoarse with excitement.

"You go, pal," I swiftly said, waving him away with the back of my hand, the soul of generosity. "Anyway you spotted 'em first and moreover I'm hungry and pooped, not to mention still a little hung over, so I'll just stay down here and see what happens."

"Don't catch 'em all," Hank said, eagerly splashing away upstream.

Half an hour later Hank had disappeared around a distant upstream bend. Meanwhile I had caught and released at least a half-dozen juvenile brookies. Dusk started falling, along with my spirits, so I sighed and plumped myself down on the damp bank and lit an Italian cigar and swatted away at mosquitoes and wondered what in hell I was doing there. Swirling bats soon joined the swarms of mosquitoes and, far overhead, I could occasionally hear the soaring screech and the diving *spung* of hunting nighthawks.

A fish rose above me, scarcely ten feet away and virtually inshore. Another junior leaguer, I thought, and I sat there idly debating whether I should bother to get up and try for it, my drowned little Adams trailing idly in the water below me. The fish rose again, making a neat little dimple and, still sitting, I executed a lazy-man's side-wheeling roll cast, flipping my sodden fly upstream where it landed in the fading circle with a genteel plop.

The fish took it underwater, ever so gently, and I flipped my wrist to set the fly and then jerked my rod to bring the foolish juvenile closer so I could release him. Nothing budged, and instead my line and leader grew taut and my rod bowed into a daisy hoop.

"Damn," I said aloud, "the little devil's got me snagged," and I wearily got to my feet to go unsnag myself.

With my first splashing step upstream my "snag" started moving out into deeper water. Curious and still unbelieving, I cautiously pumped the fish up to the surface for a look and almost swallowed my cigar when I beheld a dark dorsal fin cleaving the water at least a foot back from the end of my throbbing leader. I took another step, the fish made a powerful rush for deep water, and the battle was on.

At least an hour later Hank came splashing downstream and played his flashlight on a huddled figure still clenching a cold cigar in his teeth, his bone-tired wrist still glued to his straining daisy hoop.

"What in hell *is* it?" Hank asked in an awed voice.

"Dunno, Hank," I answered weakly, "but it sure feels like an overweight mermaid."

"Let's take a look," Hank said, holding his flash close to the dark water. We both gasped when we saw the proportions of the monster brown I was on to, its gills now gulping uncertainly, the great fish half-lying on its side. Ten minutes later I drew the fatigued creature inshore and, using both arms as a scoop—my landing net wouldn't begin to take him—somehow tossed him up on the bank and fell beside him where we both lay for a long time, panting and exhausted.

This is the second most memorable fish I ever caught. It is memorable not only because I have never before or since played any fish for nearly so long but also because I caught him on a Size 16 Adams tied onto a 5X tapered nylon leader testing to barely two pounds. How I ever held on to him I still do not quite know, but I suspect it was a lucky combination of the dreamy relaxation of a hangover plus the curious fact that this big fish foolishly failed to try to leave the pool while still fresh enough to have easily cleaned me out.

Since then I have caught several bigger rainbows and coho salmon, though how much bigger I cannot say because in all the excitement of that distant Sunday I clean forgot to weigh and measure my memorable brown. Yet this gallant brown remains memorable not because of his size but mainly because of the improbable tackle I took him on.

Today there is scarcely an outdoor magazine or fishing whatnot that doesn't regularly display small regiments of anglers proudly displaying even more "monstorious" fish than my memorable brown. Most of these pictures leave me cold for one simple reason: they rarely reveal the size and strength of the tackle they were taken on. Lacking that crucial information it strikes me this whole repetitious big-fish picture gallery is nothing more than a dreary and boring parade of champion winchers and weight lifters.

If catching this monster brown was my second most memorable fishing experience, how much bigger, one may ask, was my most memorable fish? The answer is he wasn't nearly so large, and in fact my big brown could probably have devoured him in a single gulp, sans salt or pepper. For the really memorable thing is that I took this fourteen-inch brookie last year on Frenchman's Pond (don't look for it on any map) on a Size 20 Jassid, hooking him over a tangled underwater logjam and somehow dancing him out of there and finally landing him, using a basic 5X leader with a 7X tippet testing to barely a pound. The feat was so memorable, in fact, that I finally released the tired fish as a reward for gallantry.

Any fisherman who feels proud over catching a monster fish (or indeed any game fish) on a hawser is just as deluded, it strikes me—and should feel just as ashamed—as those virile chest-thumping hunters who continue to bombard our fragile native antelopes with elephant guns. It isn't the *quantity* of the fish caught that counts; its the *quality* of the means used in catching him. To paraphrase the old jazz song, it ain't what you catch but the way that you catch it.

My old nonfishing lawyer friend, Parnell McCarthy, recently put his finger on it. We were enshrined in the Rainbow Bar having a late-afternoon quiet one together and the old boy was idly fingering a fishing catalog I'd just gotten in the day's mail.

"All a bunch of craptitude," he said, flashing me a picture of a regiment of grinning fishermen displaying their assorted Loch Lomond monsters. "The trouble with these damn fish pictures is

they fail to furnish identification charts telling who caught whom."
He wagged his head. "You fishing guys are getting as obsessed with
size as the judges of our so-called beauty contests."

"What do you mean?" I inquired politely.

"Any aspiring beauty queen may have the face of a madonna,
the soul of a swooping angel, the mind of an Einstein," he sang out
like an auctioneer, holding his empty glass aloft, "but if she don't
possess a pair of bustolas at least size 36 she ain't never gonna git
picked queen of nothin'." He banged his glass on our table.
"They're not beauty but booby contests."

"Amen," I said, banging my own glass. "You can repeat that
again."

"Coming up!" Polly the ever-alert proprietor hollered from
behind the bar.

D. McGinnis: Guide

1

Old bald-pated droopy-mustached Danny McGinnis and his "boys"—four aging bachelors who, though all younger than Dan, were either pressing or had already overtaken their sixties—lived in an old log bunkhouse abandoned by logger Andy Ferguson around the turn of the century. This rambling old structure had been christened Andy's Fleabag by the realistic lumberjacks who'd slept in it, but during the Depression Danny and the boys had changed its name to the equally realistic one of Hungry Hollow, and that it had remained.

Hungry Hollow stood on the extreme westerly rim of the Mulligan Plains where they sheer off into the valley of the Big Dead River. These broad plains had once been covered by a vast stand of virgin white pine, but all that logger Andy Ferguson had left behind, besides one bugridden bunkhouse, was miles of charred and weathered stumps looking like tombstones in some abandoned cemetery, although some occasional passing fishermen felt they rather more resembled bleak accusing monuments to man's relentless war on nature.

The only regular work Danny and his boys ever did was to try to figure out new ways to avoid doing any regular work. This sometimes proved exhausting but had for the most part always paid off because the boys pretty much lived off the land—hunting, fishing, trapping, or hopefully foraging for overlooked vegetables in their rabbit-haunted garden plot—plus pooling their several assorted pensions and social security checks and Timmy's disabled veteran payments into a common treasury jealously presided over by old Danny himself.

Trout naturally formed an important staple of the diet of the boys of Hungry Hollow because, after all, the lovely Big Dead River made an obliging U-shaped bend just below their door. And when the fishing palled, Danny and the boys could sit outside for hours on a summer evening just swapping stories and swatting mosquitoes and watching the feeding trout rising in the river below.

"Lookit dem yiggers yumping," Swan would sometimes say, pointing. "Eff Ay din't know no better Ay vould svear it vere raining hail."

But tonight no trout were rising on the Big Dead River below Hungry Hollow. They weren't because it was still not yet the end of March and snow still lingered in the valley and the river was still clogged with chunks of floating ice. Moreover, aside from the gloomy weather, a general aura of gloom pervaded the Hollow, largely because the camp treasury was not only flat broke but two of the boys were in jail—casualties of the boys' annual Saint Patrick's Day trek to the town of Chippewa. True, all such annual treks tended to verge on calamity, but this particular Saint Patrick's Day excursion had approached outright disaster.

First Big Buller Beaudin had resented some ill-timed barroom remarks concerning the genesis and possible contents of his enormous belly, and when the smoke cleared away the place had been left strewn with broken glass and inert townsmen. Then Buller had piled up the camp Model A trying to escape the cops, thus leaving the boys without transportation. Finally, old Danny had to empty the waning camp treasury paying all the assorted fines and doctor's bills needed to keep Buller out of jail.

As if this weren't bad enough, Swan and Taconite had gone on a little spree of their own and gotten picked up for drunk and disorderly and, the camp treasury now being depleted, had each drawn and were serving thirty days in jail. Only nondrinking Timmy and old Danny had escaped the clutches of the law, but Timmy had added to the camp's woes by buying and charging an expensive new fly rod he said he just simply had to have. Yes, Hungry Hollow was in a bad way: too early for fishing, no car to ride to town in, two of the boys still in jail, and the treasury not only empty but deep in debt.

So on this raw late March night as the wind grieved in the camp chimney, old Danny glumly presided over a post–Saint Patrick's Day wake. Poor Swan and Taconite were still in jail, of course. Buller sat darning his favorite sweater—the principal casualty of his barroom brawl—his moist rosebud lips working in rhythm with each darn, while slender Timmy, the camp's reigning intellectual, sat at the oilclothed table reading a dog-eared copy of *American Sportsman*. And all the while a parched and boozeless Danny, treasurer of Hungry Hollow's busted treasury, was reduced to bottling his latest batch of home-brewed beer.

Whether or not it is true that every cloud has a silver lining, as the old song says, it was at this magic moment that the great solution was born. Timmy looked up from his reading, blinking thoughtfully, and glanced over at Danny, whose cheeks were sunken like those of a victim of pellagra as he strove to start siphoning off a new crock.

"I see by an ad here, Dan," Timmy said quietly, "where some fellas down in Wisconsin is askin' twelve bucks a day for boardin' and guidin' *bass* fishermen—with boat rent extra." Timmy paused and shook his head over the wonder of it all. "Just imagine," he snorted, "payin' all that dough just to fish them lousy crummy bass! An' here we got a lovely river right outside our door fairly crawlin' with beautiful rainbows and browns." Timmy shook his head and daintily moistened his finger to turn the page.

Danny still had the siphon hose in his mouth, his cheeks bulging with raw new beer, and he frantically wigwagged Timmy not to turn the page. *"Pah!"* he finally exclaimed, extracting and pinching the hose and at the same time spewing a stream of bitter new beer across the room. Buller must have got caught in some of the spray because he quickly looked up from his darning and held his needle poised in midair, wistfully moistening his lips.

"Look!" Danny exclaimed, "lemme see that there ad!" As Timmy handed him the magazine and Danny adjusted his ten-cent-store glasses and read it, his voice grew hoarse with excitement. "Look, Timmy, Buller—if them Wisconsin birds can git sech big dough fer lettin' city dudes ketch them slobby tourist bass, why can't *we* do the same thing fer lettin' 'em fish the lovely beauties down in our river below?"

"You mean—?" Timmy began, enlightenment dawning.

"Zackly," Danny said. "Get out your paper and pencil, me lad."

While a gradually nodding Buller alternately darned and dozed, still in the grip of his Saint Patrick's Day celebration, Danny and Timmy worked far into the night on their new ad aimed at making Hungry Hollow a mecca for jaded city fishermen. Naturally they'd run their first ad in a Chicago newspaper, because naturally every small town in America has its "big town" and Chicago happened to be Chippewa's.

"How much'll we charge 'em?" Timmy asked the camp treasurer, holding his pencil poised.

"Hm, le's see now," Danny said, sipping his mustache and working his bushy eyebrows and rubbing his bald head. "Of course they's naturally gonna have to pay more gittin' way up here past them Wisconsin bass puddles. Le's see—maybe we should ought to charge 'em half price, like say six bucks a head for found an' lodgin'—with guide service thrun in."

"Six bucks it is," Timmy said, filling in the missing item and presenting the finished ad to Danny with a nice secretarial flourish. Danny again adjusted his glasses and, his voice cracked with emotion, read it aloud to Timmy by the wavering lamplight, Buller having long since crept off to bed.

NOTICE

I got brown trout and rainbows up here at Hungry Hollow big as Eskimo dogs. You capture 'em and I'll cook 'em. Rate $6 per head per day for food and lodging—with free expert guide service thrun in. Write me c/o Polly's Rainbow Bar, Chippewa, Mich.

Resp.

D. McGinnis, guide

"Boy," Danny rapturously breathed, rubbing the mist out of his eyes, "that there's so purty I'm all kinda swole up inside." He shook his head. "Timmy, you're a goddam genius an' your ad is pure American litterchewer."

Timmy's contribution to American literature worked like a charm; the first reservations came by airmail within three days of the appearance of the ad. "Will arrive on the midnight train from Chicago on May first," Dr. Sawyer's letter ran. "My three fishing pals and I plan to spend the balance of that night at your local hotel. Please await us there."

The wounded camp Model A still remained in Chippewa unrepaired, so about midafternoon on the first day of May Danny bade the boys good-bye and took off on the long hike to town to meet the first batch of city fishermen. Swan and Taconite had by now served their time and were out of jail and so a farewell delegation of all four of the boys lined up to wave him off. Luck was with Danny—or was it?—for about halfway to town he caught a ride on a logging truck and arrived in Chippewa still long before dark not only with time on his hands but a consuming thirst in his throat.

Danny would have preferred to wait in the informal atmosphere of the Rainbow Bar or indeed almost anyplace other than the fancy new Cliff Dwellers Inn where the town swells and mining crowd hung out. But Dr. Sawyer's letter had been pretty plain on that point, hadn't it, that Danny should head for the Inn? Danny reread the letter and, yes, there was no mistake. But wait! The letter didn't say *where* in the Inn he had to wait, so Danny, who always had a keen instinct for the best place to wait, smiled and headed for the street entrance to the Inn's Colonial Taproom.

The place was crowded with laggard devotees of the cocktail hour and Danny, making his first visit there and unaccustomed to the subdued lights, groped his way to an empty stool up at the bar. The dapper young bartender, fresh out of Duluth, eyed Danny up and down, from his old round undented felt hat, his aromatic plaid hunting jumper, his floppy woolen high-water stag pants, to his incredibly muddy high-top boots.

"May I be of help to you, sir?" he said with practiced disdain.

"You sure in hell kin, young fella," Danny shot back, his mustaches bristling, "an' I'd like to compliment you fer readin' my mind."

"Yes?" the young bartender said with infinite patience. "What will it be, sir?"

"I'll take a double shot of pile-run whiskey," Danny all but roared, throwing his jackknife and a pile of loose change down on the bar.

"And what would you prefer for a mix, sir?"

"Whaddya mean mix?" Danny barked, totally at sea before such esoteric barroom palaver.

"Whaddya want for a wash?" the young bartender grated, finally lapsing into the more familiar idiom of those chronic connoisseurs of pile-run whiskey.

"*Gin!*" Danny shot back, whereupon the barroom patrons giggled and roared and tossed down their dry martinis while the skimpily-gowned lady at the piano quickly struck up a tune and old Danny tossed off his drink and ordered still another double round. Spring was in the air . . .

The midnight train from Chicago duly arrived and disgorged the four Chicago fishermen and their mounds of duffel and fishing gear. The fishermen proceeded to the Cliff Dwellers Inn and searched high and low for their missing host and guide—but Danny was nowhere to be found. Finally, smelling a rat, they sensibly made their way down to the Colonial Taproom from where, putting several clues together, they extended their search out the side-street door adjoining the hotel's imposing new rock garden. There they were met by the strange midnight tableau of the Inn's little Cornish gardener trying to dislodge a snoring interloper from his pet new flower beds.

"Damme, man, you're a-lyin' all hover me crocus 'n' tulip beds, that you are!" Cooky was shouting, all the while tugging away at and trying to arouse the inert guide of the unmet Chicago fishermen. "Come aout of there, Mister Danny, you hintoxicated bum."

"Just a moment, we'll give you a hand," Dr. Sawyer said, and so the four Chicago fishermen dug Danny out of Cooky's flower beds and reverently carried him off upstairs for transplanting in a different bed.

"'E 'urted my flawers, 'e 'urted my flawers," little Cooky wailed as the procession filed away, doing a skinny dance of anger at midnight in the spring.

Danny had survived and rallied from worse adventures than an evening spent mixing whiskey with gin and sleeping in dampish rock gardens, so the next morning he was almost his old chipper self again after he had polished off a lumberjack breakfast in the hotel dining room. Feeling his responsibilities he later guided his guests over to Burke's livery stable and helped haggle over the price of the car and trailer they rented to haul themselves and their gear up to Hungry Hollow.

"How do you feel now, Mr. McGinnis?" inquired Raymond, the driver and one of the Chicago fishermen, as their cavalcade thundered across the loose planking of the bridge over Barnhardt Creek.

"Who, me?" Danny said, starting out of a little nap. "I feel like havin' another drink."

"Before *noon?*" Raymond said, aghast.

"Why not, why not?" Danny said, winking and spreading his hands. "After all, the only time I'll ever *take* a drink is during and between meals. Strickly temperance, that's me."

Dr. Sawyer sighed and produced and passed back a bottle of city whiskey upon which Danny played a long unbroken solo, deftly drying his mustaches on his jumper sleeve when he was done. "You boys havin' a little snort, too?" he finally said, remembering his manners, making as though to surrender the bottle.

"Heavens no," Dr. Sawyer said, as the others recoiled and swiftly shook their heads. "We came way up here to catch some of those gorgeous trout you described in that intriguing ad of yours. We're in training for that, see? Fishing before drinking, see?"

"You've a point there," Danny conceded after judiciously pondering. "Jest thought you might, lads. Now me, I'm used to drinkin' before fishin' 'cause our water's so fearful cold a man needs a touch to steady his castin' arm. 'Smatter of fack it gives me a little chill even thinkin' of it. Mind if I have a wee drop more?"

"Go 'head, Dan," Dr. Sawyer said, shrugging and finally surrendering. "But it would be real nice, you being our guide and all, if you'd sort of manage to stay sober enough just long enough to kind of point out the river to us."

But Danny's bald head had already sagged down on his chest in lip-puttering slumber, from which he did not rouse until they rumbled across the bridge over Mulligan Creek.

"Almost there, boys," he chirped brightly as the rented car and trailer labored up the long sandy hill to the top of the treeless Mulligan Plains. "Take the first fork to the left fer Hungry Hollow."

"What's that water I see gleaming between those tall evergreen trees down beyond that tarpaper shack?" Dr. Sawyer suddenly asked, pointing.

"That there's the Big Dead River where you guys is gonna fish," their guide explained, adding after a pause, "An' that tarpaper shack you jest mentioned happens to be Hungry Hollow where

I lives. It's also the place you boys'll be stayin'—that's unless you prefer comootin' back and forth between here an' that fancy Inn. Jest say the word, boys—"

"Oh no, no, no," Dr. Sawyer apologized, swiftly passing back the city bottle to heal the sudden breach.

"Wups, watch out fer my truck garden, young fella," Danny called out after the breach was magnificently healed. "Better park over next to the outhouse there an' have everythin' handy."

"And who are those four guys standing out in front?" Doc shrilled.

"Oh, them's jest four ol' pals who happen' to drop by one by one durin' Depression days an' who been stayin' on temporary ever since. Jest here on a li'l visit."

"But Danny, the Depression was years and *years* ago, man!"

"By God, so it was," Danny agreed. "How the bloody time flies. My, my . . . Well here we are, boys—welcome to Hungry Hollow." He held up his cupped hand and beckoned his waiting boys with five gnarled and knotty fingers. "C'mon over here, boys, an' I'll take an' interdoosh you."

2

After a quick lunch that featured Swan's fresh home-baked bread, the city fishermen pawed away at their mounds of luggage and gradually crawled into their uniforms. It was decided that all four would start fishing from the big pool below camp, flipping coins to decide which two would start fishing upstream and which other pair down. So prolonged were their preparations, in fact, that Danny was able to spear several quick drinks from the waning bottle. When at length the four were armed and ready, Carl, one of the city fishermen, asked Danny if he planned to join them fishing.

"Mebbe later, not right now," Danny said, squinting up at the sun from his seat on the camp sawbuck. "Little too bright. Anyway, ol' Danny's only the goddam guide—an' at Hungry Hollow the golden rule is 'payin' gents first.'"

"But where's your rod, your waders, and all your gear?" Raymond asked.

"No problem," Danny said, walking over to the side of the camp and taking down a battered set-up bamboo fly rod resting on two rusty nails. Each joint was held together by adhesive tape, the cracked level line tied to a coiled piece of bedspring leader to which in turn was attached a massive hair fly adorning a hook that seemed big enough to fasten screen doors.

"Won the hull outfit in a firemen's tournament raffle in Chippewa sixteen—no, seventeen years ago," Danny explained, patting his pet.

"But your waders—your net and creel and all?"

"Don't use none," Danny said, rolling his eyes. "Saves all kinds of money fer charities an' to give them missionary fellas fer convertin' heathens with."

The Chicago fishermen averted their eyes, glancing at each other with expressions that eloquently said "what have we gotten into?"

Led by old Danny, their expert guide, they slithered and slipped their way down the steep trail to the starting Big Dead pool.

"That's it," Danny said, pointing, and the four city fishermen stood gazing at the vast pool churning restlessly in the sun, hissing and boiling like some giant witch's cauldron. "Might so well give it a try here. Same price." He then leaned his ancient rod against a tree and climbed uphill and sat on a sun-warmed rock safely out of casting range.

Raymond was the first to select and tie on the maiden fly—a downy small dry—expertly placing a graceful thistle cast into the very center of the pool. There was a sudden silvery flash and the line grew taut for an instant and then went limp.

"Whoopee!" shouted Raymond, doing a clumsy little bewadered jig. "Cleaned out on my first cast! *Whoopee!*"

"Hm," Danny said, half to himself, sitting up on his sunny perch. "Mebbe they'll be on the prod after all." He then busied himself taking on and working up a new chew of tobacco while the Chicago fishermen got under way. Two of them took and returned fairish brook trout on their first pool casts—"Small fry," Danny said—and he still sat watching as each twosome disappeared around their respective bends. Meanwhile no more big fish struck.

Once alone, Danny rose and spat and reached in his jumper and pulled out a fresh bottle of Chicago whiskey he'd somehow stumbled across and played a solo in the sun. He then descended to the water, grabbed his rod, and sat soaking his leader in the pool, stripping out line, waiting for a passing cloud to come obscure the sun.

"Ah," he breathed as the sun finally left the pool, and he reached in his jumper and pulled out a slice of Swan's freshly baked bread. Breaking off and wadding a small piece, he tossed it out into the pool. There was a quick silvery flash and the bread disappeared. He then reached for his rod and casually flipped his fly where the fish had risen.

"*Clap!*" went the striking fish, and Danny struck back, and lo he was on to a real beauty. He dropped his rod and grabbed the line, calmly pulling in the threshing fish, hand over hand, deftly unhooking the fish and dropping it into the game bag of his jumper. Once again he cast his bread upon the waters and again not in vain. Before the sun emerged he had caught two rainbows and a brown, each running well over two pounds.

"Guess mebbe the big ones ain't here today," Danny remarked to himself. "Yep, yep—guess mebbe I'll have me another snort an' meander downstream."

Meanwhile, Dr. Sawyer and Thaddeus worked their way slowly downstream, fishing with the easy precision and grace of finished experts. After all, they'd waited all winter for this golden moment, and here they were fishing virtually virgin water except for the alcoholic flounderings of one old man armed with a primitive fly rod one might better beat rugs with.

The firm graveled bottom, rarely over waist deep, made ideal wading, and the air sang with the sylvan whine and whish of their lovely casts. Not a single pocket or ripple did they miss. Once Thaddeus got a boiling rise from a really big one, but missed the strike. Both took several decent brook trout, and a few juniors, all of which they carefully returned, for *they* were after the big ones. But so far the big ones were not after them . . .

Perhaps a mile below the starting pool Doc and Thaddeus paused and held a strategy council. Could it be that old Danny was right and that it was far too bright for good fishing?

"Except for Raymond's clean-out up at the pool and the one I missed," Thaddeus said, a little despondently, "I'd swear there weren't any big trout in this river."

"Let's work our way back upstream," Doc said, recalling the lovely starting pool. "Maybe old Danny can suggest another stretch."

"I'd guess our guzzling old guide is safely up in bed by now," Thaddeus said, standing on a gravel bar and playing in a seven-inch brook trout.

"That's if he's sober enough to climb the hill," Doc said, pausing on the same gravel bar and changing to another fly. "I wonder what the old goat's up to?"

Their answer came abruptly as they heard a prolonged *"Haloo-oo-oo"* and then beheld Danny rounding the upstream bend, splashing and floundering in the middle of the river, his venerable fly rod bent double before him like a graduation hoop.

"Haloo-oo," he called again, and it was then that the enchanted city fishermen saw that old Danny was being towed, hauled, and tugged downstream by the grandfather of all giant trout, the snout of which occasionally showed above the water several rod lengths ahead of Dan.

"Loo'gout!" Danny shrilled, his skinny shanks working like pistons. "Here I come—clear the goddam way!"

But the two transfixed Chicago fishermen could only stand gaping on their gravel bar as old Danny and his fish swiftly descended upon them.

"*Spung!*" went Danny's leader as it snapped and broke just as the giant fish, in the blind fury of its run, charged clear up onto the gravel bar and lay flopping and panting at the Chicago fishermen's feet.

"*Grab 'im!*" Danny cackled in cold horror, but by now the hypnotized fishermen were beyond all movement. Then, just as the giant fish made a final riverward flop, Danny sailed through the air in a superb flying tackle and landed on top of Grampaw—*whoosh!*—where both of them lay for a long time very wet and very still.

It took three drinks from Doc's emergency flask to bring old Danny around. "Who hit me?" Danny demanded, sitting up slowly and holding his side. "Who'd hit a pore sickly ol' man?"

The game bag of his jumper had come open, strewing lovely rainbow and brown trout everywhere.

"Oo me pore side," Danny said, clutching at his left rib cage. "Oo, gimme 'nother swaller of that there booze—can't even breathe withouten 'nother swaller."

Dr. Sawyer carefully fed Danny another drink and then opened his jumper and shirt and felt his left side, Danny all the while wincing and squirming.

"Do you think I'm a little pregnant, Doc?" Danny asked when Doc was done.

"No," Doc said after pondering a bit, "but I'd guess, lacking X rays, that landing your big rainbow has cost you between three and four cracked ribs on your left side."

"'Tis well worth it," Danny said, gingerly reaching over and patting his big fish and then vainly trying to stagger to his feet. "Why don't you boys fetch the fish and we'll go back to camp where Swan'll cook 'em up and we'll all sorta celebrate like? What d'you say, boys?"

Doc and Thaddeus looked at each other and silently nodded and gathered up Danny and all the fish and splashed away upstream in the dappled sunlight. Old Danny, full of visions of the frolic ahead, even managed to break into a quavering song, one of his favorite ditties:

Oh when I'm dead an' in me grave,
An' no more whiskey will I crave,
On my tombstone let this be wrote,
'Ten thousand quarts run down his throat!'

3

The next morning the Chicago fishermen awoke throbbing of pulse and coated of tongue and groped their way to the water pail in the best Hungry Hollow tradition. But old Danny soon had them relaxed and smiling with a couple rounds of Highland Flings, a potent drink of guaranteed therapy, the secret of which Danny carefully explained.

"Jest take a triple of Hungry Hollow moonshine, a dash of lemon juice, a little sugar, and add some boiling water," he explained, holding up a warning finger. "But mind, you dassen't put too much water. Yep, yep, never too much water."

After breakfast he presented his guests with some of Timmy's big home-tied bucktail flies—"Big flies fer big fish," he explained—and lectured them for ten minutes on the need for caution and patience in stalking the big ones. "Come, lads, get your gear an' let me show you."

Walking like an aging Junker general in his rigid new corset of adhesive tape, Danny led his guests down to the pool and initiated them into the ritual of casting one's bread upon the water.

"Git ready, now, one of you," he said, tossing out a wadded morsel of bread, and—*bang*—a grinning Dr. Sawyer was soon fast to a tail-standing dandy.

"Good luck, boys," Danny said, leaving them there still watching Doc fighting his fish. "Pea soup's on the menoo tonight an' I gotta go help Swan get that started."

The Chicago fishermen had a great day and each caught and

returned several lovely browns and rainbows—but none in the same league as Grampaw, of course. That night at supper they were exultant and clamored for another celebration. The next morning they even beat Danny up clamoring for their Highland Flings. And so the days dreamily slipped by.

They overstayed their leave by three days and when they left presented Danny with a brand-new fly rod and reel and double-tapered line. They also insisted upon paying double for their keep. Moreover they made solemn reservations to return the following May. "Daniel," Dr. Sawyer concluded, "we've never seen anything to match either this superb place or your excellent canny guiding."

"Thanks," Danny said, busily putting together his handsome new fly rod.

"Good-bye, Danny," they called out, waving, as they pulled away. "See you next May if not sooner."

"Yep, yep," Danny said from the camp doorway, saluting them briefly with two crooked fingers.

Buller and the boys, who'd been off cutting firewood up near Connors Creek, rushed into camp an hour later to conduct the audit. There they found an absorbed and bespectacled Danny sitting at the oilcloth table counting out greenbacks into neat little piles.

"Le's see," he was saying, "four gents fer eight days at twelve bucks a head makes—hm—what the hell *does* it make?"

"What's the verdict?" Buller demanded.

"So damn much I can't really tell," Danny said, looking up mystified and rubbing his gleaming bald head. "All I know is we jest made a fortune stayin' to home an' gittin' drunk—an' mind, gittin' bloody well paid fer it." He pointed at the opposite wall. "Buller, quick, fetch a quart of Chicago hooch hid in one of Timmy's hip boots hangin' there. Timmy, here's a brand-new fly pole fer you—I'm stickin' with my ol' curtain rod. Swan, Taconite, do *somethin'*, goddamit. We gotta celebrate. My Gawd, we's jest made a fortune. We're rich, boys, *we're really rich*!"

Kiss-and-Tell Fishermen

Most fishermen swiftly learn that it's a pretty good rule never to show a favorite spot to any fisherman you wouldn't trust with your wife—a rule that possesses the further utility of narrowing the field fast. Show your secret Shangri-La to the wrong fisherman (mercifully, or at least so I've found it, they are still comparatively few) and the next time you visit the place you are more than apt to find *him* there ahead of you, quite often leading a guided tour.

Worse yet, if the place is really good and the character knows how to spell, chances are you'll soon be reading all about *his* intrepid new fishing discovery (meaning, of course, the fabled place *you* so foolishly showed him) in your favorite newspaper or outdoor magazine. For these are the compulsive squealers on good fishing waters who keep writing those glowing confessional articles one keeps reading, typically called "The Ten Best Trout Spots in Michigan" or "Monster Browns at Your Back Door"—usually accompanied by photos and detailed maps. And I'm not now talking about those ill-disguised and often gaudily misinformed local-booster pitches, the main aim of which is to fill local coffers rather than visiting creels, but rather of hard, reliable dope about really hot fishing spots. These latter are the charming kiss-and-tell fishermen to whom I now give the back of my hand.

What it is that compels these strange characters to keep snitching on good fishing spots, especially in writing and to perfect strangers, has long baffled me. Fortunately for the preservation of my own few remaining favorite spots, I've never gotten to know one of these characters intimately. Accordingly, I can only speculate that their odd obsession must somehow accompany a particularly lardy ego, one so driven by a primitive desire to show off and be top rod at any price that its possessor is willing at one swoop to kill both his reputation for piscatorial discretion and the doomed spot he's just squealed on.

These kiss-and-tell fishermen must lead damn lonely lives, one would guess, or else have to keep moving around one hell of a lot in order to find a new batch of sucker fishermen they can con into showing them still newer spots to tell on. This is so because the normal ordinary close-mouthed fisherman need only get burned once in order to clam up and spread the alarm.

"Don't trust that squealing slob," runs some of his milder idiom. "Last summer I foolishly showed him that lovely pool below the third falls on the Middle Branch and today it's nothin' but a goddam tourist mecca. Beware of that flannel-mouthed mother-beatin' bastard an' don't show him or tell him *nothin'*!"

The nicest thing I can offhand find to say about these chronic kiss-and-tellers is that paradoxically they probably help save more good fishing spots than they ever ruin—though quite unintentionally, I hasten to add. This they do because their presence among us eventually makes the rest of us fishermen even more wary and suspicious and close-mouthed than nature has already so richly endowed us. This often means we grow slow to show our pet spots even to our tried and trusted fishing pals which naturally sharply reduces the fishing pressure on those remaining spots that have so far escaped the broadcasting flannel mouths.

Another thing the kiss-and-tellers unwittingly do is to make many of us fishermen far more likely to show our pet spots to visiting fishermen from far away than to some local worthies living on the same home grounds. One big reason is that it is far easier to hoodwink and figuratively blindfold a visiting stranger to where you are taking him than to fool a savvy local fisherman. That way, too, if the visiting stranger should turn out to be a flannel mouth, it needn't be quite so fatal as if he were a vocal local yokel, because he is far less apt to be able ever again to find the place, much less intelligently describe or identify it for others. Finally, should he nevertheless be able to find the spot again he simply won't be living so physically close to it and thus won't be around so often to help with its exposure and ultimate deflowering.

Consequently, one of the nicest compliments one local fisherman can pay another these days is to break down and actually show him a favorite spot. But even this generous gesture carries its hidden barb and it does so because if the shower fisherman can in fact trust the showee this means that henceforth the latter may never again honorably fish the place without the original shower tagging along as chaperone; either that or first giving his approval of a one-trip one-man sashay without him. Whereas if the showee *hadn't* been shown the lovely place, he just might—since both presumably haunt the same general fishing area—have stumbled across it on his own and thereafter been forever free as a bird to fish it whenever and with whomever he bloody well pleased. If this sounds a little tangled and complicated it's because it is; explaining the prevailing protocol at the Court of St. James's must be child's play compared with unraveling all the prickly nuances of the unwritten code of us crazy fishermen.

Possibly good old Hal had something like this in mind on that hot August afternoon a number of years ago when we were futilely fishing the lovely beaver dams on Anthony's Creek. As I kept vainly flailing away I became aware that Hal had stopped fishing and seemed to be watching me. At first I found his attention flattering, coming from such a savvy old master craftsman of angling, but as the surveillance continued I soon began miscasting in my nervous, glancing efforts to watch him watching me.

"What's up, Hal?" I finally said, giving up and reeling in. "You've been studying me as though you were Mr. Brinks weighing my application to drive one of your armored money vans. Did I make the grade?"

"In a way I was casing you, pal," Hal said, releasing his bomb. "How'd you like me to show you the hottest brook trout spot I know in Michigan?"

"Hal," I simpered, still in a state of shock, "that's like asking a soak if he'd mind inheriting a Kentucky distillery. When can we make the trip?"

"Right now, this very afternoon."

"You mean it's *that* close to here?"

"Follow me," Hal said, shaking his head. "And don't ask so damn many questions or I'll change my mind."

"Yessir," I said meekly, following Hal out to his four-wheel-drive fish car where we silently crawled out of our felt-soled diapers and took off, I feeling somewhat like a sheltered bride embarking on her first honeymoon: I suspected *something* real nice was going to happen to me real soon but precisely what it was I knew not.

Less than ten miles from the water we'd left, mostly over graveled country side roads, Hal stopped his bush car abruptly on a wooden bridge spanning a modest-sized stream. Several other fishy-looking cars were parked nearby, one of them bearing an out-of-state license. "Recognize the place?" he said.

"I think so, Hal," I said, quelling a low impulse to pretend I didn't. "Looks to me like the lingering remains of Strand Creek."

"Right," Hal said. "Fished it lately?"

"Not in years—ever since the tourists moved in," I said. "But I must confess I'm negotiating for the popcorn concession."

"Very funny. Where'd you used to fish it?"

"Downstream, Hal," I said, mystified over the prolonged cross-examination over a hatchery-planted stream I'd long ago abandoned to those wily angling detectives who prefer shadowing hatchery trucks. "Generally I'd shore-walk downstream and wade back fishing dry. Nice easy wading, but I finally got weary of catching hungry hatchery trout who'd rush up and fight over your fly."

"Hm . . . Ever try the water above?"

"Only once, Hal, and that was enough. Area gets real swampy and the stream narrows and dwindles fast. But the thing that really got me was crawling over and around and through all those slippery drowned cedars. That drove me up the wall—as well as fast back to my car."

"Plain chicken," Hal said, putting his car in gear. "That's the trouble with you lazy, unimaginative, rocking-chair fishermen. You just won't dream and explore anymore. Anyway, today you're again about to fish the Strand upstream."

"Yessir," I said, wincing over the prospect of once again tiptoeing terror stricken through the lovely downed cedars of Strand Creek. "Take me to your leader."

Less than a mile beyond the bridge Hal turned off on a bush-choked bumpy two-rut road, and thereafter creaked and bounced and wallowed along in four-wheel-drive until we ran out of road.

"Here we are," Hal announced, leaping out and grabbing at his fishing gear. "Let's get going."

"May I ask a question?" I timorously ventured.

"You just did," Hal said, "but live it up. Do ask another."

"Do we rig up here or pack in?"

"We pack in."

"Waders or hips?"

"Waders."

Once packed we took off, Hal in the lead, following no discernible trail but simply threading our way through dense stands of tamarack and spruce, which presently gave way to almost impenetrable cedar swamp broken by jungle clumps of tag alders. About the time I was ready to give the best trout spot in Michigan back to the Chippewa Indians we came into more open country dominated by poplars. Presently we were inching our way over and around the lush grassy tufts and mucky channels of once-flooded beaver meadows, a sure sign of the site of an ancient dam.

"Here we are," Hal said, pausing and pointing at an inky stretch of nondescript stream not more than two rod lengths wide from the surface of which protruded the bent trunks and rigid beseeching branches of a vast tangle of drowned cedars. Two blue herons suddenly rose from nowhere and undulantly flapped away in a sort of slow-motion oiled flight.

"Lovely place for an office picnic," I said. "Where do we launch the assault?"

"Right here," Hal said, plumping himself down on a fallen log. "As you can see, the place is fly-fishable only from this side. Moreover, the old stream channel's on the other side and 'way over your waders. Place is a real fooler."

"Sorta sweeps over me," I said, ruefully observing the tangle of grass and dangling bushes and overhanging brush that clotted the considerably higher limestone-layered opposite bank, the matted and tangled ruins of an inactive beaver dam some hundred feet below, and the more ominous fact that since we'd arrived there'd not been a single rise.

"What's that sound of running water I hear coming from above?" I said, wrestling into my waders.

"Possibly the sound of running water," answered Hal, occasionally no mean slouch with the deflating riposte. "It's from a series of icy springs coming out of the limestone on the opposite bank. One reason the trout are here."

"*What* trout?" I wanted to ask but tactfully refrained, asking instead, "Where does one start fishing the hottest spot in Michigan?"

"Right in front of you, man," Hal said. "This is where the little darlings live."

"But how about you?" I said, noticing Hal still hadn't his waders on and was instead sitting back indolently smoking a cigar.

"I'll fish after you get bored and weary," Hal said airily. "Anyway, can't you see there's only room for one guy at a time? Get with it, dammit—we gotta get outa here before dark."

"Yessir," I said, snubbing up the knot on my little Adams and advancing a few steps to the water's edge and barely stepping in, catching my breath over the sudden shock of ice-cold water. From that point I fed out line and gracefully fouled my forward cast on some lurking brush and my fly slapped down upon the water with a thud scarcely a rod length above me. *Clap* went a savage flash of trout and I glanced back at Hal with the inimitable silly grin of a man who's just been cleaned out.

"See what you mean," I said, imaginatively tying on another Adams, which this time I promptly lost when an even larger trout immediately took it and made a quick power dive and broke me off on a submerged cedar.

"While they scarcely teach it in fly-casting classes," Hal said, "you simply can't afford to posture and play around in these cedars with these muscular wild trout. You simply gotta skid 'em in fast as you can."

"Sweeps over me," I said, doggedly tying on another Adams.

I am not going to tell about all the gorgeous brook trout Hal and I caught and lost and broke off on that memorable evening, one reason being because we rapidly lost count. Virtually every cast with any kind of a fly ended in a savage strike, and we neither took nor saw any juniors though we did catch and return many close to and possibly over two pounds.

"Time's up," Hal announced after about a dizzy hour or so of the best trout fishing *I'd* ever seen in Michigan, at least since I was a kid. "Gotta quit now or we'll get caught in the dark. We'll return another day."

"Sorry," I said, reeling in. "I really can't make it till Tuesday."

On the slow trek out Hal told me how he'd first found the

place. He'd done it the hard way, simply by slugging his way up from the bridge through all the down cedars until he'd come upon it. "Figured there just had to be some hot spots upstream with all that cold water and natural cover and, yes, protection from rival fishermen."

"Imagination pays," I said, "especially when it's accompanied by the stamina of a water buffalo and a suicidal disdain of all slippery cedars."

"Fact is, the first time I hit the place it looked so crummy and riseless I almost detoured around it," Hal ran on. "Fact is, some of the troutiest spots I've ever known looked the crummiest."

"Shows our illiterate native trout don't read the pretty outdoor magazines," I said. "Good Lord, is it a mirage or a modern miracle and do I actually see your fish car?"

"'Tis an authentic miracle and there's still another," Hal said. "How'd you like a slug of bourbon along with a dram of water out of an old tin cup?"

"To the best trout spot in Michigan and long may it reign," I said as we solemnly clinked cups. "And many thanks, pal, not only for showing me this gorgeous place but for your tacit if misguided testimonial to my character."

"I'll chance that, chum," Hal said.

Hal and I fished the best place in Michigan together on an average of about once a season after that, generally in the dog days of August. One reason we didn't fish it more often, perversely enough, was that the place was too damn easy, destroying the fisherman's ego-massaging illusion that his own guile and craft might sometimes affect the results. These trout would probably have as avidly hit a shoehorn.

But the biggest reason we didn't fish it oftener was our guilty if unspoken knowledge that in a sense these trout were trapped, driven and congregated there during hot weather and low water in their endless quest for food, cold aerated water, and some measure of security, just as I further suspect we managed to fish it at all

216

because in our secret hearts we also knew that on this crowded planet fishermen and fish were both pretty much in the same boat.

The reign of the best place to fish in Michigan abruptly ended amidst the screaming whine and whimper of loggers' chain saws, we sorrowfully learned last August. While I was out of town Hal had hiked in there alone to case the place for our annual trip and I got the bad news upon my return.

"I heard the wailing saws even from where we park the car," Hal explained in his bleak obituary report. "Most of the cedar is already gone and they're closing in on the spruce and tamarack, evidently sawing their way straight for Lake Superior."

"Did you try fishing the creek?" I managed to say.

"Lacked the heart," Hal said, sadly wagging his head. "When I got there and saw the old beaver dam full of trailer-camp suds and beer cans and floating garbage I almost knelt and wept. The loggers came in from the other side and have unerringly built a hauling bridge right over the hottest spot. From this bridge I beheld two immaculate characters spin casting and monotonously hauling in chubs. I didn't even rig up."

One final note: I want to take back my earlier innuendo that maybe Hal showed me this once-pristine place lest I'd find it first by myself. The truth is that *both* of us knew all along that never in this incarnation would I have ever slugged my way up through all those greasy down cedars and found it on my own. Instead I give thanks to Hal for giving me a fleeting glimpse of what the fishing still might be everywhere if it weren't for our helpless lust for "progress." Sometimes in the small hours of the night I think I even prefer kiss-and-tell fishermen. For the time at least we seem to have *them* outnumbered.

Hoarding the Cast

Fly-fishing for wild trout on quiet waters must be one of the toughest and craziest ways to catch fish ever invented by man, as well as among the most frustrating and humiliating. Yet, when the omens are right, it can also be the most exciting and rewarding. I know; I've got a bad case of it.

I've been haunting quiet waters, now that I look back on it, ever since my boyhood bait-plunking days—which means a powerful lot of quiet water over the dam. But only in recent years has it swept over me that what I long regarded as a harmless predilection is really a hopeless progressive disease and that I am deeply mired in its terminal stages.

My daily fishing notes tell the whole sad story, revealing that during the last two summers I have neither fished for nor caught anything but wild native brook trout—virtually none over twelve inches long and all taken on quiet waters while using scandalously long dreamy leaders with wee flies to match. My plight becomes all the more pitiable as I contemplate all the pictures appearing lately in the local papers showing smirking piscatorial heroes all around me holding aloft almost equally burly rainbows or browns they have just derricked up or, when a block and tackle was handy, even vaster specimens of inert chinook or coho salmon—all of which I scorn.

In fact, so far sunk in sin am I that when people ask what I think of all the wondrous new fish that have invaded our waters, I am, if in a sufficiently liverish mood, apt to reply: "Simply dandy, buster. Just think of all the throngs of bait, hardware, and assorted meat fishermen these slobby new monsters are luring away from molesting my own precious troutlings."

During my long romance with quiet waters, mostly on small lakes and ponds and especially on virtually currentless beaver backwaters with which my Lake Superior country abounds, I naturally learned something about the hoarded cast. It was either that or no action, and action, I also gleaned along the way, is what this whole fly-fishing business is about. In addition I picked up some eloquent arguments to rebut the lying mythmaker who first started the rumor that our brookies are doomed because they are so easy to catch. Not while fly-fishing on quiet waters they ain't, mister, as this typical entry from my fishing notes shows: "Sunned out today. Fair rise but couldn't solve. Caught none and rose none." But before dilating further on the hoarded cast I must pause and pay my respects to the loyal order of flailers.

Flailers among fly-fishermen are so prolific that they defy accurate census, but one guesses they must be as plentiful as blackflies in August. A flailer, in case you never encountered one (or, worse yet, failed to recognize because you are one), is a fly-fisherman who casts too damn often and then compounds the felony by failing properly to fish out and retrieve the casts he makes. There are whole waterlogged regiments of them.

Speculating over what makes a flailer flail is as absorbing and, one suspects, ultimately as futile as trying to guess, say, why those queer quiet-water haunters got *their* way. Freud might have come up with some theories to make both types blush, but since he is unavailable for collaboration I must go it alone.

220

from Trout Magic (*1974*)

I have several pet theories, but my prize one is that since, under our droll economic system, the incipient flailer must, like most fishermen, work upwards of fifty weeks out of the year, once the poor pent devil finds himself actually unleashed on trout water he sort of cracks up or, to put it in more resonant five-dollar phrases, compulsively succumbs to an irresistible impulse to flail away. I call it my therapy theory of flailing.

At the risk of getting in over my intellectual waders I must unveil still another theory in which something more than simple stack-blowing therapy seems involved. It is this: Some flailers flail away so furiously that one suspects they must imagine they are beating up on someone, like maybe the boss. And I once beheld an oblivious flailer who flailed with such ecstatic abandon that I could have sworn he spied a seductive siren out there called Sade—wups, I mean Sadie—wearing only a Freudian slip.

Yet, however diversified their drives, flailers seem to share one thing in common: They all have a ball doing their thing; to a man they get a tremendous bang out of the sheer manual act of casting. Along the way they also often acquire the physiques of weight lifters, which I suppose they must in order to keep up that old heave-ho all the livelong day. Actually, they are a remarkable race of fishermen and whenever I feel a little impatient with them I recall that I too love the physical act of fly-casting, and in fact once even wrote a piece celebrating its delights that opened thus: "Fly-fishing is such great fun, I have often felt, that it really ought to be done in bed."

Flailers share one other thing in common: They rarely raise, much less ever catch, a trout. Watching one at his devotionals swiftly reveals why. After resolutely stomping up to the water he will so shortly rid of all trout, your typical flailer strips out line like an overworked barber whipping up a cold lather. Then suddenly he braces himself and lifts the accumulated mass and blindly flings it out yonder as far as he can. Then, before his fly has fairly landed, he retrieves the whole whirling mess and whales her out again. This goes on all day.

After a spell of watching such an awesome performance—*whish,
plop, wheek*—one wonders if the flailer could possibly rid the area of
trout any faster if he whipped out a pistol and fired into the water.
It could make an exciting race. Carrying on this way it is little wonder that so few trout ever disturb a flailer's reveries. The main reason they don't, of course, is that they are no longer there, my latest
research disclosing that a really distinguished flailer can chase every
decent trout into the next township by, at most, his third cast.

If I seem to be trying to reform our grand army of flailers, I
really don't mean to; first, because I doubt they can or want to be
reformed, and second, because I regard them as among our most
ardent trout conservationists and wouldn't change them for the
world. Nor am I poking fun at them, either, for in solemn truth they
should be toasted rather than roasted. So let's lift a glass to our
hardy flailers, a noble breed of abstentious souls who so rarely ever
raise a trout, let alone take one home. After all, think of all the trout
they save!

If the very fishermen who stand most in the need of the
hoarded cast are beyond redemption, then, as I've just implied, to
whom *does* it apply? Could it possibly apply, say, to such suave and
crafty old fly-fishing hands as you and I, who cast with such consummate grace and precision, and who invariably work our fly out
of the magic hot spot before going into our lift retrieve?

The answer, alas, is yes; the hoarded cast applies to you and me
and to all other wistful souls who fish the fly. In fact I sometimes
suspect that a failure to use the strategy of the hoarded cast may be
the biggest single lack in the arsenal of most otherwise competent
fly casters. The merest glance at some of the unique problems facing the fly-fisher should show what I'm driving at.

Fly-fishing is first of all a combined act of high deceit and low fakery aimed at creating the illusion that a bent pin adorned with
assorted fluff is something good to eat. Next, nothing good to eat in
a trout's natural habitat comes equipped with a strange light-refract-

ing gut or synthetic tail at least seven feet long. If I've made sense so far then it follows as the night the day that a fly-fisherman should do only those things that heighten his illusion and disguise his fakery, which, in turn, put another way, revolves around his eternal battle with light.

Though there are few rules in fishing that nose-thumbing trout haven't riddled with exceptions at one time or another, if any ironclad rules do exist my guess is that high on the list is one running something like this: Light is the most constant problem facing the fly-fisherman and glaring sunlight is the worst possible light he has to face. The reason, of course, is that the stronger the light the weaker the illusion, and by definition glaring sunlight is the glarin'est. Which is probably why virtually all fly-fishermen pray less for salvation than for solid overcast.

Why their prayers are so seldom answered is a question vexing experts, some claiming that God conducts an impartial head count and there are simply more tourists praying the other way. In any case, during the average trout season a fly-fisherman is lucky to draw one really overcast day out of ten. So unless he stays home and sulks the other nine or else takes up night fishing (which I happen personally to abhor), he must on most days bravely sally forth in the jolly sunshine prepared to battle his enemy Light.

But how does he fight light? one may ask. The answer is by waiting. Waiting for what? Waiting for any number of things. Like what? Well, waiting for a passing cloud bank to come obscure the sun; waiting for a breeze to spring up and create a protective ripple; waiting for a bank of fog or mist or even smog; waiting for a gentle shower; in short, waiting for anything that will help heighten his illusion and hide his fakery. But what if nature fails to cooperate? Then he simply sighs and ties on a finer tippet and commands himself to wait longer between casts, always slowly retrieving the fly virtually to his feet before going into the pickup. He practices, in short, the discipline of the hoarded cast.

The hoarded cast, then, is not a method of casting but a

method of not casting; not something the fisherman should do but something he shouldn't do. Its whole rationale is bottomed upon trying to circumvent or mitigate the illusion-shattering hazard of light. It is a doctrine of restraint and self-discipline, of simple waiting and biding one's time. It is to take it slow and easy; that is, to use the hoarded cast. One of these fine sunny days I think I'll even try it.

Morris the Rodmaker

Fly rods are like Cornish pasties—both are best made for love rather than for money. And where love is missing the cost of the rod is often irrelevant. I've owned several expensive "name" rods that turned out to be magnificent tent poles, and one of the loveliest rods I ever owned was a dreamy old prewar Granger that cost a mere twenty-five bucks. (It now stands retired in my den window cross-sworded with a gallant old Paul Young.) While most good fly rods are also expensive, alas, without care and love one can easily wind up flailing a mere ornate broomstick. All of which brings me to Morris the Rodmaker.

Morris Kushner and I first met when he stopped off one summer while driving to Montana on a fishing trip. He'd spent the night at our town's only hotel, having driven the day before from his suburban home near Detroit—almost as far from where I live, believe it or not, as I in turn live from Hudson's Bay.

So the next morning all Morris had to do to find me was to walk across the street to the Rainbow Bar, where I'd earlier written him he might find me if I wasn't home. I was absorbed playing cribbage when he walked in, but since we small-towners always case every stranger, when I glanced up at Morris I saw what I guessed was a retired bourbon-bibbing Irish railroad man: sturdy, ruddy, blue eyed, smiling, cigar smoking and radiating a kind of tolerant good will.

I can't recall whether I won or lost at cribbage that morning, though I must say, like most fishermen, I tend to forget my bad days. Anyway, when the game was over Morris came over and introduced himself (I never did ask him how he recognized me) and we had a draft beer and naturally I asked him if his travel plans allowed him a few hours off to join me in fishing. "Do they, Mr. Kushner?" I repeated.

"Of course," he said, removing his stogie with the loving reluctance of the inveterate cigar smoker. "And don't keep mistering me, old fisherman, 'cause we aren't all that far apart."

"Righto, Morris," I said. "Let's go get your gear and go fishing. Where's your car?"

"Behind the Inn."

"Then come ride with me in my bush car."

"Don't mind if I do," said my smiling Irish railroader with the fairly un-Celtic name of Kushner.

Morris was toting almost as much fishing gear in his big shiny car as I do in my bush car—which is one hell of a lot of gear—including what seemed stacks and stacks of fly rods, from which he selected three—the only time before or since that I've accompanied a man fishing who carried so many rods on a one-day trip.

We headed for a beaver dam up on Deer Creek (the name of which I think I can safely mention since, at last count, I'm sure there are more Deer Creeks in Michigan than ever there were deer). On the way Morris told me he was a retired tool-and-die maker who'd made his bundle by finally forming his own company and making whatever it is master tool-and-die makers make for the big Detroit auto firms—which Morris carefully explained to me but which fell upon the helplessly blocked ears I seem to get in the face of anything faintly technical.

"Where'd you ever pick *that* up?" I wistfully inquired, wondering if there were any cram courses an old fisherman might take in a subject that allowed him to drive a big roomy car full of fishing gear all the way out to Montana.

"Mostly being a helper to men who already knew," Morris explained, adding that he'd been at it virtually since a boy, when his parents brought him over here from Russia.

"Oh," I said, pensively reflecting that tool-and-die making probably wasn't my cup of tea anyway, since I had yet to learn even to tie a decent fly.

When finally we bounced our way into the lovely old dam, Morris nimbly leapt out and rigged up all three fly rods. "Well," I could not help remarking, "I must say you come well prepared, Morris."

"They're all brand-new and I wanted to try them out actually fishing," Morris explained, and once again I wondered why fate had denied me the career of a tool-and-die maker.

Few fish were rising during the heat of the day, but while waiting for Morris to assemble his bamboo arsenal I spotted a nice riser on the far side and pointed it out to him.

"Why don't you try for him while you're waiting?" Morris suggested.

"Too big a deal to cross over," I said.

"I mean try from this side."

"Thanks, chum," I said, "but I'd be lucky to lay out a decent fly half that distance."

"Then I'll try," Morris said, unhooking a fly from a set-up rod and quickly working out line and, before my unbelieving eyes, laying out a superb cast about ten feet above the steady far riser.

"Lovely, lovely," I murmured.

The fly floated over the fish; the trout rose; and Morris struck.

"Clean missed him," Morris squealed, grinning from ear to ear, thrusting his new wonder rod out at me. "Here, you try for him when he starts again."

"No way," I said, shaking my head. "I'd need a slingshot ever to cast a fly that far."

"But maybe you can with my rod," Morris insisted. "I built lots of power into this one."

"*You* did?" I said, puzzled. "You mean you *made* the rod I'm holding?"

"Of course. Made all three of 'em. In fact, made all the rods you saw back in my car."

"Oh," I said, a light dawning. "You buy the blanks or kits or whatever and then assemble them?"

"No," Morris said, shaking his head. "I build all my rods strictly from scratch and I even designed and built the machine I make 'em with."

"Oh," I said, completely awed, recalling a wobbly wooden stool I'd made in high school that nobody has yet ever quite dared actually sit on. "Oh."

Morris's trout had meanwhile obligingly resumed rising, so with much trepidation I went through the motions of trying to cast a fly over him. I succeeded, of course, or I wouldn't be telling the story now, doing it with more ease in fact than I usually cast half the distance. The whole thing so stunned me that when the trout quickly rose and took I reared back in amazement and cost Morris a favorite fly.

"Wowie!" I hollered. "That's gotta be the longest cast I ever made." I hesitated, groping for the right words. "Morris," I finally ventured, "do you make rods like this—er—professionally?"

"You mean do I make 'em to sell?"

"Well, yes."

"No," Morris said, grinning. "I only make 'em because I love to make nice things for myself and my friends."

"Oh," I said, crushed.

from Trout Magic (*1974*)

"And since we're now old friends and you've found a rod of mine you like, keep it, my friend. It's all yours."

"Oh," I said faintly, torn between hugging my lovely new rod and the generous artist who made it.

This took place, I'd guess, about five or six years ago. For several summers after that Morris would stop off on his way to more distant fishing climes to spend a day or so fishing. And, despite my feeble protestations, never once did he leave without leaving behind still another magic Kushner rod in which he'd mingled both his genius and his love.

The last time I saw Morris he was accompanied by his wife, Fannie, a warm-hearted, attractive, and friendly woman who blushed like a girl when Morris insisted over dinner on telling me how he had courted her during their early Detroit days by taking her out riding on his very first motor vehicle—a brand-new Harley-Davidson motorcycle.

Then, about two summers ago, came my last letter from Morris saying he didn't think he could make it up my way that season. "The old Harley is clunking on about half a cylinder," he wrote, "and just may be running out of gas." Even more depressing were the implications of his scribbled postscript saying he'd decided to sell all his rods.

That was in June and my fears were not groundless. The following month I got a thoughtful letter from his son Victor that his father had passed away. Since then I've heard from another son, Seymour, which so eloquently confirms my suspicion that fly rods are best built for love rather than for money that I'd like to quote from it.

"It is my opinion," he wrote, "that the reason my dad's rods are so excellent is that he was a master craftsman and built them with endless care in an effort to achieve his dream of perfection.

"The machine he built was ingenious and his own creation, but still it was only a milling machine. Just as all violin makers use chis-

229

els, gouges, and saws, yet not all violins are comparable in quality
. . . His fly rods were truly a labor of love."

I still have and treasure my Kushner rods, of course, and sometimes it seems when I use one of them I see out yonder over the
water the smiling smoke-wreathed face of the immensely gifted
Russian-Jewish genius whom I once mistook for a retired Irish railroader.

The Fishing Story Life *Missed*

After writing three books, the cheering throngs of readers of which I could have accommodated nicely in a two-car garage—no, better make that one—I wrote my first novel, and all hell broke loose. While I still wonder what *that* book had that the others didn't, the fact is that my *Anatomy of a Murder* almost overnight got itself glued to the best-seller list, tapped by Book-of-the-Month, knighted by Otto Preminger (whose subsequent movie was graced by the presence of that gentle man Joseph N. Welch, who became a dear friend) and, as the royalties rolled in, blessed by the Internal Revenue Service.

Now the only reason I'm mentioning this is not to brag, heaven knows, but because the following story would be rather pointless if I didn't, since this background was the basis for there being any story to tell. For the painful truth is that, for all its material rewards, there is much about the trauma of bestsellerdom that is eminently forgettable. In fact if it weren't that my own immersion in it freed me to fish, for which I am eternally grateful, and allowed me to get to know some talented and lovely people I would other-

231

wise have missed, I doubt I would ever again mention it, even to myself.

Anyway, as my orbiting book and I joined hands and soared through the blazing hoops of national notoriety, I was naturally invited to appear and brandish my book on all manner of shows— talk shows, quiz shows, panel shows, possibly even dog shows— though here the memory bobbles a bit. Most of these bids I managed to turn down, especially after I discovered that a fisherman was more likely to raise a dead cat than a trout on the pastoral East River. But I did accept a few, and one of the most pleasantly memorable of these was when *Life* photographer Bob Kelley phoned me one day and asked if he might come up and follow me around fishing a few days, thus furnishing me with this story and starting a lasting friendship.

"You a fisherman, Mr. Kelley?" I parried cautiously.

"Yup," he said. "And I sure liked your book."

This was by now a familiar gambit that accompanied most of these invitations, and I tried not to wince. "Tell me, Mr. Kelley," I said, ever the tease, "and how did you like the movie?"

"Oh, that. I don't mean your courtroom yarn, though it wasn't too bad," Kelley said. "I mean your fishing book, *Trout Madness*, which I really liked. Main reason I called, in fact."

"Well, well," I said, beginning to purr.

"*Life* wants you to write the story to go with my pictures, for which they'll naturally pay," he ran on, naming a figure so generous it stunned me into silence. "Hello? Hello?" he shouted, clicking the phone. "You still on?"

"Barely, but rallying," I managed to say, already putty in the man's hands. "When would you plan to come up?"

"Midafternoon plane tomorrow," Kelley said. "How about it?"

"Fine, fine," I said before he could change his mind. "I'll meet your plane tomorrow."

So the next afternoon I met Bob Kelley's plane, then smiling, crew-cut, trench-coated Bob himself, who in turn presented me to a curly-headed towering young New Englander called Robert Brigham. "Moose is the reporter assigned to this one," Kelley explained as I pumped Moose's big paw.

"But I thought your magazine wanted me to write the story," I said, a little shaken.

"It still does," Bob Kelley said, shrugging and widening his hands. "But when our boss assigns a reporter to a case"—Bob rolled up his eyes and snapped his fingers—"*that* reporter tags along."

"Maybe Moose was sent to translate my stuff into English," I said, a little thoughtfully.

"Barely possible," Moose admitted in his Down East drawl. "That remains to be seen."

"Well, well," I said, rubbing my chin. "I'll try not to overwork you, Mr. Moose."

Clanking with cameras, luggage, and assorted equipment, the two Bobs and I repaired to the Mather Inn in my town and then for refreshments down in the bar, where Bob Kelley proceeded to outline his general plan. This, he explained, was for us somehow to try and show in words and pictures just what magical lure there was about trout fishing that would make a presumably intelligent man, one endowed with a four-karat legal education, quit a more or less permanent job on his state's highest court and flee home to chase trout and write yarns about it. "What did make you do it?" Bob concluded.

"Just lucky, I guess," I said, "as the whore lady told the social worker when asked how *she* got that way."

"But seriously," Bob pleaded.

"That, Robert," I said, "is something I've been trying to explain to myself ever since—not to mention to my wife." I sighed. "But I'm willing to give it another try."

For the next three days Bob Kelley and I gave it the old college try, accompanied by our reporter, Bob Brigham, who had nothing to report, and whom we accordingly pressed into service as a combined rod bearer, camera toter, and ambulant bar. How did we make out? As my old fishing pal Luigi might have put it, "Lat me try an' tole you, my fran."

Part of the charm of trout fishing is that trout, unlike people, will respond only to quietude, humility, and endless patience, and as far as I was concerned Bob Kelley's trip richly confirmed that fact. It also proved some things trout will *not* respond to, one of them certainly being any fisherman who tries to show off and glorify himself at their expense. This sort of thing they seem to sense almost instantly by some mysterious telepathy running up through the rod and down the line and leader to the fly. Once this message is flashed, the trout seem to conspire to bring the poor wayward fisherman back to humility; either that or to the brink of nervous breakdown.

There was one other lesson all of us learned: that my Upper Peninsula of Michigan trout, at least, wanted no part in appearing on any photographic command performances ordered by anyone called Henry R. Luce. *That* message came through loud and clear.

Those first three days of fishing were a disaster as far as fishing pictures were concerned, and though I took the boys to some of the hottest spots I knew, I did not catch a single really decent trout. It seemed that I was so eager to provide Bob with a thrilling picture that I spent most of my time posing and posturing, either overstriking the few decent trout that did rise or, in my preoccupation with being photogenic, striking too late.

On the evening of the second day I did get on to one decent fighting brown when fate had poor Bob reloading his camera. By the time he'd shed that one and grabbed and focused another—he bristled with them—the bored brown had wound itself around an underwater snag and, as we heard my leader go *ping*, was merrily off and away.

In retrospect, as I write this it sweeps over me that this sort of thing has happened so often, not only then but since, that I'm prepared to swear that a fisherman is only at his relaxed best when he knows that nothing is watching him except the scampering chipmunks and God.

Bob was most understanding and nice about the whole thing, being a fisherman himself, but by the end of the third day the strain began to tell and even I could sense—in fact *that* was a good part of my trouble—that *Life* fully expected Bob to come up with at least one thrilling picture of a trophy trout being caught by that best-selling fly-casting author of *Trout Madness* because, after all, *Life* dealt in *success*.

When on the evening of the third day we finally gave up we found Moose awaiting us back at the jeep deep in a novel, to which he'd sensibly turned on the morning of the second day when he saw how sad the fishing was.

"Any luck?" he dutifully inquired, pointing at the clinking drinks awaiting us on the hood of the car.

I widened my eyes and shrugged and raised my outstretched arms in the international sign language of defeat, and reached for my drink. "*Ah* . . ."

"Where to tomorrow?" Bob inquired glumly, still shedding cameras. "It better be good, for tomorrow's our last day."

"Really don't know yet," I said, "but I'll brood over it during the night. Meanwhile, if you will, Moosie boy, please pass the bourbon."

During the night inspiration struck—why hadn't I thought of it before?—and early the next morning we parked the jeep on the south side of the top of a deep valley through which ran one of the most sporting and wadable stretches of the entire Big Dead River. Though I rarely fished the place any longer because of my growing infatuation with brook trout, I had long known it harbored some of the biggest browns around.

"We rig up here, Bob," I said, leaping out and grabbing my waders and fighting my way into them as Bob did likewise while Moose yawned and settled down with his book.

"Moose," I said, when Bob and I were just about armed and ready for the last day's fray, "it's going to be a long day. Bob and I have a lot of river to cover. Wouldn't you like to tag along?"

"I'd sure like to," Moose eagerly said, "but I don't have any waders."

"No problem," I said. "I've got an old emergency pair way too big. Wear them."

My inspirations were coming in clusters and as Moose writhed his way into my old patched waders I had another. "Hell, Moose," I said, "there's a nice big pool where our trail hits the river. Why don't you take one of my extra rods and try for a trout while we do our stuff?"

"But I never fly-fished in my life," Moose confessed.

"Incredible. I thought all New Englanders were born holding a fly rod."

"Not this one. Only a little surf casting as a kid. Never held a fly rod in my hand."

"Then why did you and Kelley bother to buy fishing licenses?"

"Routine magazine policy to appease the local gendarmes. But I still can't cast a fly."

"Tell me, can you lace your shoes?" I asked.

"Of course."

"Then you can cast a fly," I said airily. "I'll rig you up a fiber glass nymphing rod you could heave a polecat with along with a stout leader and some big flies. All you got to do is keep pelting away. What do you say?"

"I'm game," Moose said, shrugging. "Beats reading bad novels."

So I rigged up Moose and handed him a tin box of faded and tattered old bucktail streamers and the three of us slid and slipped our way down the steep river trail to the first pool.

The omens were good. While no trout were rising in Moose's shaded pool, we soon spotted several spunky risers working between us and the first bend below.

"Let's go, master angler," Kelley said, champing at the bit.

"Bitterness will get you nowhere, Kelley," I said. "But first I got to give Moose a quick lesson." So saying, I towed Moose out into the current to give him casting room and, taking his rod, gave him a short cram course in casting a fly without impaling one's ear. "Now you try it," I said, handing him a rod, and Moose grabbed it and lashed out—and narrowly missed impaling *my* ear.

"Wait till we get out of here," I shrilled, scrambling, and Bob and I quickly splashed across to safety above his pool. "If time palls there's beer in the car icebox and you know where we hid the key," I called out to him above the sound of the current.

Moose nodded grimly and lashed out again, caught a dead branch behind him, jerked on it mightily and broke the branch, lost his balance and, amidst the crashing of falling timber, fell on his face in the river. "C-c-cold!" he sputtered, floundering to his feet and again falling, threshing and blowing like a beached whale. Bob and I averted our eyes and—it seemed the only decent thing to do—silently slipped away downstream on a worn fisherman's trail.

I shall mercifully spare any detailed account of the next four hours. It is enough to say that I fished over dozens and scores of rising browns, by far the best fish we'd seen on the trip; in fact, some of them real lunkers. But it was the same old story: in my zeal to please and play the role of master angler I kept striking too soon, too late, too hard, too soft, too something . . . Box score: no trout. After about two frustating miles of this I looked sheepishly at Kelley and Kelley looked at his watch and shook his head.

"Too early for cocktails, Robert?" I inquired softly.

"I'd say just about four hours too late," Kelley said. "Let's get the hell out of here."

We took the shore trail upstream, resolutely ignoring all the lovely rises we saw along the way, and presently emerged on a high shaded bank overlooking Moose's pool.

"*Look!*" Kelley tensely whispered, pointing, and there in the middle of the pool, far over his flooded waders, stood an intent Moose fast to a simply massive rod-bending trout. Oblivious to our presence, Moose worked the threshing creature in, lunged at him with the net, missed, and as we watched, the big brown made a mighty flop and threw the fly and dashed away.

"Oh my Gawd," Kelley moaned in anguish, bowing his head.

Moose heard Kelley's lament and looked up and waved. "Hi, fellas," he called out cheerily. "How's the ol' luck?"

"Lousy," I said, "How about you?"

Moose turned his head and pointed inshore. "Got five dandy browns dressed out there in the ferns on account of no creel. Caught 'em the first coupla hours."

"*What!*" Kelley gasped.

"Lost three or four before I got the hang of the thing, one far bigger'n the slob that just got off."

"*What!*" I gasped.

"Lost track of how many I've caught and put back. Great fun, this fly-fishing." With that he slapped his big fly down on the water with a tidal splash, there was a savage roll and take, and Moose reared back like a bee-stung shot-putter—and naturally snapped his leader and lost his fly on another lunking trout. "That's it," Moose said, splashing his way ashore, dripping like a tired water spaniel. "There goes my last fly."

"*My* last fly, you mean," I pensively corrected him.

"Let's go get a drink," Kelley said in an awed voice. "I need the therapy."

Hours later, back around my kitchen table, I had my final inspiration. "I've *got* it!" I said, slapping my leg.

"What's that?" Kelley said. "That we go make a midnight raid on the local fish hatchery?"

"The idea for your real fishing story," I ran on, all aglow with my vision. "Look, fellas, it's simply perfect. Here's this master fisherman you came a million miles to photograph, the wily angler, the old fox, the guy who writes books about his art—who after four days of flailing falls flat on his—"

"Yes?" Kelley inquired silkily.

"Keister," I said, glancing over at my ironing wife.

"Go on."

"And there's good ol' Moose, who never held a rod in his life, who threshes around like a mired mastodon in one solitary pool, heaving out harpoons and flailing away for hours like a man beating a rug—and who makes the old master look like a bum." I spread my hands. "That's your *real* story, boys. It's beautiful. I love it. And God knows it's fishing."

Moose wagged his head. "We'd be fired," he said.

"What do you mean fired?" I said, looking at Kelley for support.

"Moose is right," Kelley said, "We came here to do a success story about a best-selling author and expert fly fisherman. That is our mission."

"So-called expert," I amended.

"No matter. Anything that tarnishes that halo of success—or maybe haloes don't tarnish—or dims the glittering image of our star is bad and verboten. The magazine'd never stand for it and we could indeed lose our jobs."

"Yes, I guess I see," I said after a spell, shaking my head. "In fact I'm awfully afraid I do see what you mean. But someday, I warn you, I'm going to tell it the way it was. And I do hope it won't get you boys fired."

"I'll drink to that," Bob said, and all of us clinked glasses and were shortly off to bed.

So the next day the boys caught their plane and I began working on my dubious success story, the main thing I recall about it being, as I brooded and pondered, that I came up with a thing I suspect more nearly expresses why *I* fish, at least, than anything I've written before or since. It was called "Testament of a Fisherman," which, I'd almost forgotten till now, first appeared in *Life* before it came out in Kelley's and my subsequent book, *Anatomy of a Fisherman*, now out of print.

That was at least a dozen years ago. Since then *Life* has folded its tent, of course, and Bob and Moose have moved on to greener pastures. But as I look back on it and consider my small part in it I can't help wondering whether *Life* wasn't sealing its own death warrant even then by so endlessly spinning its gilded fairy tales of "success," instead of telling it as it was. At least in its heedless death flight after this elusive will-o'-the-wisp I know of one grand fishing story it surely missed.

First Day, Last Day

Fishing is essentially a lonely pursuit I have learned; best enjoyed in solitude, one's sense of isolation from the scurrying man-swarm being in itself a good part of the fun. And since I go fishing almost every day all summer long while most other fishermen have to work, I would naturally find myself fishing alone a lot anyway, whether I happened to like it that way or not.

Even when I'm accompanied in my fishing it's usually by but one other fisherman, only rarely by two, and even then we quickly separate when we get there, often never to see each other till it's time to quit. And yet this persistent aura of unsociability that attends fishing lies less in any ingrained aloofness of us fishermen, I suspect, than in the nature of the sport itself, and I'd like to offer some evidence to prove it.

A gang of us local fishermen gets together at least twice a year and sometimes oftener, solitude be damned. Our set dates are the first and the last days of fishing, with an occasional spontaneous get-together in between (maybe to escape traffic) on such holidays as July Fourth and Labor Day. Our only bond is that we are friends and fellow fishermen, and our ages are often as disparate as our trades, the latter currently ranging from bartenders to chemists. (I tried for an A to Z thing but couldn't quite make it, because, drat it, our lone zebra breeder has moved away.)

And what do we do? Well we fish, of course, but not too seriously, and like mostly to sit around an open fire and compare and exchange flies and fishing fairy tales and generally frolic and overfeed (and drink) and, when the day is far spent, grope our way home. If one of us has faltered and soared heavenward on creaking wings since our last session, we'll raise a cup to his memory, less in a spirit of melancholy, I swear, than in wistful regret that he can't be there to enjoy the day.

Some of the fishermen at these sessions I fish with regularly, others occasionally, and some but rarely during the regular season, if at all. And the gap in our ages, if not quite nine to ninety, is sometimes marvelous to behold.

At one such recent conclave, for example, our youngest fisherman was but nineteen and the oldest eighty-nine (my old friend and cribbage partner, Gurn S. Webb), followed by the late L. P. "Busky" Barrett, then in his early eighties, with Hal Lawin and I running neck and neck, closing in fast on our three-score-and-ten.

Then came the younger set, such as Don Anderson crowding sixty and, one of my oldest living fishing pals, "young" Hank Scarffe, reaching an incredible fifty, followed by such fumbling adolescents still in their thirties and forties as Ted Bogdan, Anthony "Gigs" Gagliardi, Mike Kelly, Harry Koenig, Joe Overturf, Lou Rosenbaum, John "The Builder" Walbridge (he built my fishing shack and bridge), and Jerry Wozniak (notice how slyly alphabetical the old fisherman is), our "baby" being bearded Tom Bogdan in his teens.

How these droll sessions ever got started is lost in the mists of memory. But I can recall, not without a pang, that over the years I have moved from being one of the youngest to attend them on to being one of the very oldest, a wry circumstance I choose to ignore (perhaps itself a sign of galloping senility) just as long as I can still look forward to celebrating the First and Last Day along with my fellow fishermen.

Some Early, Some Late

Fishermen at Night

Story, May 1938

We left the camp and cut down the hill into the waving grass of the ancient beaver meadows. My father pointed at a fresh deer track in the soggy trail and kept walking, his long legs swishing the wild grass. He was carrying his fly rod, set up, slowly smoking a briar pipe—an old, caked one with a hole worn through the bit. I drank in the fine smell and it was mixed with smells from the damp earth.

Over the little log bridge at the creek and at the far edge of the meadows, in the young poplars, we flushed two partridges, and we kept raising the rooster, who would fly ahead of us and land, and then turn, ruffling and bobbing like a young prize fighter, until we got too close. Finally it sped in heavy flight over a little hill and we could hear it drumming on the next ridge.

My father could step over most of the charred, weather-worn logs, skeletons of the giant white pines, while I had to climb up on each one and stand there for a little while as tall as my father, and then jump down and run after him, my leader box rattling against my creel.

245

We came out of the poplars and down below us there was a series of beaver ponds and a big beaver house stood in the reeds. There were no beaver. The sun going down made a reddish color on the water. The water was quiet except for the ripples of the trout rising to the flies. A mist was beginning to spread over the ponds, and it was still, there was no noise, except for the frogs croaking and whistling and the splashing of the water spilling over the beaver dams into the ponds below.

My father stood there and packed and relit his pipe. He said, "Next year, son, I'll put in a system here to furnish electric lights for the camp."

I said, "Yes, sir." Then I said, "Don't you think it's more fun to have kerosene lamps? Honest, Pa, I don't mind tending them. Don't you think machinery and things would sort of spoil it here— it's so pretty-like."

My father laughed and walked ahead and I followed him along the edge of the ponds as we walked up to the big pond at the head of the dams. We worked through a thicket of willows and came out in the reeds at the edge of the big pond. The ground was soft and it shook when we moved. My father touched my arm and pointed across the water. A deer stood looking at us, standing in the tall reeds, its big ears up and forward, then one ear, then the other, sort of moving its head in the air, all the while looking at us. Then my father clapped his hands and the deer blew and wheeled, and I saw its white tail straight up, bouncing and bouncing over the fallen old pine logs, and it was gone.

"A beautiful running shot, son," my father said.

The trout were rising and my father knelt and looked at the water and then tied on a leader and a little black fly. I stood watching him. I watched his easy spiral casts as he worked out the line, straight up and forward to avoid catching the thick willows behind us, and then he placed the fly, and it floated down into the water like a thistle. There was a quick roll, and my father had him, the rod bending like a buggy whip, and I watched my father smile and he smiled so that I could see his teeth closed over his pipe and little lines by his eyes. My father slowly worked him in, smiling that way, until the trout lay still at his feet, and my father, not using the net, reached down and took him with his hand.

"Pretty tired trout, son," my father said.

I could hear a whippoorwill make a noise across the pond.

I found a little black fly, and I fumbled in my hurry to tie it and pricked myself and my father said, "Be deliberate, son."

"Yes, sir," I said.

On my first cast I hooked the willows and snapped the leader, and my little black fly was twenty feet up in a willow. My father laughed and I could feel my cheeks burning as I searched in my kit for another black fly but there were none.

I said, "Have you any more of these black flies, Pa?"

My father said, "Sh—don't talk so much. Work your own flies, son." He cast his fly again, so easily, and just missed a beautiful strike.

I fouled my second cast in the willows and I had to bite my lip to keep the tears back when my father laughed again, showing his strong teeth clenching his pipe.

"You'd better go around and get out on the raft," my father said, pointing across the pond.

In the twilight I saw the logs of an old raft lying in the water amid the reeds. I scrambled through the willows and made my way across the matted arc of the beaver dam. I did not look at my father. It took me a long time to get around the pond and I could hear splashing and my father chuckling and I knew that the fishing was good.

I found a long jack-pine pole. I did not look across at my father, but quickly pushed the raft off into the deep water. Just as I was about to cast, the raft started to sink, over my ankles, my boots, up to my knees. I tried to push it back to shore and the pole caught in the mucky bottom and pulled me into deeper water. It was then that I heard my father laughing and I looked over at him and he was slapping his leg and laughing loudly with his mouth open. I worked hard with the pole, and then I couldn't touch the bottom. I tried to paddle with the pole, and it snapped off, and I held a little piece in my hand. The raft started to tip and the water was over my hips, and I saw that the sun had gone down. And all the time I could hear my father laughing and laughing, roaring with laughter. Then I saw him holding his stomach, laughing, and I began to cry, I could not stop, and I stood looking at him, laughing so that the tears rolled down his cheeks. Suddenly I shouted, "You standing there laughing and watching your own son drown . . . you—*you go to hell!*"

I started striking the water, the tears running down my face, and the raft started to rise and move slowly across the pond toward my father. He stood there holding his stomach with both hands, bending up and down, laughing all the while.

"You go to hell!" I shouted again, crying harder than ever, and then he doubled up and leaned against the willows, shaking like he was crying. As I wildly threshed the water I prayed over and over for a gun so that I could shoot my father.

The raft was across the pond and I stepped off the raft on to the boggy edge of the pond and stood there dripping, looking up at my father, my fists clenched at my side. My father had stopped laughing and he looked at me, and we stood there. I was not crying. Then he smiled a little and said, "That's a hell of a raft for a fisherman, son. We'll have to get us a real boat. Come on, we'll get back to camp and dry out and have a damn nice drink of whiskey—what do you say, John?"

"We'll sure have to get us a boat. That raft's no good. And we'll have a fine drink of whiskey, Pa—a hell of a big drink, you bet."

It was dark on the way back to camp, and the meadow was thick with the mist. I did not mind shivering at all, and I whistled to imitate the frogs. "Tomorrow," I thought as I walked behind my father, "Tomorrow I'll sure in hell get hold of the old man's pipe—and smoke the damn thing right in front of him you bet."

Showdown at Cedar Swamp

Rod & Reel, May/June 1981

For many years over countless beers in nearly as many bars I've listened to the triumphant chants of our local anglers—in which I confess I often joined—proclaiming our unswerving ability to beat the pants off of any brave city fisherman who ever dared to challenge us. And since all of us lived and fished within virtual casting range of Lake Superior on the remote Upper Peninsula of Michigan, simply "U.P." to its inhabitants, for a long time our challenges went unheeded. But as our brags grew in pitch and volume and were finally heard below the Straits of Mackinac, and ever farther away, more and more curious city anglers began filtering up our way to discover what inspired them—and the battle was joined and merrily continues. And with good fishing waters everywhere receding as their fishing tribes increase, I'd guess our rivalry must be typical of that going on most everywhere.

And what are these piscatorial advantages we locals so modestly keep admitting? First of all we live much closer to the magic waters, don't we, and so naturally get to fish more often and grow ever more proficient. Naturally we also get to "know" our local waters far better, including the patterns and rhythms of our local fly hatches as well as the best and most productive wadable stretches—along with the barren or tricky ones to avoid. Especially do we get to know the favorite lies of the biggest and boobiest dappled mermaids, we tell ourselves—and the list runs on and on. And lately, thanks to our Arab cousins, it seems we've gained an added advantage: naturally our poor city rivals get in even less practice these days what with the price of gas closing in so fast on bourbon. . . .

The first treasonable doubts about our unbeatableness began to assail me when I got to know and even fish with some of these city anglers, a meeting prompted by propinquity and their ever-increasing numbers. An added reason, in my case, may have been the three books I'd meanwhile written on the delights of our U.P. fishing, which seemed to act as a magnet for some, attracting them up here to see for themselves whether my tales were true or were instead by far my finest fiction—as some of their less enchanted reviewers claimed—quite a heady compliment, come to think of it, considering the three novels I'd also written. . . . But whatever drew them, the more I watched these city anglers at work the more I began wondering whether we locals were really all that good, a subject I'd now like to explore, first defining and confining the terrain.

By fishermen I mean only fly fishermen—in case the rumor has gotten around that there are other mentionable ways to woo a game fish. Next, by game fish I mean only trout, in case a companion rumor has spread that there might be other mentionable varieties inhabiting our planet. Finally, by fishermen I include the ladies, bless them, clinging to the archaic term not out of chauvinism, I swear, but rather because I tend to gag over calling any fisherman a fisherwoman much less a fisherperson. . . . I'd also like to confine my exploration only to "good" fishermen, excluding chronic duffers and beginners, not so much out of compassion but simply to narrow the field. Just what makes a fisherman good has long both intrigued and baffled me, so I'll now take a deep breath and give that another try.

First I'd guess that any good fisherman should possess the knack of occasionally getting on to and landing a trout; either that or going back to golf where, I'm told, the proof of one's proficiency is neither as tangible nor demanding. Next I suppose he should be able to cast and present a fly without producing an accompanying tidal wave—though all of us doubtless know habitual tidal-wavers who on some days manage to top the field. Finally I'd guess that casting an occasional glance to see what the trout are feeding on before casting the fly could rate fairly high on the list—though once again I suppose we all know those lucky souls who keep doggedly tying on old mops when only midget flies are popping—and still leave our faces red. In summary, then, it seems fair to say that a good fisherman is any angler who can with some consistency choose and present a decent fly and at the same time remain conscious of what county he's in and avoid too often falling on his can.

Perhaps a few questions here might help speed the exploration and bring me to the point. Granted the local advantages of which I speak, if both the city and country fishermen are equally savvy, one might ask, what real difference can it make where they hail from? Doesn't a good fisherman remain a good fisherman whether at home or abroad or whether he lives next to a silo or a skyscraper? Something, say, like a good sprinter or boxer or tennis player?

My answer, after years of research—*too* many, my wife has often claimed—runs something like this: Fishing is unlike any other sport in the world, indoors or out—all of which, indeed, is a good part of its mystique and charm; further, no two fishermen's "playing fields" are ever quite alike, even the same ones constantly shifting and changing before his very eyes. Fishing, when it's done for fun—and what other reason is there?—has really little or nothing to do with athletes or their little games.

Along with this revelation it has also gradually swept over me that the so-called advantages we local lads are believed to possess can just as often become disadvantages when we face a savvy city angler on the local waters we think we know so well. Thus, to take a common example, we locals often rig up and race—where we tend to remain glued—to the same magic spot where we caught that dappled beauty umpteen years ago, while our rival city anglers, unimpeded by such nostalgic dreams, remain free to explore and play the field.

What I'm saying can perhaps best be summed up in the phrase: familiarity breeds contempt, by which I mean we home-grown fishermen too often become slaves to the past, sometimes even passing up feeding trout in our dash to reach some former Shangri-La, as I've just said. We also seem to suffer from the very ease and availability of our local fishing, developing a sort of spoiled-brat indolence, which happens to rhyme with insolence, far too ready to shrug and go over our fly boxes once again if things aren't going our way. Maybe, the sulking trout aren't rising as they should or it's too damned hot or bright out there or it happens to be raining buckets or the wind is raising whitecaps—all part of the passing scene to our undaunted city fishermen who, far from ever going through *their* fly boxes when there's fishing to be done, rarely ever glance at the weather or miss a single cast.

This brings me to something else going for our city fisherman, an intangible something that may best be called the Beckoning Finger of Time. For in my recent research into what makes the urban angler tick I've also observed that when *he* goes fishing always before him there seems to dangle an invisible sign, big as a Rolaids ad, upon which is emblazoned a message that seems to shout: "Look, Buster, time's a-wasting and you've got only so many hours left, so keep a-casting, brother, ever pelting and flailing away."

It is precisely this hang-in-there quality that separates the city men from the country boys, I do believe; the presence of a sort of inspired itch that gives his fishing the intensity and drive and almost fanatic concentration that distinguishes the two—granted both are otherwise equally "good." And while I've never yet quite caught a city lad fishing in a full-blown typhoon, I've often peered out of my bush-car window and marveled to see my city pals still out there stoically casting away during the damndest weather—akin to the fabled postman who still delivers the mail come hell or high water—while I, so snug and dry, keep groping for that trusty six-pack. I've also observed that this bug-in-the-britches intensity has the added utility of keeping his fly on the water, no small advantage in this era when flying trout are getting so scarce—except on the covers of the more imaginative outdoor magazines.

As if all this were not enough, our city fisherman possesses one final advantage. For not only does his sublime itch goad him on when he is fishing but seems endlessly to spur him when his rural parole is over and he's once again back home. For even there, my roving agents keep informing me, he spends most of his leisure hours plotting his next assault: once again poring over everything ever written about fishing from Izaak Walton down to the latest word on the relative merits of graphite and boron. Or else kept blissfully chained to his tying vise. Or trying out his latest fairy wand down at the old club swimming hole. Or joining his fellow addicts over at their favorite sport shop comparing notes and strategies. Or listening to lectures by our traveling fishing gurus as they fly in with their slides and props to divulge the latest dope.

In fact I've lately started wondering just how lucky can a fisherman get, fishing so fiercely when he *is* there, ever in training when he *isn't*, Spartanly girding for the next assault—while we carefree country lads once again raise high our steins and voices as we croon and croak how good we are. And yet, and yet—I feel a final confession coming on—I still can't seem to make up my mind to pack my gear and move to sylvan Flint. Just plain chicken, I'd guess, plus the gnawing fear that by moving I might miss one of our cheery beery U.P. tavern chorales celebrating how good we are.

Gamboling at Frenchman's

from *Waters Swift and Still*, 1982

Show me a fly fisherman who's still out there flailing away—after all, a few faint-hearted ones occasionally do go back to golf—and I'll show you one of the biggest gamblers outside Las Vegas. And one just as heedless of the odds against him. For who but a real gone compulsive gambler would continue to stand for hours, often up to his whizzle-string in ice water, pelting out a series of bent pins adorned with bits of fluff and tinsel, all in the wistful hope that some hungry fish might finally mistake one of them for something good to eat?

My fishing pals and I know quite a bit about all this, for not only do we pursue one of the wariest creatures in all fishdom, the wild brook trout, but we do so in one of the toughest spots we've run across in the whole Lake Superior area of the rugged Upper Peninsula of Michigan, good old Frenchman's Pond, simply Frenchman's to the sturdy crew who regularly haunts the place, of which I am a charter member.

Just to list a few of the odds against fishing Frenchman's is enough to drive the average fisherman back to his golf cart—if not up one or the other of the tall spruces and tamaracks that line the rear margins of its boggy banks. First of all it really isn't a true pond at all—which are quite tough enough to fish anyway, heaven knows—but rather a shallow, crystal-clear and long-abandoned old beaver dam, which, with the aid of our annual patching jobs, still backs up its chilly waters for nearly a mile.

The moods of this pixilated pond are as variable as its width and winding course, and both are as eccentric as a midwinter rabbit trail through a cedar swamp. At one point it's but an easy fly cast to reach a riser on the other side; at another, both luck and prayer must accompany the final heave.

Wading is out because of the generations of accumulated silt, which must date clear back to the last glacier. Canoeing we quit when it early swept over us that in all that clear, shallow water any half-decent trout promptly spooked and went into a sulk at the first dip of the paddle. Floating in an inflated tube we put on probation for a spell, despite the accompanying clouds of churned up silt, till the day we flatly banned the tube when a nodding Hal had to be lassoed and towed ashore still bediapered in one, where it took most of a bottle of bourbon to start him cussing again.

"Wee touch of hypothermia from all those cold underwater springs," Doctor Lou diagnosed as he administered still another belt of bourbon to his shivering patient.

"Whatever in hell I've got, Doc, the treatment's too damned expensive," Hal finally croaked. "Imagine flooring nearly a bottle of *that* and not even knowing it."

Short of fly-casting from a balloon, an idea we periodically dallied with, this left us only the pond's boggy banks from which to fish. These ran virtually the length of the pond on both sides, and while there was generally room enough to cast a fly without snagging one of those rearguard spruces or tamaracks, the big feat was to work oneself successfully into position to attempt one.

For both shorelines are composed almost entirely of countless wobbly hummocks rearing their grassy heads out of a hidden multi-tude of lurking mudholes, still further disguised by blankets of low matted bushes, each tentacled branch endowed with a passion for snapping off artificial flies or weaving eccentric spider-web patterns out of fragile leaders and tippets.

Lloyd summed it up the day we finished building our log cabin on a bare granite knoll overlooking the pond, a cabin complete with an old school bell that would tell even the farthest-wandering fish-erman that the late-afternoon cocktail hour had arrived. "Fellas," Lloyd said, pointing pondward during a between-drink lull, "trying to cast a decent fly out there is tougher than playing that old kid's game of rubbing your belly while patting your noggin."

Still we persisted, and the sight of all six of us engaged in our fishing devotionals at the same time moved some of our nonfishing cronies to occasional bursts of poetry.

"Know what you guys look like?" one of them one day sud-denly cupped his hand and hollered from the open camp doorway.

"No," one of our struggling band hollered back, "I've often wondered."

"Like a herd of stampeding water buffalo."

"Dead wrong," Hal hollered back. "More like a bunch of drunks on a trampoline."

Why would a crew of canny old fishermen continue to haunt such a crazy place, let alone build a camp there? It would be nice to say we were continually drawn back by its sheer rugged beauty, peeking up like a glittering jewel out of those low wooded serpen-tine hills with their occasional reddish gleams of ancient granite; by the continued ignoring by the choosy trout not only of our favorite flies but of our years of accumulated lore; yes, by the very dare and difficulty of the place—wups, I almost said challenge, a close call.

All this was indeed part of its charm, no doubt, for one likes to think there's still a touch of Thoreau in every fisherman. But the big lure of Frenchman's was something else—its big wild brook trout, mermaid-plump trout we'd known all along were there, trout almost spectral in their taunting elusiveness, ghostly trout we could so rarely lure or ever land when we did. Yet scarcely a day passed when we failed to behold one of their wave-rippling rises—*kerplonk*—and scarcely a week when one of us wasn't left blinking by being abruptly cleaned out—*ping*—surely two of the most exciting sounds in all fishing.

The presence of these magazine-cover trout in our pond was contrary to all the sacred precepts of fishing we'd picked up at our fathers' knees, of course. For hadn't every savvy fisherman learned from boyhood that few wild brook trout in our northern bailiwick ever grew to be more than twelve inches long? Especially when confined to living in old shallow beaver dams where they were so constantly vulnerable to their many natural enemies? And especially those haunting forsaken old beaver dams fed by dozens of bubbling underwater springs pumping gallons of ice water which, as anybody knew, sharply lowered a trout's metabolism, and therefore his appetite, and therefore the growth of any poor stunted creature forced to dwell there? To all of which certified scrolls of fisherman's wisdom Frenchman's continued to have but one teasing response: *kerplonk!*

As for our prevalence of *pings*, these with true fisherman resourcefulness we managed to blame on everything but ourselves: the difficulty of ever luring a really big trout in all that stereopticon-clear water; the companion difficulty of successfully playing and landing one with all those hidden logs and ancient beaver cuttings and miscellaneous snags and roots and weeds and gobs of tenacious algae lurking in all that silt and along those snaggy-bushed shores, especially when fished from a swaying trampoline; the weirdness and unpredictability of the pond's natural fly hatches and the consequent difficulty of ever consistently matching them. On and on our excuses ran. Finally there was our almost helpless tendency, so common to prideful action-hungry fishermen—especially when the fishing is lousy—to keep tying on still more fragile tippets, so that we generally wound up being chronically underleadered.

This fine-leader syndrome that afflicts so many fishermen is not quite as sporting as it sounds. For the longer an angler fishes, the stronger he's apt to feel that the finer his leader the more follows and hits he's likely to get, probably because so few flies in nature come tethered to nylon tails upwards of umpteen feet long. By and by it sweeps over him that his leader might be one of the weakest weapons in the whole fly-fishing arsenal; that, alas, the sad truth is that as yet there *are* no perfect leaders—that is, both perfectly invisible and unbreakable—(though he nightly prays that Dan Bailey or someone out yonder is working on them) and that any leader he uses is an inevitable compromise between attracting more fish and the increasing risk of losing those he attracts.

Good old Hal put it more tersely. "While there's no damn question that our hawser-leadered buddies stand a far better chance of landing a slob once they're on to it," he one day declaimed, "there's also no question that the fine-leadered boys who prefer action over avoirdupois will get on to far more biggies in the first place." He raised his glass. "Maybe the old poet fellow said a mouthful when he wrote: ''Tis better to have lured and lost than never to have lured at all.'"

So the *pings* continued merrily until, following a particularly frustrating day five summers ago, we tolled the camp bell and met in an emergency session and vowed to try to solve some of the problems that afflicted us. One of the more obvious ones, of course, was the constant physical difficulty of fishing the place. So we had another round of drinks and talked away and finally passed the hat and, presto, in a matter of weeks had installed twin rough-plank boardwalks running practically the pond's length on both sides. We also built a narrow footbridge to get across on without having to boat or walk way down around the dam. Finally we fashioned and set out a series of wooden casting docks, Lloyd surrendering his precious collection of old wooden beer crates for us to squat on during the frequent ritual of tying on still more tippets.

All this measurably improved both our balance and tempers as it also increased our *pings*, alas. But our growing frustrations kept pace, for in making our improvements we'd also managed to lose our pet alibi for so regularly falling on our fannies—the now largely vanished difficulty of fishing the place. Some elusive thing was still lacking; we knew not what. Things came to a head just four seasons ago last July, on a memorable Saturday. To save time and rhetoric I'll swipe most of the account from my old fishing notes.

Today we turned Frenchman's into a genuine gambling casino lacking only dice girls and slot machines. Here's how it happened.

When we reached camp around noon the pond had gone crazy. Trout were rising and rolling everywhere: big, little, medium. Hal said it looked like a hail of golfballs with a few bricks and horseshoes thrown in. We quickly rigged up and raced for the boardwalks and our favorite casting stations—mine being at a tangled jumble of ancient submerged logs which, in an inspired burst of creativity, we had labeled the Log Jam, located in the narrows just above our new footbridge. Naturally the Log Jam was a great hideout for big trout since they, like their human pals, generally grab up the best spots. Naturally the Log Jam was also one of the main *pinging* centers of the pond.

All of us fished like mad all afternoon until around five when someone mercifully tolled the camp bell. After the first round of drinks we took a creel census, followed by a stunned silence, for nobody but nobody had caught a decent trout. All of us had had plenty of action, though, either being cleaned out at least once on the strike or busted or pulled off during the play.

"Fine bleeping state of affairs," Hal finally said. "Guess we gotta mend our ways."

"How?" somebody asked.

"Like maybe talkin' things over to see what in hell we can do about it," Hal said. "But first another round."

So we had another round and talked things over and were well into the second fifth when we arrived at an intriguing plan.

Beginning the very next day and from then on we agreed to place a standing bet on each fishing trip, every time out. The rules were as simple as falling off a trampoline: The guy with the biggest trout ten inches or over would win a buck each from all the others. That was it. All had to be taken on flies, of course, and the fly produced.

During our huddle we kept reassuring ourselves that we weren't even faintly commercializing our favorite sport. Perish the thought. Merely trying to chase away boredom and stimulate zeal in what we all agreed was one of the toughest spots we'd ever fished. Then we had another round and huddled some more and, to add spice to the roll of the dice, further agreed that the losers would pay two bucks a head when the winning trout reached twelve inches or better; three bucks at thirteen and so on into the higher realms of fantasy. We'd simply gamble our way into a state of mingled bliss and more fish.

There were a few miscellaneous odds and ends: A guy could keep his qualifying trout in a live trap, if he liked, and return it after the showdown. Or sooner if meanwhile a pal happened to catch a still larger trout.

"But suppose I catch a twelve-incher and Hal noses me out with a thirteen?" I inquired. "Don't I deserve a two-dollar credit for coming so close or must I also pay Hal three bucks along with the poor guys who only caught a chill?"

"Close don't count, lads," Hal argued in rebuttal. "Main reason I gave up dancing."

So my suggestion was voted down with only my lone dissent. Next we agreed a guy couldn't hog a hot spot all day but was limited to a half-hour at a stretch if another guy showed up and wanted to give it a try. Finally we agreed that each day's betting would end with the ringing of the camp bell, summoning all parched fishermen to the first round of drinks, generally around five.

"To Frenchman's!" Hal toasted at the end of our historic huddle.

"Transformed from pastoral boardwalk to roaring gambling hell all in one afternoon," someone said.

'Twas the last day of fishing and all up and down the pond my pals and I scurried against the deadline at five. Four summers had fled since we'd started gambling at Frenchman's and as I took up my stand at the Log Jam and sat tying up a new tippet my thoughts wandered over the intervening years.

Our fishing had picked up remarkably from the very first day, whether from avarice or added concentration I cannot quite say. One thing was plain: All of us fished longer and harder and with far more intensity. That very first Sunday I'd started at this same spot, hadn't I? Ah, yes, it was all coming back. We'd begun fishing around noon and on just about my first cast at the Log Jam I'd hooked and landed a plump twelve-incher—my first decent trout in weeks—and had admired and calibrated him and reverently placed him in my brand-new live trap.

I recalled how, in my excitement, I'd spent most of the rest of that first afternoon boardwalking up and down the pond proudly telling my pals about my prize—and also making sure that none had excelled me. Then, only minutes before five, Hal had come ambling along and paused to admire my fish.

"Any more luck?" Hal softly inquired.

"Couple small passes," I lied softly, as I'd actually just busted off on an even bigger trout.

"Mind if I give it a try?"

"My pleasure," I further lied, resignedly reeling in and moving away. "Don't catch 'em all."

Before I'd retreated ten paces along the boardwalk Hal had made a few false casts and popped out a little dry over my hot spot and—presto—hooked and splashily fought and landed what turned out to be that first day's winning thirteen-incher. Meanwhile, I, always slow at math, stood there stupidly figuring out that instead of just winning ten bucks (five guys at two bucks a head) I'd just lost three, all in one lousy cast, a total net loss—let's see—of thirteen whole bucks, almost the price of two bottles of our favorite hypothermia therapy.

During those years I'd occasionally won a few bets, of course, for it's hard for anyone to lose all the time at anything, even when the cards do seem stacked against you. And after all, wasn't it just as egotistical to believe in consistent bad luck as in good, both carrying their self-absorbed assumption that someone out there gives a damn? Yes, but wasn't it still mighty curious that most of my few winnings had either been on under-twelve-inch days or only when a few guys showed up? And wasn't it only last summer that I'd caught that dreamy plus-fourteen-incher when *none* of my pals had shown up?

I finished tying on my new tippet, then a small dry, at the same time ruefully wondering whether that distant first day of betting hadn't set the tone and pace of my piscatorial gambling career. True, our fishing had sharply improved, mine included, but why in hell did I so rarely win a bet and so often merely come close? Was it some sort of punishment for ever daring to suggest allowing that betting credit? Had my fate as our gang's favorite pigeon frozen me into a permanent role as runner-up?

Kerplonk, I suddenly heard, scrambling up so rapidly I kicked over one of Lloyd's beer crates, stripping and whipping out line, finally lofting out the little dry, which sang past my ear, poised for a fleeting moment, and then settled like a wisp of thistle in the middle of the lovely ebbing circle left by the rising trout.

The trout instantly rose and took the fly. I struck—lo, there was no *ping*—and I all but skidded it out of the danger zone—the narrow Log Jam where all of us so regularly lost so many fish and flies—and in moments had landed it and stood hefting it in my hand—a nice drippy twelve-incher. I glanced at my live trap, and then almost furtively up and down the pond—no pals in sight—and suddenly knelt and slid it back into the water, where it lay working its gills for a moment and then, presto, was gone.

"Maybe that will break the spell," I murmured out loud, feeling for a moment like one of those legendary millionaires lighting up his cigar with a ten-dollar bill.

In the next hour at the same spot I took and returned two more trout about the same size, one possibly larger. Then I sauntered back to camp and sipped a slow can of beer, listened to a couple of innings of baseball, then sauntered down below the bridge to check on my pals. Also to see what in hell was keeping them glued below. Also to show them I hadn't used up my current half-hour at my favorite spot.

Fishing had been good below, too, I discovered, Lloyd having just been cleaned out at the Big Spring and Lou a little earlier at his favorite Weed Patch. Ted and Gigs were still out of sight, probably in the deeper water down at the dam, a sporty big-fish spot the two often shared, while, as usual, good old Hal stood teetering and casting away on a rickety wooden platform on stilts that we called the Diving Board, so I moved down his way.

"Any luck, pard?" I inquired. Hal grunted and gestured at his nearby live trap. "May I sneak a look?" I said, and Hal nodded and I sneaked a look. "Hm," I said, for my hunch had been right: There lay a gorgeous trout, at least a fourteen-incher.

"Want to give my spot a whirl?" Hal said as I turned to leave.

"No thanks, pal, just came down slumming to see what I had to beat."

"Better get going," Hal said, glancing at his watch. "And don't catch them all."

"Have a nice day," I said as I got going, "as total strangers keep chanting at check-out counters as they heist our dough."

Once back at my Log Jam I saw it was already past midafternoon and that time indeed grew short. Play it cool, I told myself. So I sat on my beer crate and went through some of the more chaotic of my fly boxes. Then I heard a good trout rise and glanced upstream and saw its circle spreading over the Top Log area.

Remembering our half-hour rule, I glanced at my watch and headed for the Top Log, pausing a good cast length below the sunken log, which today I could plainly make out running straight out and downward from the brushy shore where, in the distant days when it was still a tree, it had once proudly stood.

First glancing back to make sure my favorite spot wasn't being invaded, I worked out line, false-casting, and finally sailed out a sizable dry just beyond the deeper end of the sunken log over one of the bigger springs. I glanced around to check on my pals and inadvertently twitched the fly and heard a watery explosion and then a sharp *ping*—and ruefully saw I had not only lost my fly but nearly half my lovely tapered leader.

Again I glanced at my watch—my, my, how the time flew—and stood there debating whether I still had time to tie on a brand-new leader or at least a couple of lengths of new tippet. Better get back there first, I told myself, and then we'll see.

Back at the Log Jam I'd barely sat down on my beer crate when I almost fell over backwards as a simply whopping trout rose, sending out wavelets in all directions. Once again I glanced at my watch and emitted a whistle—make that a low whistle—and mentally shrugged and found and managed to tie onto the remaining half of my shortened hawser leader a duplicate of the big feather-duster fly I'd just lost.

"Only minutes more," I kept whispering as I whipped the fly back and forth, back and forth, my fly darting like a hummingbird, all but closing my eyes as I finally released both fly and whirling hawser in the general direction of the Log Jam, where it landed at the far end with a watery *plop*.

Nothing happened and then I remembered the magic twitch, so I gave my fly a little twitch and a trout rose. I struck, and to my dismay saw I was on to a plucky junior-leaguer that seemed scarcely larger than my fly. Again a glance at the watch—only two minutes more—someone campbound waved at me from the footbridge—so I reeled in furiously, hoping to get in at least one more cast before the final bell.

I'd skidded the small trout almost to shore when I saw and

heard a sudden surging *kerplonk*, and I reared back and struck more out of shock than anything, and found myself latched on to an epic rod-bender that thrashed and churned like a retrieving spaniel.

The camp bell was still ringing as I finally towed him in close and batted him ashore with my net, for no way would he fit, falling on him and wrestling him just as he disgorged the smaller trout with my fly still in its jaw. Still wrestling, I managed to unhook my fly and slip the still-wriggling junior back into the pond.

"Looks like a dandy," Hal hollered across from the camp doorway, shading his eyes.

"Not bad," I modestly hollered back. "May need a licensed surveyor to measure 'im."

I left my big trout crammed and sulking in the trap, eyeing me balefully, and headed back to camp, now wrestling not with any trout but a flood of vexing questions. Had I really caught this monster on a fly? I asked myself. Or merely on a midget trout I'd already taken on a fly? But we had no rule against trolling or baiting our fly, had we, and wasn't this really akin to maybe adding a lone kernel of corn or a wee salmon egg to one's adroitly maneuvered fly? Or wasn't all *that* a lot of bull and shouldn't I confess all and leave the verdict up to my pals?

"Looks like it's between us," Hal said after we and the other boys had downed our first round. "How big is your baby?"

"Don't know yet, Hal," I answered honestly enough, "but I'd guess at least somewhere between eighteen and twenty inches, maybe more."

"Wow! Whadya catch'im on, man?"

I glanced down at the pond for a spell and turned and answered Hal.

What do *you* think I said?

Loon Calls on the Polecat

Fly Fisherman, May 1984

Hal and I have fished together for quite a few years—just over 20, according to my old fishing notes—drawn together by whatever mystic bond it is that turns lone fishermen into fishing pals. In our case part of it doubtless sprang from our shared passion for pursuing the elusive brook trout; that plus our common devotion to the consoling properties of sour mash bourbon.

Our first meeting took place under rather droll circumstances. It happened on one of those deep, cold, serpentine, heavily-wooded, rocky-shored, Canadian-type lakes that still dot the more wildly glaciated crannies of my native Upper Peninsula of Michigan.

Luckily for us and for its trout the lake still remains nameless on most maps, but shortly after we met, Hal, an old map collector, finally dredged up an old one that called it Polecat Lake, of all things. Though by now there are probably more Deer Lakes in Michigan than there are deer, this was the first Polecat I'd ever run across in all my years of fishing—and also the last.

Hal proudly showed me his old map one day as we sat on a log after a long afternoon of fishing, watching the trout rising and the sun setting over Polecat, enjoying our usual post-fishing reward of a few belts of bourbon to fortify ourselves for the long hike out.

"Picked up this treasure at a garage sale," he said, carefully folding away his prized map after I'd finally tracked down Polecat nestling there amidst a maze of lakes and streams. "A guy can sure pick up the damndest things at these garage sales."

"Poe-ole-cat," I said, reverently rolling out the prolonged syllables like a southern colonel presiding over a friendly neighborhood auction. "Real poetic name. Wonder how they ever dreamed it up?"

Hal reflectively rubbed his chin, as he often does. "Probably because any fisherman crazy enough to keep fighting his way in here soon gets to smell like one," he said.

"I see," I said, remembering the dense tangle of cedar swamp we still had to grope our way through to get back to our car. "Damned efficient name," I said. "Combines the romantic with the aromatic."

"Tell me something," Hal said as we finished our drinks and began stashing our gear for the hike out. "Did you ever hear the one about the persistent guy that tried to buy the garage at one of these garage sales?"

"No," I admitted, "but I'll bet the poor guy fainted when the owner said yes."

"Dead wrong. Instead he up and sued the garage owner for false advertising when he wouldn't sell."

"Pooh-ole-cay-at," I said, holding my nose.

This is how Hal and I sometimes carry on under the stress of fishermen's fatigue mixed with bourbon. But getting to that droll first meeting. . . .

On that distant day I'd been fishing alone off of one of Polecat's many submerged rocky points, a trick I'd early been forced to learn in order to make a half-decent backcast without losing still another fly or snagging still another tree. I had just missed the strike of a nice trout when I froze in mid-cast, listening to the haunting faraway call of a loon. I peered out over the lake but couldn't locate it. Then it called again—this time there was no mistake—the same shrill, wavering, lunatic trill.

Now if you've never heard the call of a loon, there's no use in my trying to tell you about it, and if you have I mercifully needn't bother. In either case, whenever I hear the call of a loon I invariably get an attack of the chilblains running up and down my spine. It's not so much a feeling of fear as a sudden sense of the remoteness and solitude of both men and loons mingled with the uneasy feeling that maybe both of us are but fleeting pauses in the immeasurable unraveling of time. Loons, you see, not only give me the chilblains but small attacks of wrestling with destiny.

This particular loon had finally fallen silent, so I quit peering and once again cast my fly just as the loon sent forth another distracting call. Again I peered, teetering and balancing on the slippery rocks, and this time finally spotted it—a dark floating object on the far side of the lake, dwarfed to a speck by the range of low rocky hills with their sparse rows of sentinel pines looming behind it.

Then a good trout rolled right out in front of me so I went back to work, on the first business cast barbing and busting off on a heavy threshing strike. Again I heard the loon call, this time, I could have sworn, with a small overtone of derision. So once again I paused and peered, almost slipping off my slippery rocks when I saw that my loon had drifted much closer and this time looked for all the world less like a loon than a floating hat.

This naturally gave me more chilblains, so after that I merely pretended to fish, all the while keeping a weather eye on this strange apparition, which kept calling all the louder and oftener the closer it got. In my panic I even thought I detected the outlines of a face under the floating hat, so I gave up all pretense of fishing and stood gaping and debating whether to stay and face the music or wade ashore and grab my gear and get the hell out of there.

Then I saw the approaching apparition slowly rising up out of the water—first a man's upper torso, then what seemed a dripping

269

tire or something wrapped around its middle, then a smiling man splashing his way up to me, holding a fly rod in one hand and the other held straight out toward me.

"Hi," my loon man said.

So that's how Hal and I first met. It was also the first time ever that I'd beheld one of those then new-fangled fishermen's floats I'd lately been hearing about and which, upon closer inspection, turned out to be little more than a pregnant rubber inner tube covered with canvas along with a sort of diaper arrangement across its middle to accommodate the floating fisherman's bewadered legs.

Hal had added one ingenious innovation: He'd tied on a pair of ping-pong paddles, one on each side, the better to propel himself as well as steer. "Lets me go first class full speed ahead and also travel steerage," is the way Hal explained it.

"Did you hear that bloomin' loon calling?" I asked Hal after we'd exchanged names and lodge grips and had recovered a little from the mutual shock of finding an intruding stranger invading the other's favorite secret trout waters. "Loons always give me the willies," I confessed.

"*I* was the loon," Hal said, giving me a wink, and with that he tilted his head back and opened his mouth as wide as Pavarotti's on the home stretch and let out the looniest lunatic blast I'd ever heard. "Learned to do it as a kid summering up in Minnesota," he explained as I stood gaping. "Wanna try it?"

While I never did learn to sound like an authentic loon, Hal and I began "going steady" after that, fishing together every chance we got; this despite the fact that we lived and worked nearly a hundred miles apart. But this still gave us those long northern evenings after work as well as occasional weekends—that's when we didn't find it more expedient to stay home and mend our frayed domestic fences. Another small impediment arose when our needy Arab cousins raised the price of gas to rival bourbon, and for a spell we even discussed going hardhat and switching to motorbikes.

Then late last summer came the magic day when both of us

woke up to find ourselves retired. Never again would we have to waste a single day of fishing by having to dress up in the mornings and go to work. We celebrated our parole by spending a long week-end camping on the shores of old Polecat, and fetching along a skil-let and, after swallowing hard, for the first time breaking our sacred vows of never keeping any of its trout and instead went on a retire-ment binge.

That first night we dined on fried trout and wild mushrooms (chanterelles) garnished with wild watercress. Hal, a sort of all-around outdoor Audubon, had gathered the latter two items on our long hike in. All this we washed down with bumpers of bourbon diluted with discreet dashes of Polecat water, a heady mix.

"Just think, Hal," I said after supper as we sat batting mosqui-toes and sipping our bedtime bourbon and once again watching the sun slowly sink as the bigger trout started to rise. "Isn't it funny, now that we're both retired and can fish all the more, that the big shots in Lansing up and cut the cost of our fishing licenses to peanuts instead of raising them."

I'd struck a responsive chord and Hal went into one of his declamatory arias. "It's par for the political course," he said, holding one hand up in the air and dolefully wagging his head. "Now that we're deemed to be too old to work and are free to fish *all* the time instead of only on holidays, evenings and weekends—besides hav-ing oodles of leisure to vote—the clever bastards up and cut the price instead of doubling it."

"Or maybe even quintupling it," I said.

We sat in silence until Hal reached over and clinked my cup with his. "Here's to three of nature's loveliest creations," he intoned in the voice of a Sunday morning TV preacher once again unveiling his zip code road to salvation, "who will only live—indeed, *can* only live—where beauty dwells."

"Hm," I mused. "And here I thought those three babes jumped bail and fled to Flint after their last raid."

"*Babes*, hell!" Hal said. "I mean the white-tailed deer, the ruffed grouse—partridge to you untutored U.P. natives—and the wild brook trout that we're so lucky to live among."

"Hear, hear," I said, glancing at my watch and reaching for my pack basket. "Better we get rolling, man, else we may have to spend the night in a cedar swamp sleeping with two of your brand of lovelies."

Two weeks ago Hal and I made it back to Polecat on our first trip since our trout binge of the year before. While we probably preferred to view our long absence from the place as a kind of guilty atonement for the breaking of our no-trout vows of the year before, I also suspect that part of it sprang from our increasing lack of enthusiasm for making the exhausting trip in there and back.

We arrived at old Polecat shortly before noon, this time sans skillet, puffing and blowing like a pair of beached whales. For a long time we just sat on our favorite log, staring out over the water, occasionally congratulating each other like reunioning old grads over how good it was to be back.

Once our rods were rigged, Hal helped me get into my waders and I helped get him into his—both new firsts—and then, reciprocity running rampant, also for the first time I helped Hal unpack and inflate his fisherman's float.

"I'd give you a tip, boy," Hal said with a smile, "if it weren't for these tight waders making it so hard to get at my cache of dimes."

Hal balked a little when I also helped wrestle him into his float— "I feel like a fat lady trying to try on her kid sister's girdle," he said— and we all but shook hands as I finally helped launch him out to sea.

"Thanks, pal," Hal waved and called back, once afloat, cupping his mouth like Captain Bligh. "Don't ketch 'em all."

"Aye, aye, Sir," I hollered back, making a two-fingered salute.

I stood watching Hal paddling himself away until all I saw was the floating cowboy hat, which soon magically looked more and more like a retreating loon. Then I found and trimmed a long tag alder branch to use as a wading staff—another new first—and gingerly waded out on my slippery rocks, teetering and balancing like a drunk walking a line for a skeptical cop. On my very first cast I got a magnificent strike—one of the topmost branches of one of the many tall Norway pines lurking so sneakily there behind me. . . .

Since I am not here spinning one of those gripping sagas about how Hal or I caught—or lost—The Big One (though I'll confess I've spun my share), I'll spare the details of how many branches I caught or flies I lost during that long afternoon. I was busily tying on still another fly when I heard the nearby call of a loon and I almost cheered when I looked up and saw Hal paddling himself ashore for our first bourbon reward of the day.

Once unwadered and duly rewarded, we sat on our log and sipped away, gathering ourselves for the hike out. Then I barely stifled a yawn but the ever alert Hal caught me at it in mid-stifle.

"You a little pooped, man?" he inquired ever so pleasantly.

"Just a wee bit," I confessed. "How about you?"

"I'm *real* pooped," Hal in turn confessed, yawning unabashedly. "Chronic pooptitude seems to be the price of—how shall I put it?—overripe maturity."

I shrugged. "Maybe we're both getting a little too stiff in the joints for these long trips."

Hal suddenly giggled a little and held out his cup in front of him, both hands, in an attitude of adoration. Then he daintily dipped his little finger in his drink and, again ever so daintily, sipped the lone bourbon teardrop off his finger, at the same time giving me an elfin sidelong glance. "And then again, pal," he said, "there's always the chance that maybe we're getting stiff a little too often in the wrong joints—like sitting here boozing on this bourbon-soaked log."

"Could be," I said, "but at least we can still enjoy a drink or two and occasionally manage to make a decent cast."

Once again we sat sipping away until Hal lowered his drink and turned and faced me. "Tell me, pal," he finally said, "whether you believe it is possible for any savvy and moderately sane fisherman to stand up to his whizzlestring in icewater for hours vainly casting flies at the trout he simply *knows* are there before it finally sweeps over him that he might better have stayed home that day and mown the hay on his neglected lawn?"

"Well," I said, after dutifully pondering, "I s'pose it *could* happen at times to even the best fisherman—ahem—maybe even to old masters like us. Seems as though on some days the trout do go into a sort of a sulk—"

"Sulk my foot," Hal broke in. "It happens all the time to any honest fisherman over the age of four. Moreover it's just happened to us, here, this very day." He pointed an accusing finger at me. "Confess," he said. "How many trout did you catch today?"

"Um—well now—let's see,—"

"How many, damn it?"

"None, damn it."

"How many strikes or passes?"

"None, come to think of it."

"How many rising trout did you see?"

"Not a bloomin' one. How about you, Izaak Walton?"

"Same score all the way."

"Then what's the big deal?" I demanded. "All you're saying is that for once both of us happened to get skunked at Polecat."

"Skunked at Polecat," Hal slowly repeated, savoring each word, "*Skunked at Polecat!* Did you just dream that up?"

"Blame it on the bourbon," I said. "But you still haven't answered me. What's so new about a fisherman occasionally falling on his prat and getting skunked?"

"That's exactly my point," Hal came back, eyeing me accusingly. "But it seems to take *some* fishermen I know one hell of a lot of years to get the message."

"What message?"

"That chasing trout and chasing women have one big thing in common—both can be all but impossible to catch when they're not in the mood."

"My, my," I said, blinking. "Really never thought of it *that* way before."

"Except that trout have far more character," Hal pushed on.

"*Sh*," I whispered, cupping my ear and glancing over both shoulders. "I think I hear the distant tramp of advancing feminist feet. Lower your voice, man, and tell me what the hell you're driving at?"

"By character I mean that trout are far less apt than some ladies to be lured into a change of mood by the piscatorial equivalents of glittering jewels and gold and by the subtle purr of dyed fur and all the other dependable mood-switchers of the past."

"My, my," I said, groping in my pack basket and pulling out a bottle and pouring us another healthy belt of bourbon. "Maybe you got something there," I said as we touched cups. "But what are we going to *do* about it man, now that we're a couple of old birds free to fish night and day? Consult tea leaves or the Zodiac or something every day before we dare go fishing? Or else donate our rods and gear to the Boy Scouts and take up golf? *Tell* me, man?"

"I mean I think it's high time both of us faced up to it," Hal quietly said, momentarily shifting from oratorical high gear.

"But I still don't follow."

"That when we find that the trout aren't in the mood that we find something else to do."

"Like what? Go through our fly boxes for the umpteenth time?"

"No, simply put down our rods and go gather mushrooms," Hal said.

"Mushrooms?" I said in a small voice.

"Mushrooms," Hal repeated like a benediction.

"But where?"

"All around us," Hal said sweeping out his arm in a half moon, once again back in oratorical high gear.

"But where?" I repeated.

"Look, man, we're lucky enough to live in one of the best and most varied wild mushroom spots east of the Mississippi. And most of them like the very same places that trout crave. Remember those chanterelles you slavered over when we broke down and banquetted here last year? And that I found and gathered in less than a mile from here?"

"I sure do. But what's the big point?"

"Simply face up to it, as I just said, and when the trout aren't in the mood, quietly put down out rods and go gather mushrooms instead."

"But suppose the mushrooms aren't in the mood?"

"Ah, you finally asked it," Hal said like a gloating D.A. closing in on a witness. "Chasing trout and chasing mushrooms have one vast difference between them."

"What's that?"

"When the mushrooms are there the pursuer can always catch 'em if only he stirs his butt!"

"Yes?"

"While if the trout are there, but not in the mood, his troubles have only begun—as it's taken both of us all these years and once again today to rediscover."

"Well I'll be damned," I finally said, and with that we finished our drinks and arose and shook hands and wrestled ourselves into our packs and stood taking a long farewell look at the evening mists settling over Polecat.

"Two old fishermen embarking on new careers on the distant shores of Polecat," I heard Hal muttering, as much to himself as to me.

It was then that we heard the loon calling—prolonged and wavering, both gleeful and achingly melancholy, sounding ever so close and yet ever so far away.

"Was that you?" I finally turned and asked Hal in wonderment after the first wave of chilblains had subsided a little.

"Not this time," Hal said, shaking his head. "*That*, pal, happened to be the real McCoy."

My Friend, My Friend

from *Seasons of the Angler*, 1988

Some of the loveliest places I know to fish are also some of the toughest, and for many years Frenchman's Pond was one of them—that is, until Jim the Indian came along.

The pond is fed by a narrow stream that begins in a sprawling cedar swamp lying several miles north of it, as well as by the many underwater springs that line its entire length. These springs keep spouting ice water all year round and doubtless account for the joyous fact that only wild brook trout dare live in it. Their presence also explains why my fishing pals and I are so drawn to it, despite the many hazards of fishing the place.

The pond's swamp-fed feeder stream joins it about half a mile above our fishing shack. There, it suddenly swells into a wide and mostly shallow body of crystal-clear ice water, hazard enough in itself—as all chronic pursuers of the elusive brook trout well know or must soon learn. There were still more hazards to face, though.

The entire camp side of the pond is lined, up to the water's edge, by a dense growth of tall trees, mostly spruces and tamaracks, extending clear down to the old beaver dam. And each one of these many trees seems to take a special delight in parting fishermen from their favorite flies.

Consequently, we learned early to fish from the open bog on the other side, where there was plenty of room to cast, and to which we soon built a wooden footbridge at a narrow spot just below the camp. But the boggy side, though easier to reach, presented plenty of problems of its own. For the entire bog was covered with a tenacious growth of swampy bushes that extended clear back to the low glacier-honed granite bluffs that run a serpentine course along both sides of the pond. This growth was not only a hazard in itself but also served to cover the many hidden water holes that lurked beneath its course.

This treacherous growth grew right up to the water's edge and down into the pond itself, causing a constant danger of snarling lines and leaders, not to mention lost tippets and flies, as well as trout. For a time we tried trimming these bushes, especially along the water's edge, but this only seemed to stimulate their growth; so we sighed and put down our shears and took up our rods again. We also tried wading or floating in rubber tubes to avoid the bogs, but soon gave that up because of the treacherous bottom, an incredible snarl of silt and slippery rocks and sharp-edged ancient beaver cuttings that had evidently been accumulating ever since the last glacier passed that way. A further reason, in fact the main one, is that we soon discovered that any fisherman who dared to expose or suspend himself in all that ice water for more than a few minutes risked freezing his (here the appropriate idiom is optional), leaving him in a semicomatose state that doctors more elegantly call "hypothermia." We also soon discovered that ice-water fishing gravely depleted our bourbon budget in our efforts to revive each other.

For a spell we tried boating, but soon abandoned that for both practical and aesthetic reasons. Practical because the minute one stepped in a boat and started clanking one's way among all those wily trout in all that clear water seemed only to scare the hell out of them. Aesthetic because sitting in a rocking boat attempting to cast a decent fly possessed all the charm and grace of trying to court a reluctant mermaid in a slippery bathtub. So back to the bogs we went, teetering and floundering, once again stoically losing leaders and flies, along with trout and our tempers—that is, until that lucky day when Jim the Indian came along and saved us.

I'd been fishing alone for hours, teetering and balancing my way from one boggy spot to another, lurching and stumbling along like a drunk on a trampoline. Thus far I'd only snarled my leader three times and lost two flies. The trout were occasionally rising, mostly out of range off the opposite shore, and I was having trouble finding the magic fly. Just then, a nice trout rose right off the boggy bank where I stood, so I swiftly changed to that season's favorite fly, called—my, my, I plumb forget; our favorite flies change so often.

First, I deftly fed out enough line to reach the trout, all in accordance with the latest dope in the casting manuals; then I made a quick double-haul and went into my business cast. Out, out sailed the line, the leader and fly following because they had to, the latter two finally folding forward with the grace of a ballerina's arm, the fly coming to rest upon the water's surface with the elfin lightness of a windblown wisp of thistle.

The trout rose; I struck; *ping* went my flyless leader as it raced back toward my ear. I stepped back to avoid it, and found one leg bogged down in an unseen water hole up to my thigh.

"Hi!" I heard a voice calling as I wallowed to extricate myself. I paused to look, and standing on the old boat dock across the pond was a smiling bear of a man carrying a loaded packsack, holding a rod case in one hand, and saluting me with the other.

"Hi!" I managed to croak.

"I'm Jim Washinawatok, from Wisconsin," he called across to me. "I live on the Menominee Indian reservation down there."

"Oh," I called back, still trying to extricate myself. "Give me a minute—or maybe an hour—and I'll be right over."

I finally made it and wallowed my way down to the bridge, where a smiling Jim met me, and we shook hands. He was a powerfully built man with sloping shoulders and straight black hair framing a handsome, carved-looking face, much like that of the man who once modeled for the old Buffalo nickel.

"How'd you ever find your way, way back here?" I asked when at last I'd caught my breath.

Jim explained that he'd read some of my past yarns about Frenchman's and had long wanted to visit both it and me. But he didn't quite know where to write me, so he finally decided to come.

"But how did you track me down?" I repeated.

"Got hold of a county plat book with all the township maps showing land ownership, and finally tracked you down."

"My, my. I feel like a dismounted John Wayne. First time I've ever been tracked down by a real Indian," I said. "Welcome to Frenchman's Pond."

Just then, there was a whoosh of wings as a pair of ducks flew over us, upstream bound, veering upward and then down once again, barely skimming the water, like a pair of practicing jets. As if by signal, a nice trout rose in their wake, and at the same time we heard the haunting cry of an unseen loon. I glanced at Jim, whose lips seemed to be moving as if in silent prayer.

"Like the place, Jim?" I asked.

Jim nodded before he spoke. "Being in this place at this hour is like coming home after a long absence," he said. "Not only do I like the place, but I've already fallen in love with it."

Another good trout rose off the boggy shore to our left, and as we watched its outgoing ripples, still another trout rose just above where we sat.

"Better get rigged up, Jim," I said, getting up and grabbing for my rod. "Those rises seem to have revived me, so let's go give it a try."

After Jim had rigged up, I took him on a quick tour of the place: the camp, with its long folding bed that was a couch during the day; the crowded toolhouse; the winding trail to the outhouse. Then we hiked down to the dam along the wooded granite bluffs on the camp-side trail. We found the trout rising and fished for an hour or so, returning all the fish except two, which I insisted Jim keep for his breakfast. (I, still a slave to indoor plumbing, preferred to sleep at home.)

We crossed over on the arc of the dam, gathering a batch of wild watercress on the way, and then hiked back toward the bridge on an old needle-carpeted game trail, picking a mess of chanterelle mushrooms to go with Jim's trout and watercress breakfast. We had almost reached the bridge when Jim, who was behind me, touched my arm.

"Look," he whispered, pointing to where a lovely buck deer, its horns still in velvet, was standing under a giant lone white pine tree in an open patch of granite. The deer stood facing us with large unblinking eyes, looking as still and frozen as a statue on a lawn.

"Whew!" Jim blew, sounding like a deer himself, and the deer wheeled and leapt and suddenly was gone, leaving only a lone pine tree growing out of an open patch of granite.

"Great place to put a tepee," Jim said, staring at the scene.

"Great idea," I absently said, my mind more on a certain six-pack that awaited me back in the bush car.

Once across the bridge, Jim cleaned out his trout while I raided the six-pack and turned on my battery-run tape player. Then we sat outside batting mosquitoes and watched the sun go down and the trout begin to rise, all to the piano music of Claude Debussy.

It was then that Jim, almost shyly, broached the subject, asking me if I'd ever thought of building a few rustic wooden platforms out from the water's edge on the boggy side. "Might make casting easier and also save some leaders and flies and possibly even a few trout," he smilingly explained.

"Never really thought of it," I confessed. "Maybe someday I'll give it a try."

"Mind if I try making a model," Jim said. "Saw a lot of old rough boards and two-by-fours piled behind the toolhouse."

"Fine, Jim," I said, finishing my beer and reprieving Mr. Debussy and heading for my bush car to take off for home. "See you tomorrow. Can I bring you anything?"

"Maybe two or three pounds of mixed spikes," Jim called after me as I left.

The next day I arrived at camp around noon, bristling with spikes. As I rolled down the hill, there stood Jim across the pond, calmly fly-casting off a brand-new platform that he'd already built and anchored in place since we'd parted the evening before.

"Great idea, Jim," I hollered across to him, walking down to the dock.

"You ain't seen nothing yet," Jim hollered back. "There's two more new ones just below the bridge. Rig up and come give 'em a try."

"But you should have waited for me to give you a hand, Jim. How'd you ever get them across the narrow bridge?"

"Boated 'em across."

"But the old boat leaks like a sieve," I hollered, coining a phrase.

"Not any more. Caulked it last night with some of the bags of unused cement I found when I cleaned out the toolhouse."

"Well, I'll be damned," I said, hurrying back to camp to grab my already rigged-up rod. Once there, I found a spotless camp, even to freshly baited and re-set mousetraps. "Place hasn't been this clean since it was built," I murmured to myself as I grabbed my rod.

Jim's love affair with Frenchman's Pond began the time he built those first casting platforms on his first trip there nearly twenty years ago. Since then, he's come back every chance he's had, which is at least once a season, and usually more. During that time, he has transformed the place from a bog-teetering sanatorium for frustrated fishermen into a kind of sylvan anglers' paradise. All this he has somehow managed to do without much changing the wild and unkempt look the place must have had from the time of the last glacier.

I could probably write a fairly hefty book about all the things that Jim has done to improve the fishing at the old pond. He still prefers to work alone; one of the reasons, I suspect, is so that he can continue to surprise me. There are now over a score of casting platforms along both sides of the pond, all joined together by boardwalks of rough planks. All he seems to want or expect from me is to keep him well supplied with spikes and planks and two-by-fours.

One morning when I arrived at camp, I found him toting an entire tree down to the narrows, just above the bridge, as the starting "anchor" of still another protective brush pile for the trout, of which he had already built several.

The tree was a "leaner," Jim explained, that is, one already uprooted by age or the wind, and he had sawed off the uprooted bottom and trimmed the branches and lugged it at least a half-mile, a feat roughly akin to carrying an upright piano across a freshly plowed field.

He has also built a series of anchored rafts at strategic spots, not to fish from, but as protection and cover for the trout, many if not most of whose enemies seem to come from above, ravenous creatures like ospreys, eagles, kingfishers, and loons—as well as us loony fishermen. He has also built several extra-long casting platforms from the tree-lined side to allow for guarded backcasts at persistent rises that could not be reached from the boggy side.

Then came the summer when I arrived at camp and found still another big surprise: Jim had brought his wife, Gwen. I had known he was married and had two daughters, but he had neglected to tell me that he had wedded a woman who looked like an Indian princess. With her gleaming black hair framing her large dark eyes and comely face, she also conjured up boyhood pictures that I still carried in my mind of the beautiful Pocahontas.

Gwen did not fish, but preferred to sit outside and watch our antics while she sketched or sewed or worked on the studies she had brought along from the state university. She had already graduated in nursing but was continuing to take courses in medical and related subjects, so that she might one day permanently return to the reservation and both teach and spread her knowledge among her own tribespeople, particularly in the world-afflicted area of alcohol and drug abuse.

The first evening, after fishing, all three of us sat outside and watched the sun go down behind the ancient granite bluffs across the pond, a scene broken only by the rising trout and the evening flight of birds and the call of the frogs. The sight was so primitively beautiful that I overstayed my leave and, instead, sneaked up to my bush car and brought back my tape player and a favorite cassette.

It was well I did, because as the sun finally sank and darkness began to take over, the sky slowly began to brighten and glitter, suddenly becoming aflame with a series of eerie lights: the first northern lights of the season. I reached for my tape player and sat and watched the strange lights shifting and melting across the sky in great dripping organ pipes of silent melody.

Listening to Anna Moffo singing the haunting "Vocalise" by Rachmaninoff on the tape player was moving enough in itself, but doing so while beholding such a rare heavenly spectacle left us frozen in the grip of ecstatic chill. Even after the music had ceased and the lights in the sky had faded, we sat there in silence. Finally, I heard someone speaking, or half murmuring, in an awed, feminine voice: "I love this place."

After that, Gwen accompanied Jim on his annual trip to the pond as frequently as she could. Often, instead of fishing, the three of us would go exploring the back roads in the bush car, pausing to pick whatever wild berries or cherries or mushrooms might be out, sometimes winding up dining at some obscure rural café on such neglected "gourmet" delights as genuine Cornish pasties or Italian polenta—rarely found anymore in even the fanciest franchised restaurants.

Then came the recent summer when, for family reasons, I had

284

to be away during the last few days of Jim's annual visit. When I returned home, I quickly mounted the bush car and headed for the pond, rarin' to go, hoping that Jim hadn't left yet. But he and his car were gone, and instead I found a note pinned to the camp door written in Jim's beautiful script.

> *Before entering this castle, sir, please cross the bridge and start down the deer trail, pausing at the lone pine.*
>
> *Jim*

I followed orders, wondering what new surprise was coming this time, pausing at the lone pine, and there, standing next to it on the bare granite rocks, was a beautiful towering Indian tepee, the tall slender trees that supported it reaching witch-fingered out of the top.

Back inside the camp I found a note lying on the table:

> *I did it myself, using only "leaners," and I hope you like it because it's the first one I ever built.*
>
> *Jim*
>
> *P.S. Take a look behind the camp door.*

I looked and found a fresh strip of white birch bark framed in birch twigs hanging from a nail. There was writing on it, so I sat at the camp table overlooking the pond, the better to see, and this is what I read, written by my friend and fellow writer Jim the Indian, out at Frenchman's Pond:

COME BACK, GRANDFATHER

We walked here once, Grandfather.
These trees, ponds, these springs and streams,
And that big flat rock across the water over there.
We used to meet with you over there—
Remember, Grandfather?—and
We would smoke and talk of many things.

We would drum and dance and sing
And after a while make offerings.
Then we would sing the travelling song
And would go our ways
And sometimes we would see your signs
On the way to our lodges.

But something happened, Grandfather.
We have lost our way somewhere and
Everything is going away.
The four-legged, the trees, springs and streams,
Even the big water where the Laughing
Whitefish goes, and the big sky of many eagles
Are saying goodbye.
Come back, Grandfather, come back.

Treed by Trout

Michigan Natural Resources magazine, July/August 1989

It took me many years to learn that some of the most memorable rewards of fishing possess neither gills nor fins. Granted such a miracle, one old fisherman will in what follows try to share some of the nonfinny rewards he's collected over the years while pursuing his trouty obsession. (Lest I risk leaving the impression that my using the word "obsession" here implies that I think all of us fishermen are a little daft, and to avoid distracting debate or even a poll-losing fate, I think I'd better replace it with "craft.")

These unusual sights become even more bountiful when the fisherman happens to live in such an unusual place as the Upper Peninsula of Michigan, where this lucky native does, a sprawling tangle of hills and swamps and endless waterways. The few scattered towns and assorted gasoline, six-pack and lottery-ticket stops are but isolated scars in the woods and together harbor fewer people than do some modest single towns "down below," which happens to be an authentic bit of U.P. idiom meaning the Lower Peninsula or "below the Straits." These sights seem to abound all the more if the fisherman is also obsessed (there, I finally said it!) with the pursuit of the wild brook trout, a shy reclusive creature which, unlike its pursuers, will not live, indeed cannot live, except where beauty dwells. And since we fishermen also happen to belong to a species which seems increasingly hellbent on chasing all natural beauty still farther down the pike, it follows as the night the day that fishermen must range ever farther in their quest for the trout of their dreams.

One more thing. Fishermen who choose to chase the wary brook trout early learn that their chase is eerily akin to pursuing an aloof and shy fairy princess; there's damn little chance of catching either when they're not in the mood. All this is lucky for the dwindling brook trout, naturally, but also quite frustrating to the baffled fisherman, and probably accounts for most of the impromptu detours we fishermen keep taking while waiting for the trouts' unpredictable moods to change.

I was still an unshaven lad when, in an outburst of national virtue, the entire country went dry in a venture called Prohibition. Though the experiment failed, and the daring law was eventually repealed (actually it was a formal constitutional amendment), it changed the course of American life in many ways.

One thing it did was to create an avalanche of native home brewers and backwoods distillers most of whom, at least up my way, sought to conceal their naughty ways by practicing their craft either on or near remote trout waters. (Possibly this poetic propinquity inspired the birth of the then common expression "watered booze?")

Though I managed to survive that tumultuous era with a few taste buds left, looking back I would guess I could probably fill a wing of the Smithsonian Institution with all the remains of the abandoned backwoods breweries and distilleries (mostly broken barrels and kegs and jugs and bottles and yards of tangled piping) I've run across and stumbled over during my quest for trout. And still do.

Then there was that distant late summer afternoon when I startled a convention of lovely brook trout at the chilly mouth of an unknown feeder creek while floating my way down a branch of the Escanaba River. The wedge of trout seemed to explode and disappear in a single Houdini flash, all heading up the mystery creek, so naturally I beached my boat and grabbed my rod and splashed my way upstream after them.

After wading half a mile or so up the shallow, sandy-bottomed creek itself, I came upon the sun-bleached grassy-strewn ruins of a once vast beaver dam. To avoid perhaps once again disturbing the siestas of all those fleeing trout, I left the creek and took to the heavily beferned and wooded creek bottom, soon confirming a long suspicion I've had that along about August most U.P. woods become jungles, particularly moist creek bottoms, all striving to imitate tropical rain forests.

But I sighed and pushed on, daintily balancing my rod before me. Suddenly I stumbled—yipes—and abruptly found myself seated amidst a pile of hidden rocks. Mercifully my magic wand—I mean my fly rod—was still intact. Peering further I discovered that these mossy rocks simply had to have been piled there by human hands because the crude pile was unmistakably and deliberately made to face the ruined beaver dam to form a kind of squat, miniature fort.

Old prowlers soon learn that the best way to learn the perils of prowling is by prowling. (All of which reminds me of the old Saturday movie serial we kids used to attend for a nickel called "The Perils of Pauline." Then, of course, there's the well-known dietary Perils of Pralines). Anyway, I craftily took down my rod and warily pushed on through my native rain forest.

This all happened way back when I was still a bumptious adolescent in my fifties, but I still recall that in less than the length of a football field I came upon four more crude rocky forts, all in turn facing the old backwater of the ruined beaver dam.

Then I noticed one more macabre thing: that the rocks on the upstream end of each fort curved around inward. This set my imagination tingling along with my spine. Could these rocky inward curves have been designed the better to hide the armed occupants of each fort as they awaited their unsuspecting victims as they airily floated their way downstream?

Pushing on, I soon discovered that I had not only run out of forts but was both parched and pooped (something that adds up to an advanced state of "pooptitude," as my old friend Sunny calls it). So I left the creek bottom and climbed up on a rocky ridge behind it and got back to my boat and finally to my bush car before any wayward mermaids waylaid me.

That night I had a long, tortuous dream that went something like this: Once upon a time a band of Indians began feuding over wine, women or pelts, pretty much the same things our species has endlessly fought each other over ever since we shed our tails.

Several things seemed clear: the big old beaver dam must have still been intact; the crude forts were fashioned from the scattered glacial debris fallen from those mossy granite cliffs behind them; and the armed occupants of those forts calmly awaited their victims firm in the knowledge (as every tenderfoot Boy Scout knows) that no matter how many canoes might descend the creek, or however heavily armed, each occupant simply had to leave his canoe to portage it, one canoe at a time, around the unnavigable arc of the beaver dam spillway itself.

The fact that the forts are still there seems strong proof, however negative, that there were probably no survivors among the canoeists on that distant bygone day when all hell broke loose on a secluded and nameless trout stream in the Upper Peninsula of Michigan. Sometimes I think of it as the Massacre of Mystery Creek and someday, with luck, I may even write a two-pound novel about it bearing the novel title *Anatomy of A Massacre.*

Switching from forts to fireplaces, there was the day I found myself stalking black morels down a steep, leaf-strewn hill in early May. The morels kept eluding me, as the little rascals so often do, when once again the stalker stumbled—this time upon a narrow leaf-strewn pile of rocks that turned out to be a long, narrow, squat-chimneyed, carefully fashioned outdoor oven built of native rocks.

Though now almost totally hidden by generations of matted leaves, closer looking showed that the heavily besooted oven had been much used in the past. Moonshining or the making of maple syrup seemed unlikely because, in the latter case, the surrounding trees were all wrong and only a sap would have lugged sap that far, while back in the moonshine days the many family catalogues abounded with all manner of stoves that sold, it seems in rueful ret-rospect, for roughly a dime a dozen.

I've never disturbed the place or tried to date the ashes (Busy tonight, Honey?) or probed the place with metal detectors and the like. In fact, I rarely revisit the eerie place, but sometimes at night I wake up and wonder just what it was they cooked on that ancient oven—whoever *they* were.

Possibly a deer? Or perhaps even a person? Or in our unbridled passion for creating all manner of religious rituals, perhaps used it in the exercise of their own religious rites, whether weirdo or other-wise.

Or, more recently, since he seems to be having quite a revival lately, perhaps used it to warm up the old guitar once plucked by Elvis Presley who, as the cover of a magazine I recently beheld at one of those modern cultural centers called a checkout counter assured me, may even be our next president. An absorbing prospect, but since then I've heard that already there's at least one busy string-plucker hovering over Washington who is also rumored to possess a latchkey to at least the back door of the White House.

So far I've mentioned only sights created by the hand of man. But I've also run into many natural sights that in their way are even more intriguing. Especially is this true of trees, which in their way can be even stranger than people. Which, by the way, gives trees one hell of a lot of latitude.

I could probably fill a coffee-table-sagging book with pictures of all the memorable trees I've seen if only I'd been manually adept enough to ever learn how to work a camera. Or mentally adept enough ever to learn how to translate the baffling factory instructions on how to work the things. But many of these trees are still there and so I thought that, before the roving loggers reduce them to chips, I might try to preserve just a few of them in mere words.

On the way to my camp out at Frenchman's Pond stands a giant gnarly solitary white pine that must have been around when Abe Lincoln was a lad. Isolation and a squat trunk that splits in two less than half the way up probably saved it from the loggers, but just seeing it silently standing there, day after day, makes even some ancient fishermen realize how fleeting human life really is compared with that of many trees. In fact sometimes, spurred by a shot of bourbon or two, I'll even bet my favorite fly rod that this old tree was probably already a sapling when a young George Washington chopped down all those cherry trees. Or was it only one lone cherry tree?

Once out at the pond, just across on the footbridge from camp, stands a lone perky white pine on top of a squat, rounded outcrop of lichen-strewn ancient granite. When I say ancient granite here I mean it's billions not mere measly millions of years old. (Sounds like a politician carrying on about the budget.) The thing that makes this tree so special is that it was once a lower limb of an older and larger pine that somehow grew out of the debris accumulated in a narrow crevice in the granite; the older tree blew down in an ancient storm and eventually appeared to have died; but, and here's the mystery, was somehow reborn and somehow still survives as a sturdy tree magically transformed from a former single projecting limb.

Quite a lesson for old fishermen on the tenacity of trees.

On with the prowl.

Then there's that giant white pine that still bravely stands alone near the lower main Escanaba River, leaning over at almost a forty-five degree angle, another mute monument to the tenacity of trees, leaning at an angle so accurate that a mariner could probably set his course by this statuesque proof of our prevailing northwest winds.

Then there's that giant elm I once encountered on a prowl that goes back to Model A days. The tree was deeply riven from top to bottom by a bolt of lightning during an ancient storm. Though the scope and depth of the gash was ghastly, and the elm's toppled top hovered only inches from the ground, the wound had somehow healed and the tree was in full leaf and appeared vibrantly alive. So I stood there and toasted it with a warm beer and then quietly stole away, wondering even as I write this if it can still possibly be around.

Last May I was slowly cruising a heavily wooded winding two-rut road in my bush car looking for what, in my scholarly fashion, I call the Oyster Mushroom. Since I've forgotten its Latin nicknames I'll instead give this clue: it grows in lush creamy-white layered patches on the outer bark of certain poplar trees, the Latin names of which shall in turn remain nameless and I equally blameless.

After years of research I've discovered that mushrooms, unlike trout, can only be "caught" if they're there, while with trout, alas, even when they are there, one's troubles often only begin. Anyway, my mushroomy meditations were abruptly interrupted when I suddenly came upon a single strand of heavy metal cable strung across the narrow road in front of me, surrounded as usual by a rash of hearty, home-made, hand-painted Upper Peninsula welcome signs. "Private property—no trespassing," read one of them. "Violators will be prosecuted to the full extent of the law," warned another. "Stay the hell out!" tersely said another, which at least probably saved a dab or two of paint.

So I grunted and stirred and finally got out to find out whether

I could turn around or else be reduced to gnawing the cable. Traffic had been sparse but I finally found a small break in the crowded woods where my trusty four-wheeler might ultimately see-saw its way back to freedom. So the see-sawing began until "plop" went the motor as it coughed and died while I sat there softly coining a few colorful new swear words, when suddenly the creative cursing ceased and I sat there staring at the scene before me.

For there dead ahead of me stood one of the strangest woodland sights I've ever seen—two young white birches caught making love in a remote wooded retreat where leering old fishermen seldom roam.

Dangling Angling Genes

Fly Rod & Reel, May/June 1990

If ever there was a pollster clever and nimble enough to round up 10 fishermen at one time in one place—especially during the fishing season—the chances are great that when he started quizzing his captured quizlings nine of them would confess under fire that yes, they guess they first got hooked on fishing when daddy took them out when they were boys. And the chances are equally great that the lone one-out-of-10 escapee either didn't have a daddy around to corrupt him or else he was one of those rare genetic mutations who had somehow just missed the boat.

For a long time my own mother held out such a ray of hope for me. Though my two older brothers were already hooked, my mother still clung to the hope that her own part of the genetic pool might still save her youngest son. After all, hadn't her own father managed to escape the piscatorial allurements of the Hudson Valley village where he was born? And hadn't her own two brothers also sturdily remained unhooked?

She drew further comfort from the fact that I had already safely passed the age my own brothers were when they had first gotten hooked. And that I seemed to share her love of music, the thing that had first drawn her to our northern Michigan town to teach it in the public schools—that is, until she finally collided with and married the mad fisherman who, between his endless fishing trips, somehow found the time to become my father.

She also knew that I shared her love of books and stories and had already written a story of my own that had won a prize at the Ridge Street School—a box of colored crayons. "Lost Alone All Nighty In a Swamp With A Bear" I had called it, and when my father heard the news that night at supper he pondered a moment and said, "With a story title like that, son, about all you really had to add was 'Woof.' Next time try not to blow the suspense before the opening line."

"You men!" my proud mother said, arising and hurrying out to the kitchen.

My mother also knew that not only had I so far remained unhooked but that I was actually growing to hate the whole idea of fishing, a distaste stimulated by all the trout my father kept lugging home and dumping into the kitchen sink for his youngest son to clean—and for which my sole reward was the privilege of living almost solely on trout all summer long; that and standing in the backyard waving my father and his pal, Danny, away as they took off on still another trout safari without me.

Things reached a climax one Saturday morning as once again I stood in the backyard and waved my father and Danny away in the old Model T.

"Don't ketch 'em all!" I hollered after them.

"Don't forget to mow the lawn," my father hollered back as they rolled away.

"Damn!" I hollered after them, suddenly turning and running into the house and raiding our wooden icebox of all its trout and peddling them around the neighborhood for a nickel apiece. Then I ran downtown with the money jingling in my corduroy knickerbocker trousers and went on a banana-split binge at Gill's Kandy Kitchen.

That evening my mother watched with growing concern as I languidly picked and nibbled away at my supper. When I started hiccupping and finally pushed my plate away the questions began. Was I ill? Was it something I ate? And what happened to all those lovely trout in the icebox? Oh, so you were a good boy and distributed them among our neighbors? My, my, you mean you sold them? And what in heaven's name did you do with all the money, son?

Full confession followed, and instead of scolding me, my mother surprisingly smiled and hugged me. When she further promised not to tell my father what I'd done, I hugged her in return, for both of us knew that the obsessed fisherman in our family possessed a temper as short as his legs were long.

To this day I don't know what, if anything, my mother ever told my father about my icebox raid, but the following Saturday, as I was getting ready to join my school chums on our weekly trek to the Butler Theater to see if our latest movie queen had once again survived the latest horrifying dilemma the villain had left her in the week before, my father arrived home early and sought me out.

"Grab your toothbrush, son," he said. "'cause I'm taking you fishing for the weekend out at the old South Camp."

At that point my mother inquired whether there would be enough room for me in the old Model T along with Danny and all of his bottles and gadgets and gear.

"Danny can't make it today," my father said.

"Why not?"

"Hangover, Annie—just a plain old-fashion hangover."

"Oh," my mother said, and I can still see her standing there in the backyard pensively waving to us as we roared away, my father (as usual) gripping the wheel of the Model T with all the hunched intensity of a novice making his first roller-coaster ride.

That weekend I got hopelessly hooked on the pursuit of trout, and when we arrived home late Sunday night and my mother sat listening to me running on and on about my new obsession and how daddy planned to take me out along with Danny the next weekend, she finally turned to my father and spoke.

"Congratulations, Nick," she said, her eyes flashing, "Congratulations on finally landing our youngest son in your fishing net."

"Aw, now Annie, don't take it so hard," my father said. "After all, a lad can't get into too much trouble goin' fishing with his old man."

"That's what you said about the older boys," my mother said, biting her lips as she rose and left the room.

Time passed, as it has a droll habit of doing, and one summer my mother took her first trip back to the Hudson Valley village where her father was born. There for the first time she met a number of cousins of varying degrees who told her much about the Traver family background and the area where they had long abounded, and seven offered to sponsor her for membership in the local D.A.R., whenever she felt that she cared to join.

More time passed and I somehow forsook fishing long enough to finish both college and law school and met and married a girl called Grace who hailed from a nearby Chicago suburb, winding up, of all things, working for a big downtown Chicago law firm that contained so many caged lawyers that in the general confusion they sometimes even sued their own firm's clients.

When, after several years of that, I discovered that a fisherman was far more apt to latch on to a dead cat than a trout in the Chicago River, I quit my job and fled north and ran for D.A. of my home bailiwick, a job I somehow won and held onto for 14 years. Since it's a long time between fishing seasons up my way—a place father north than many points in Canada—to pass the time I began scribbling stories and then several books, two of them about my D.A. job.

Then came the chilly fall election day when I found myself abruptly paroled from my D.A. job by the unappealable verdict of the voters. So I soon began popping up on the other side of the courtroom barriers, this time defending cases ranging from drunk driving to first-degree murder. But it was still a long wait between fishing seasons, so one winter I wrote my first novel—to pass the time—and finished just in time for the eve of the fishing season.

Twice it was swiftly rejected by two of our country's canny publishers, so one night out fishing I remembered an editor who'd worked on my last D.A. book and liked it, so the next day I baled it off to him at the new New York firm where he worked and, presto, both Sherman Baker and St. Martin's Press promptly grabbed it. Though my first three books had raced each other to out-of-print oblivion, almost overnight *Anatomy of a Murder* caught on and became glued to the bestseller list.

Ironically, about the time I thought at last I was free to go fishing whenever I wanted, instead, for the first time. I became too busy to even think about fishing. The book got the full treatment: Book-of-the-Month Club, made into a movie by Otto Preminger, into a play by Elihu Winer—while meanwhile I woke up one morning and found myself appointed to our state's highest court and faced with not one but two hotly contested statewide elections.

I mention all of this not only to brag but because it is necessary to the yarn I'm spinning. Perhaps the best thing I can say about the trauma of best-sellerdom is that I somehow survived it. And I still didn't think that my idlest scribbling should henceforth be cast in bronze or that my most casual rhetorical burps were now worth a buck a burp.

Meanwhile I was invited all over hell, which is par for the course, I guess, complicated by the fact that this latest sacrificial lamb on the altar of fleeting notoriety was not only a chronic scribbler but also a fisherman, lawyer, ex-D.A., judge and battle-scarred politician all rolled into one.

Fortunately, I was kept so busy on my new court job that I had to turn down most of the avalanche of invitations. But some I simply couldn't decline and one day such an invitation came from my publisher and that following Friday night found Grace and me adrift in a downtown New York hotel where a note at the front desk informed me that due to a sudden change in plans, we had the entire next day free to ourselves.

Thus it happened that at breakfast the next morning (Saturday) I slyly suggested to Grace that we rent ourselves a car and maybe drive somewhere out of town.

"Good idea," Grace agreed. "But where?"

"Maybe up to West Kill and visit my old friend Art Flick," I said after a careful pause. "Maybe Art could lend me a fly rod and we could even visit the hallowed trout waters he's so often talked about."

"I think I smell something fishy," Grace said, delicately sniffing the air. "I further think it would be far more appropriate if we instead drove up the Hudson Valley and visited the village where your mother's non-fishing father was born as well as some of the non-fishing relatives you've never met." She paused before making her final cast. "In fact, it would be a real treat for me to for once meet a branch of your family not reeking of fish or hopelessly afflicted with trout madness."

"Yes, Ma'am," I said, bowing my head.

So Grace and I soon found ourselves whirling up the beautiful Hudson Valley, Grace studying a borrowed road map and I at the wheel of our rented car.

"Turn left at the next sign," Grace said, and sure enough, the sign read "Rhinebeck," and in only minutes we found ourselves in another country, driving up a narrow but bustling main street that looked all the world like a scene out of a pre-Revolutionary oil painting.

"Maybe we should stop somewhere and phone the cousins Albertina Traver and Beth Lown that your mother especially knew and so often spoke of," Grace suggested.

"Good idea," I said, and soon we had parked the car and found ourselves standing together on a quaint, weathered sidewalk upon which I nostalgically reflected, my own non-fishing maternal grand-father might once have trod.

"Maybe your cousin Sam might let us use his phone," Grace softly said, pointing at a narrow brick building next to which we just happened to be standing.

"Sam Traver, Barber" read the sign in the window, so I tried the door and found it locked. A note was pinned to the door which I read and then carefully pinned back.

"What did the note say?" Grace inquired, ever so softly.

"Shop's closed," I said, shrugging. "Guess we'll have to try phoning from some other place."

"What did the note say?" Grace repeated, more firmly, and when I hesitated she went to the door and unpinned the note and, clearing her throat, proceeded to read it aloud.

"Sorry, gone fishing for the weekend. Back Monday. Sam." She read it in a firm, clear voice.

"But I just told you that the place was closed," I said, blushing and fumbling for the car keys.

Grace stood studying me for quite a spell before she spoke. "You sly, deceitful fishermen are all alike," she finally said with a certain smile. "For a long time I've suspected it but only today do I now know for sure that neither your mother nor I ever really had fighting chance."

Two Profiles

If Trout Could Talk

A Talk delivered at the 4th Annual John D. Voelker
Foundation Meeting at Northern Michigan University on
June 25, 1993

Norris McDowell

Renowned author, respected jurist, champion of his beloved Upper
Peninsula, master of the roll cast and king of the cribbage board;
Michigan's John Voelker left his inimitable mark in many ways and
on many people. But perhaps the most remarkable thing about this
rare man is that through it all—from one accomplishment to
another and even in the winter of his years—John remained at
heart a little boy who liked to go outside and play.

There's a narrow, winding road near a place in the woods that
was dear to John and his playmates; a place known by his readers as
Frenchman's Pond. The old road runs doggedly through rock-
strewn gullies, up and around conifered crests, and under towering
hardwoods. John knew these rocks and trees well, often slowing his
old Jeep wagon "fish car" to admire them and share witticisms and
wonder about them with his traveling companions.

If they could talk, those rocks and trees, what stories they could tell about John, who so often spoke of them as he prowled the backwoods.

And what of the feisty chipmunks at Frenchman's Pond, whose under-foot scurries were predictably entertaining on warm days? What would they say of this man whose wry "50-cent epigrams" and laughter so often rang from the cabin, to the boulders, then across the shimmering waters?

If trout could talk, the brooks at Frenchman's could spin the best yarns of all about John, who wooed them patiently, wrote of them passionately and spoke to them pleadingly. Yes, he talked to trout, this Voelker. And when they shunned him he would marvel at their intelligence and call them graduates of the Harvard Business School. When he did catch a trout, he was apt to apologize to the fish for the inconvenience, then release it "with only its feelings hurt."

When fishing was slow it became cribbage time, and countless games were played in John's tiny cabin by the pond. The contests were spirited in more ways than one, thanks to the maestro's patented Old-Fashioneds—the fabled "bourbon from a tin cup that always tastes better out there."

Losing a cribbage game to John cost his opponent a quarter, upon receipt of which the former Supreme Court justice would cackle appreciatively. Then came his famous down-the-nose, blue-eyed leer and the "beeg" question. "Care to try another, lad? I do believe it's your deal."

Regrettably, I knew John neither long nor well, although I feel blessed to have known him at all. Our friendship grew from a note he sent me early in 1986, while I was editing *Michigan Natural Resources* magazine. He asked why we were offering his book *Trout Madness* for sale, but not his more recent *Trout Magic*. John's note, from green felt-tip pen on yellow legal paper, was the first of many he sent me over the following five years. I was surprised and delighted to hear from him, having heard that after *Anatomy of a*

Murder made him famous, he became reclusive or, as he put it, "fled the baying hounds of success."

We began listing *Trout Magic*, and a few months later, on October 28, John wrote to say thanks. He enclosed the latest issue of *Rod & Reel* magazine, which contained both an article about him and an announcement that he had been named Angler of the Year. The article mentioned John's love of cribbage, my favorite card game.

Call it fate, coincidence or whatever, but just two hours after receiving that copy of *Rod & Reel* from John, I saw the first perfect cribbage hand of my life. At lunch that day, I dealt it to my friend Larry Folks, with whom I had played the game for 15 years. The chance of holding a perfect hand is so slim that a player who does get one often frames that lucky jack and four fives.

Euphoric that afternoon, I wrote John to tell him of Larry's good fortune. A few weeks later I received the following response, which Larry framed along with his perfect hand, and which has hung in his den since:

"I've been playing cribbage since the early 1920s and consider two-handed cribbage the most fascinating card game dreamed up by man, mostly a game of luck, alas; but, in a class game, often decided by skill, a game not only of position but essentially one of *relative* position, something even a lot of old timers never quite learn.

"Some old timers never held a 29 (perfect) hand; I've held three, the last one out at fishing camp 10 years ago. Even holding the chance for it is quite a feat. I dealt the last 'biggie' and held three fives and the jack of hearts; Hank sighed and cut and, presto, I turned over the five of hearts. The hand is now immortalized and framed under glass and hanging in camp, and do come up sometime and behold it and then take on the sly U.P. cribbage champ—sometimes spelled 'chump.' Regards, John Voelker (Robert Traver)."

And so it was that I accepted John's invitation and drove the following spring from Lansing, where I live, to his hometown of Ishpeming. He suggested that I meet him at the Rainbow Bar, where he liked to start the day with a few games of cribbage. It seemed strange to walk into a bar at 9 A.M. but I did and, sure enough, there he was, playing cards with pal Ted Bogdan. The only other person there was Pollie the bartender, absent-mindedly polishing glasses as he watched John and Ted peg their way around the cribbage board.

Soon it was my turn to face the maestro, who quickly trounced me twice and took my pair of quarters. "'Tis mostly a game of luck, lad," he said graciously, perhaps trying to make me feel better about losing, perhaps setting me up for further drubbing later.

Then, he rose and announced that he was going to the post office to get his mail, then "out to the camp." Would I like to ride along? "I'd love to, Judge Voelker," I said. He nodded, turned for the door then spun around to face me. "Do call me John," he said softly, "it's been a long time since my days in the black nightshirt." Then he smiled and placed a hand on my shoulder. "I was paroled," he explained.

Any self-respecting crow could make it from Ishpeming to Frenchman's Pond in 45 minutes. Our trip that morning took John and me about three hours. As promised, he stopped at the post office. ("I still get a royalty check from 'Anatomy' now and then. When you write your best-seller, lad, make sure to nail down a good deal on the movie and TV rights.")

Next, he stopped for gasoline. Then he pulled into the parking lot at a new supermarket and asked me to go in with him. Inside the store, John led me to a long produce counter brimming with leafy rows of cabbage, lettuce, celery and other vegetables. He paused and surveyed the bounty. "The Russians would love to have something like this," he exclaimed.

Following him from aisle to aisle, I began wondering what, if anything, he was after. Finally, he stopped at the meat counter and carefully selected a package of side pork. When we returned to the Jeep, John wordlessly stowed the pork in a Tupperware bowl behind the driver's seat. It took him a few moments to find the bowl, which he finally spotted then dug from a mound of assorted cardboard boxes, fishing gear, clothing, glass bottles filled with dried pussywillow along with other flora, and other treasures.

John offered no explanation for his side pork purchase, and I was not about to seek one. Later I theorized that it was contraband, destined for consumption at Frenchman's Pond or on some remote trout stream where John's blood pressure and cholesterol levels were of little concern, at least to him.

Back on the road, he drove at a possum's pace, straddling the white line on the right side of hard-surface byways, which he avoided whenever possible. He said he would drive for miles out of the way on a two-track road to avoid stop lights. I thought he was kidding. But after an hour or so of bouncing along rutted logging roads and across rickety bridges, it became clear that he was serious about pursuing the least-traveled passages. More than once on our way to camp we were stymied by tree trunks that had fallen across the road, which I jumped out of the Jeep and dragged aside while John sat patiently behind the wheel.

He talked throughout the journey, sometimes to me and sometimes to himself, as if there were a third passenger. "Why did you take the right fork back there, John?" he asked. "Well, we've turned there before and never been last in here," John replied.

As we bounced along, he pointed out unusual rock formations and ancient white pines reaching for the clouds. Stopping beneath one, he led me to its massive trunk and declared: "This one was here before Washington, Jefferson, the Revolutionary War . . ."

Pushing on toward the pond, John continued his gentle, rambling commentary about the wonders of nature, all the while scanning the wooded road sides. At one point he reined in the Jeep, handed me a bucket and sent me toward a clump of ripe blueberries. "Looks like we beat the bears to those," he laughed. "Go get 'em, lad."

Finally, after unlocking a thick steel cable that hung across the road, we chugged round a bend and down a steep hill and there, glistening in the late-morning sun, was Frenchman's Pond. While I explored, John got out his fly rod and fished silently from shore, clearly at home in this "solitude without loneliness."

We lunched on pasties I had bought that morning in Negaunee, then played several games of cribbage, all at my expense. John sat facing a window on the pond, watching for rising trout. As we took turns shuffling and dealing, my mind kept returning to the words of something he once wrote: "I fish because . . . I suspect that men are going along this way for the last time, and I for one don't want to waste the trip." It struck me that of all the things this man had done in his life, wasting the trip was not among them.

I went up to see John again in the fall of 1987, and each spring and fall through 1990. We corresponded regularly during that period, and I will always treasure his letters. Following are excerpts from a few of them:

"I'm getting so much mail to answer about that article Dixie Franklin wrote [about John] that I'm worried whether my writer's cramp will cramp my fly fishing . . . and lately I'm even dabbling with running for president."

"Wishing you all the joys of Christmas and the chance to get back up here for a low-tuition graduate course in cribbage!"

"Storm's over, sun's out; John's rarin' to prowl through a newly plowed tunnel of white. Snow in a city is an affliction; up here, poor city lad, it's a glittering trip through fairyland."

"I once knew places where dozens and scores of wild orchids once grew but the loggers—softer tissue for milady—have chased most of them and most of the mushrooms far far away."

"Opening day was typical: cold, damp, boozy and virtually fish-less. Picture 17 adults loaded with fortunes in gear and fly patterns but not catching even *one* adult keepable trout! I love it. P.S. I won a little at cribbage after thawing out."

"The Utica lads have come and gone and we had a ball and I showed them some of our trees. Tomorrow five fishermen arrive from sylvan Chicago."

"Yesterday Paul Grant and I went morelling near a secret spot where we often fish, and fortune smiled, and we emerged parched from the search with visions of six-packs dancing in our heads and damn near a half-bushel of prime morels in our baskets, the biggest and most exciting find we've had in years."

And, finally:

"The more I prowl the woods the more I realize how little we people really know about the planet we vainly think was made for us to tinker with and plunder."

In fairness to John, it should be noted that he usually beat me at cribbage. He was the best player I've ever encountered. But on the other hand, it should also be noted that when I did beat him I did so soundly. He hated to lose, perhaps even more than he loved to win. After one of the few games I won, he said: "It's tomorrow you're heading home, right?" I nodded. "I suppose you plan to go out tonight and spread humility all over the peninsula," he said, trying in vain to hold back a smile.

John invited photographer David Kenyon and me to his home one day to photograph him for an article written by our Marquette friend Dixie Franklin, which was later published in *Michigan Natural Resources* magazine. The day before, I had come out ahead of John at cribbage, and I knew he was still smarting from it as Dave asked him to sit at his big oak desk and pretend to write something;

in green felt-tip on a yellow legal pad, of course. "But what shall I write?" John asked.

Ah, it was the perfect opening and I pounced. "How about an affidavit?" John looked puzzled, but only for a second. Then he smiled and mumbled that he had not written "one of these things since my days in the black nightshirt." And, as Dave snapped away with his Nikon, John wrote the following:

> "John D. Voelker being first duly sworn on oath deposes and says that prior to yesterday he reigned as the undisputed Cribbage champ of the U.P., that during yesterday those downstate eliters sent a crafty man called Norris McDowell up here to beat me; and beat me the man did, winning games and quarters and even skunking the deposed champ, who, with lumpy throat, now signeth off; further deponent sayeth not, dammitt.
>
> "Signed this 20th day of August, A.D. 1987, John Voelker, former chump."

Whenever I read those words it is my throat which grows lumpy, and it is my heart which fills with hope that sometime, somewhere we will play again. And it is my soul that longs to hear those words, "I do believe it's your deal, lad."

On His Own Terms

Rich Vander Veen and Fred Baker

John Donaldson Voelker led his life as many wish they could—on his own terms. He was one of those singular men who knew who he was and lived his life as he chose. The foundation named in his honor pays tribute to John as a renowned fly fisherman and philosopher, an eminent member of the bench and bar, and a novelist and outdoor writer.

Voelker spent most of his life near his 1903 birthplace of Ishpeming, Michigan, and left his beloved Upper Peninsula only when forced to do so. No one understood the stouthearted people of the Upper Peninsula better than Voelker, who set many of the plots of his eleven books in the rugged land near Marquette, including *Anatomy of a Murder*, his greatest literary success. He wrote under the pen name Robert Traver (Traver was his mother's maiden name), because his early works were published when he was the Marquette County prosecutor, and he did not want to create the impression that he was "spinning yarns on company time."

Voelker's roots were firmly established in Michigan's north

country. His grandfather, a German immigrant, landed at Sault Ste. Marie in the 1840s, and crossed the Upper Peninsula by oxen team, settling near Copper Harbor, where he built the first of three breweries. Voelker told a newspaper reporter, "My father, George, was born at Ontonagon in 1860. He learned to speak Chippewa Indian before he talked English." In his day, George owned the saloon with the longest bar in Ishpeming, no small distinction in a rough-and-tumble mining town that, to this day, has more saloons than churches.

Voelker was the last of six sons. Like his father, he took to the woods and streams at a young age. His talent for trout fishing came from his father, who taught his sons how to hook a trout with a hand-tied fly. Voelker often said they brought back so many trout that his mother grew sick of frying fish.

Voelker's mother, a teacher, wanted her youngest son to have a formal education, but her husband disagreed, saying that knowing how to tramp the woods and draw a stein of beer was education enough. Voelker followed his mother's wishes however, and after graduating from Northern Michigan University, he worked his way through the University of Michigan Law School as a waiter. "When I got my degree and was elected [Marquette County] prosecutor in 1934, dad was so proud he cried."

Following his graduation from law school, Voelker married Grace Taylor of Oak Park, Illinois, a young woman he met in Ann Arbor. Shortly after his marriage, Voelker went to work for the Chicago law firm of Mayer, Meyer, Austrian & Platt, where he worked in the bowels of the firm's law library, putting in his time as what he called a "law looker." He lasted three unhappy years in the Windy City before returning to the U.P., telling Grace that it was better to starve in Ishpeming than to wear emeralds in Chicago. In 1934 he was elected Marquette County prosecutor, the first Democrat to win the job since the Civil War. He served fourteen years.

Voelker flourished in the prosecutor's office; his family grew to include three daughters and he began publishing stories crafted from his experiences, including *Trouble Shooter* and *Small Town D.A.* He became a respected trial lawyer who had the instinct to go for the jugular of a lying witness. During his last ten years in this office, Voelker lost only one felony case. Although reelected six times, he was hardly a typical politician. He hated campaigning, preferred instead to tell Finnish dialect stories in backwoods towns or play cribbage with his cronies.

Eventually, he was defeated at the polls, and went into private practice. He observed philosophically that sooner or later it is pretty much inevitable that a prosecutor will wear out his welcome in a small community like Marquette County, because with the passage of time you eventually prosecute enough defendants to turn a majority (consisting of their friends and relatives) against you. "Being voted out of office probably turned out to be the best thing that could have happened to me," he said, "because if I hadn't been I would have had to prosecute a certain case instead of defending it." Some say that "certain case" was the basis for his bestselling novel, *Anatomy of a Murder*.

In January 1958 the Book-of-the-Month Club featured his novel *Anatomy of a Murder* as its main selection. Voelker dryly observed that, "At 52 I'm a promising young author." *Anatomy of a Murder* quickly became a national best-seller, and established Voelker as an author of international stature. Otto Preminger secured film rights to the book in July 1958. While visiting the Upper Peninsula in January 1959, he decided to shoot the entire film on location in Marquette. The movie and book were based on a case thay Voelker defended in 1952, and told the story of a small-town attorney's successful defense of a serviceman who was charged with killing a bar owner who had allegedly raped the soldier's wife. The movie starred Jimmy Stewart, Lee Remick, George C. Scott, Ben Gazarra, Eve Arden, Joe Welch (of McCarthy Trial fame) and included a musical score by Duke Ellington, who composed it in Marquette while the movie was being filmed. The movie received six Academy Award nominations.

On January 1, 1957, Governor G. Mennen "Soapy" Williams appointed Voelker to the Michigan Supreme Court to fill a three-month vacancy. Voelker ran twice for reelection and won both times, leading the judicial ticket after a campaign managed by John's dear friends, Bill Ellman and the Honorable Damon Keith. The dynamic team of Ellman and Keith was the pattern for Emil Hornstein and Leon Falconbridge in *Hornstein's Boy*, Voelker's political novel. We consider this 1962 work, written in ninety days, concerning civil rights and nuclear warfare, to be required reading every election year. The experience gleaned from his many campaigns is reflected by Hornstein in this fifty-cent epigram: "In a democracy those most gifted to govern are all too frequently those least gifted in the dark arts of ever getting to govern."

During Voelker's 1957-59 tenure with the Supreme Court, he wrote more than one hundred humorous and well-crafted opinions. "For years I have cherished the dream of assembling Voelker's opinions and editing them for publication," wrote Gerald Elliott of the *Grand Rapids Press* shortly after John's death. "It's a task that's crying to be done before those sparkling words become buried in a ton of dust." His most famous case involved the arrest of eight nudists near Battle Creek. In a dissent so persuasive that it garnered a majority, Voelker threw out their convictions, scornfully observing that "It seems that we are now prepared to burn down the house of constitutional safeguards in order to roast a few nudists. I will have none of it." With an epigram characteristic of his pithy humor, he observed of the odd cult to which the defendants belonged that "If eccentricity were a crime, then all of us were felons." *People* v *Hildabridle*, 353 Mich 562, 579 (1958).

On November 24, 1959, Voelker resigned from the Court, pro-claiming that "while other lawyers may write my opinions, they can scarcely write my novels." He returned to the solitude of his beloved Upper Peninsula to craft seven more books. Voelker wrote all of his books laboriously in longhand, most of them on yellow legal pads with a green felt pen. He did most of his writing during the winter months when thick ice covered his favorite fishing spots.

Laughing Whitefish, Traver's only historical novel, is a courtroom drama based on three nineteenth-century Michigan Supreme Court cases. This novel captured John's profound respect for Native Americans and the way they sustained nature before the arrival of the white man. In *Laughing Whitefish,* he observed:

> The law—and only the law—[keeps] society from coming apart at the seams, the world from reverting to a jungle. No other system than the law [has] yet been found for governing men than raw violence; it [is] society's safety valve, the most painless way for men to resolve their differences, and achieve some sort of peace-ful social catharsis; any other way [lies] anarchy and chaos . . . The very slowness of the law, its massive impersonality, its neutrality, its calm insistence upon proceeding according to settled proce-dures and ancient rules, its tendency to adjust and to compro-mise, its very delays if you will—that all of these act to bank and cool the fires of violence and passion and replace them with order and reason.

Laughing Whitefish tells the true story of an Indian woman and a frontier lawyer's fight for elemental justice. Can Laughing Whitefish, a Chippewa Indian, collect a debt owed her father, the late Marji Kawbawgan? She has unimpeachable proof—a tattered document giving Marji a share in the fabulous Jackson Iron Ore Mine to which, years before, he led the white men who developed the mine. And no one denies the validity or authenticity of the document.

Yet—as he passionately and brilliantly illustrates—law and justice do not always coincide. Marji was a poor, uneducated man who followed the ways of his people; the mine owners were powerful and educated. Laughing Whitefish's attorney, William Poe, had to find a way to use the same law that had kept Laughing Whitefish from her inheritance to restore her to her rights, an old man to his honor, the Chippewas to hope, and himself to renewed faith in his profession. *Laughing Whitefish* would make an excellent movie, with its conclusion filmed in the historical Supreme Court Chambers in which the cases were actually held.

Among Voelker's legions of admirers was CBS news correspondent Charles Kuralt. When informed of Voelker's death, Kuralt spoke fondly of his friend,

> Every Christmas, author John Voelker sent a sprig of cedar to his city friends. I thought it was an attempt to remind people who live in the cities, like me, where they should live. I was thinking I won't be getting any more cedar sprigs at Christmastime . . . [John] was really about the nearest thing to a great man I've ever known. He changed my life directly. I was so enchanted by his fly fishing, especially the way he did it. I took up the pursuit myself and have become an enthusiastic fisherman.

The late Arnold Gingrich said that if he could only read one fishing book, he would choose one of Traver's.

Dave Richey, writing in the *Detroit News*, recalled Voelker as the

> Poet Laureate of the Upper Peninsula and the Bard of Frenchman's Pond. As Man measures time, Voelker led a long, full life. But now his cheerful grin, twinkling eyes, short snappy one-liners delivered around a Parodi cigar or an old tin cup of bourbon old fashioned, are a thing of the past . . .
>
> Voelker could put into words the inner thoughts that few trout fishermen can express. He could draw word pictures of rising

trout, the slash of a brookie to a fly, and the mystery of what trout fishing is all about.

Johnny Voelker played the game well. He lived for trout, loved them, and fought for their natural reproduction and their environment in a manner other anglers would be wise to adopt before it's too late.

His rich legacy will live on in the memory of millions of friends. His words and deeds touched all trout fishermen, and among those people whose lives he personally enriched, he will be sorely missed. I toast your memory, old friend.

Detroit Free Press outdoor writer, Eric Sharp asserted that Voelker

Won't be forgotten for a long, long time—not even after they bury him near Ishpeming—not far from the calm waters of French-man's Pond where he spent thousands of hours casting flies to brook trout and thinking about his next book. . . . I often wondered what made him special, why people fell under the spell of this gentle, compassionate, and yet incredibly worldly person who combined scholar, poet, and hard-eyed realist in the same complex mind.

In *Laughing Whitefish*, speaking through Willie Poe, Voelker observed the following about his mother's death:

I learned in a rush one of the stark and bitter lessons of human existence; with terrible clarity I learned that all the places I would ever see, the books I would ever read, the music I would ever listen to, the people I would ever love—that all would one day disappear leaving nothing behind, nothing at all. If this gave me resignation and humility I hoped it also gave me a kind of daring, a daring to live to the hilt one's little span.

And live he did. On his own terms. The John D. Voelker Foundation was incorporated in 1989. John said it made him feel "a wee bit embalmed" to have a Foundation named after him. We of the John D. Voelker Foundation are proud to have known him and are privileged to honor his memory.

The John D. Voelker Foundation confers scholarships to Native American students who plan to attend law school, and confers the annual Robert Traver Fly Fishing Fiction Award for "a distinguished original work of short fiction that embodies an implicit love of fly fishing, respect for the sport and the natural world in which it takes place, and high literary values." For further information on the John D. Voelker Foundation and how to join, write to P.O. Box 15222, Lansing, Michigan 48901-5222, or visit the Voelker Foundation website: www.voelkerfdn.org.